# NEPAL
## The Making of an Inclusive Constitution

*Demands, Debates, Dissents*

# NEPAL

## THE MAKING OF AN INCLUSIVE CONSTITUTION

*Demands, Debates, Dissents*

Nihar R. Nayak

MANOHAR PARRIKAR INSTITUTE FOR DEFENCE STUDIES AND ANALYSES
मनोहर पर्रिकर रक्षा अध्ययन एवं विश्लेषण संस्थान

PENTAGON PRESS LLP

First published in 2025 by
PENTAGON PRESS LLP
206, Peacock Lane, Shahpur Jat
New Delhi-110049, India
Contact: 011-26490600

Typeset in AGaramond, 11.5 Point
Printed by Aegean Offset Printers, Greater Noida, U.P.

ISBN 978-81-982857-3-7 (HB)

***Disclaimer:*** *The views expressed in this book are those of the author and do not necessarily reflect those of the Manohar Parrikar Institute for Defence Studies and Analyses, or the Government of India.*

**www.pentagonpress.in**

*For my daughters, Debolina and Upasna*
*With all my love and admiration*

# *Contents*

# *Acknowledgements*

This book would not have been completed without the unwavering support and encouragement of numerous well-wishers. I am profoundly indebted to the many individuals who have assisted me throughout the various stages of my writing endeavour.

First and foremost, I extend my heartfelt gratitude to Sujan R. Chinoy, Director General of the Manohar Parrikar Institute for Defence Studies and Analyses (MP-IDSA), whose steadfast encouragement and support were instrumental in completing this volume.

I am also sincerely thankful to Group Captain (Dr) Ajey Lele (Retd.), Deputy Director General of MP-IDSA, for his invaluable support in ensuring the timely publication of this work. His willingness to extend deadlines whenever sought, was crucial to completing this book, and his interest in my project is greatly appreciated.

My sincere thanks go to Dr. Uttam Kumar, Coordinator of the Non-Traditional Security Centre, MP-IDSA, and my mentor, for his selfless guidance during the formative stages of my writing.

The publication of this book would not have been possible without the diligent supervision and support of Dr. Ashok K. Behuria, Coordinator of the South Asia Centre, MP-IDSA, who generously provided insightful suggestions throughout the process.

I am grateful to Dr. Uddhab Pyakurel, a faculty member at Kathmandu University, for his valuable recommendations regarding the book's structure and content.

I would also like to acknowledge my colleagues in the Non-Traditional Security Centre and South Asia Centre and Vivek Kaushik, Associate Editor at MP-IDSA, who offered timely and meaningful support during the writing phase.

I express my special appreciation to all the scholars, policymakers, and journalists from Nepal and India who shared their insights during our discussions, which significantly aided in formulating my thoughts and ideas.

My deepest gratitude goes to Dr. Krishna Bhattachan, Prof. Krishna Hachhethu, Dr. Nishchalnath Pandey, Prof Rajesh Kharat, Mr Chiran Jung Thapa, Mr Chandra Kishore, Mr Dipendra Jha, Mr. Shankar Limbu, Mr Jay Nishant, Mr Debendra Yadav, Amb. Vijay Kant Karna, Mr Ajay Bhadra Khanal, Mrs Akanshya Shah, Mr Parshuram Kaphle, Mr Bishnu Rijal, Mr Sunil KC, Mr Sandeep Rana, Dr Pramod Jaiswal, Mr Devesh Jha, Mr Anil Giri, Mr Parushottam Paudel, Mr Sidharth Agarwal, Mr Chandradev Bhatta, Mr Sundar Khanal, Mr Roshan Khadka, and Mr R. B. Khadka for their valuable time in clarifying my doubts and for sharing their diverse perspectives while I was drafting this book.

I appreciate the anonymous referees' comments and constructive suggestions, which have greatly enhanced the quality of this work.

I must also extend my gratitude to Mr Rajan Arya of Pentagon Press and his dedicated staff for their support in publishing this volume.

Furthermore, I would like to thank the MP-IDSA library staff and all others who contributed to this project at various stages.

It would be remiss of me not to acknowledge the sacrifices and unwavering support of my wife, Swetalina (Jolly), and my daughters, Debolina and Upasna, during this writing journey.

I sincerely hope this volume will benefit all stakeholders and stimulate a healthy discourse on enduring peace and political stability in Nepal.

Any oversights in this book are solely my own.

**Nihar R. Nayak**

# *List of Abbreviations*

| | |
|---|---|
| ADB | Asian Development Bank |
| AIM | Alliance for Independent Madhes |
| AJRA | Adibasi Janajati Rastriya Andolan |
| ANJTMM | All Nepal Janatantrik Terai Mukti Morcha (Vivek group) |
| BOG | Basic Operating Guidelines |
| CA | Constituent Assembly |
| CBES | Chure Bhawar Ekta Samaj |
| CIDCA | China International Development Cooperation Agency |
| CIEDP | Commission of Investigation on Enforced Disappeared Persons |
| CM | Chief Minister |
| CNIE | China NGO Network for International Exchanges |
| COD | Commission on Disappeared Persons |
| CPA | Comprehensive Peace Agreement |
| CPN | Communist Party of Nepal-Chand led |
| CPN-UML | Communist Party of Nepal (Unified Marxist–Leninist) |
| DANIDA | Danish International Development Agency |
| DDCs | District Coordination Councils |
| DFID | Department for International Development |
| EC | Election Commission |
| EIDHR | European Instrument for Democracy and Human Rights |
| EP | European Parliament |
| EU | European Union |
| EUEOM | EU Election Observation Mission |

| | |
|---|---|
| FDI | Foreign Direct Investment |
| FICCI | Federation of Indian Chambers of Commerce and Industry |
| FNCN | Federation of National Christians-Nepal |
| FONIN | Federation of Nepalese Indigenous Nationalities |
| FPP | First-Past-the-Post |
| FSF | Federal Socialist Forum |
| FSFN | Federal Socialist Forum Nepal |
| GDP | Gross Domestic Product |
| HLPC | High Level Political Committee |
| HUGOU | Danida Human Rights and Good Governance Advisory Units |
| IED | Improvised explosive devices |
| ILO | International Labour Organisation |
| INGOs | International Non-government Organisations |
| INWOLAG | Indigenous Women's Legal Awareness Group |
| IPMF | Indigenous Peoples' Mega Front |
| ISI | Inter Services Intelligence |
| IWGIA | International Work Group for Indigenous Affairs |
| JSP | Janata Samajwadi Party |
| JTMM | Janatantrik Terai Mukti Morcha |
| KNF | Kirat National Front |
| LAHURNIP | Lawyers' Association for Human Rights of Nepalese Indigenous Peoples |
| LCCs | Local Coordination Councils |
| LeT | Lashkar-e-Taiba |
| LNLF | Limbuwan National Liberation Front |
| LSG | Loss-of-gradient |
| MBA | Maithili, Bhojpuri and Abadhi |
| MJF | Madhesi Janadhikar Forum |
| MLM | Marxism, Leninism and Maoism |
| MNLF | Magar National Liberation Front |
| MNLT | Madhesi National Liberation Front |
| MoFA | Ministry of Foreign Affairs |

| | |
|---|---|
| MRMM | Madhesi Rastriya Mukti Morcha |
| MW | megawatt |
| NA | Nepali Army |
| NC | Nepali Congress |
| NCP | Nepal Communist Party |
| NEFIN | Nepal Federation of Indigenous Nationalities |
| NEOC | Nepal Election Observation Committee |
| NGOs | Non-governmental Organisations |
| NHRC | National Human Rights Commission |
| NIWF | National Indigenous Women's Federation |
| NMSA | Nepal Magar Students Association |
| NNC | Nepali National Congress |
| NPTF | Nepal Peace Trust Fund |
| NSP | Naya Shakti Party |
| NSP | Nepal Sadbhawana Party |
| NSP | Nepal Sadbhawana Party-Anandi Devi |
| NSPN | Naya Shakti Party Nepal |
| NTSG | Nepal Tamang Student Ghedung |
| ODA | Official Development Assistant |
| OHCHR | Office of the High Commissioner for Human Rights |
| PCCs | Province Coordination Councils |
| PLA | People's Liberation Army |
| PLC | Para Legal Committee |
| PP | Parliamentary Party |
| PR | Proportional Representation |
| PW | People's War |
| RIM | Revolutionary International Movement |
| RJP-N | Rastriya Janata Party-Nepal |
| RNA | Royal Nepali Army |
| SDC | Swiss Agency for Development and Cooperation |
| SLMM | Samyukta Loktantrik Madhesi Morcha |
| SPN | Samajbadi Party Nepal |

| | |
|---|---|
| SWCN | Social Welfare Council Nepal |
| TAR | Tibetan Autonomous Region |
| TEL | Terrorist Exclusion List |
| TMDP | Terai Madhes Democratic (Loktantrik) Party |
| TNLF | Tamang National Liberation Front |
| TRC | Truth and Reconciliation Commission |
| UCPN | Unified Communist Party of Nepal (Maoist) |
| UDMF | United Democratic Madhesi Front |
| UK | United Kingdom |
| UN | United Nations |
| UNDAF | United Nations Development Assistance Framework |
| UNDP | United Nations Development Programme |
| UNDRIP | United Nations Declaration on the Rights of Indigenous Peoples |
| UNHCR | United Nations High Commissioner for Refugees |
| UNICEF | United Nations International Children's Emergency Fund |
| UNMIN | United Nations Mission in Nepal |
| UNPFN | United Nations Nepal Peace Fund |
| UNPO | Unrepresented Nations and Peoples Organization |
| UPF | United People's Front–Nepal |
| VHP | Vishwa Hindu Parishad |
| WCCs | Ward Coordination Councils |

# *List of Figures and Tables*

*Figures*



*Tables*

# *Introduction*

In the post-colonial period, many Afro-Asian countries struggled to institutionalise a responsive and representative form of government. After years of struggle and experiments, many of these countries settled for notionally democratic governance systems. However, due to political instability, lack of economic growth, and improvement in democratic norms, many states switched from one form of government to another, which, in most cases, gave rise to severe social and political conflicts.

Central-eastern Himalayan countries—Nepal and Bhutan—were not excluded from the waves of change that were taking place around them. In this context, these countries have been undergoing major political transformations since 2008. The diversity of ethnic composition and demands of marginalised communities suffering from economic, political, and social discrimination have complicated the political transition process in these Himalayan countries.

The democratisation processes continue to be marred by political violence, mainly due to the emerging system's inability to adopt an inclusive order and resorting instead to questionable coercive measures to counter the demands for devolution of power. In Nepal, the Constituent Assembly (CA) took seven years to complete the constitution-making process by holding two CA elections.

Nepal has had a history of recurring conflicts since 1950. Modern Nepal has witnessed conflicts[1] every ten years or less than that. For example, there was the anti-Rana movement led by the Nepali Congress (NC) in 1950; the anti-Panchayat system protests in 1960; the Jhapa uprising in 1974; *Jan Andolan* I in 1990; the Janajati movements in the 1990s; Maoist insurgency in 1996; *Jan Andolan* II in 2006; the Madhesi movement in 2007; and the anti-constitution protests in post-2015 period.

Barring the Maoist insurgency, the span of these conflicts has been relatively short and of low intensity. The state often responded by suppressing the disputes rather than addressing the underlying issues. The 2006 Comprehensive Peace Agreement (CPA) was the first significant attempt by the state to resolve the civil conflict in which an alliance of seven political parties signed a historic agreement with the then Maoist rebels. As a result, the level of violence went down significantly in the post-CA period. As per the CPA, some ex-Maoist combatants were re-integrated into the Nepali Army, and a new constitution[2] was adopted.

Unfortunately, even after a decade of signing the CPA and nine years of adopting a new constitution, uncertainty still looms large over political stability and permanent peace in Nepal. Large sections of society, mostly marginalised groups[3] (Dalits-Adivasi-Janajati-Madhesi) who constitute around 70 percent of the total population of Nepal, are not satisfied with the new constitution. 'Despite some progress in institutional development and peacebuilding, Nepal remains vulnerable to different manifestations of violence and fragility.'[4]

More than 100 people have died, and an equal number of persons have been injured in the anti-constitution protests since June 2015. There was a trust deficit between the marginalised groups and the Prachanda-led NC-Maoist coalition government because of the delay in making the second amendment to the constitution. The Communist Party of Nepal (Unified Marxist-Leninist), then the main opposition, opposed the bill presented in Parliament on 8 January 2016. The bill sought to amend the September 2015 Constitution for the second time to address the demands of protesting groups. As part of the Madhesi[5] and NC-Maoist agreement in July 2016, the government had assured that it would bring a second amendment 15 days after government formation to address the remaining demands of the marginalised groups.

Since the government failed to keep its promises, the Madhesh-based parties decided not to participate in the first phase of the local body elections held on 14 May 2017 unless the government passed the amendment bill. The Madhesh-based parties felt that the people might reject them outright at the polls if they contested the elections without ensuring the amendment.

Moreover, the Nepal Federation of Indigenous Nationalities (NEFIN), in a statement on 23 February 2017, condemned the government's decision to hold elections in May by disregarding the marginalised groups' demands. NEFIN Chairman Jagat Bahadur Baram said, "The newly adopted Constitution of Nepal has failed to ensure the rights and identity of indigenous, Madhesi, and oppressed communities. The government unilaterally announced the date for local polls conspiratorially by ignoring the serious demands raised by the NEFIN."[6]

The NEFIN threatened a phase-wise agitation[7] in alliance with the Adibasi Janjati Rashtriya Andolan (AJRA) Nepal and Madhesis if the government failed to address their demands by passing the Second Amendment bill before the second phase of local body elections.

The Madhesi and Janajati parties' non-participation in the local body elections raised questions regarding the durability of the CPA and the legitimacy of the new constitution to prevent recurring conflicts in Nepal. A new set of dissenting groups has emerged in the post-constitution period. This might plunge Nepal into another round of political conflict because the failure of moderate parties to bring about changes in the constitution and implement the CPA could create a space for radical groups to start a new movement against the state.

Many studies on peace agreements have found that despite the best efforts, peace processes often fail to bring about enduring peace in post-conflict societies. Even if there is not a full-scale resumption of war, violence, insecurity, and instability pervade many post-war societies.[8]

According to a World Bank report of 2010, of the 103 countries that experienced some form of civil war between 1945 and 2009 (from minor to significant conflict), only 44 avoided a subsequent return to civil war. That means that 57 percent of all countries that suffered from one civil war during this period experienced at least one conflict after that.[9] A 2011 World Bank report further found that 'a high level of criminal violence can follow successful peace agreements.'[10]

These studies have identified that the absence of good governance, slow implementation of agreements between the state and marginalised groups, weak institutions, delay in delivering transitional justice, absence of neutral peace mediators, absorption of rebel leaders by ruling elites through alluring through power or money, and lack of an influential role played by the international community have all contributed to the relapse of conflicts.[11]

Moreover, high-altitude mountainous countries like Nepal, with multi-ethnic groups and weak governance systems, could be prone to conflicts or recurring conflicts in the post-peace agreement period. The conflict could be prolonged if a particular ethnic group gains a majority in that society. Given their dominant position in society, they manipulate the internal system and the external support to rule over minorities. Therefore, implementing the peace process becomes more difficult in the case of the multi-ethnic and smaller states surrounded by large countries with whom they share ethnolinguistic borders.

In May 2008, the first Constituent Assembly of Nepal began writing an inclusive constitution to institutionalise the peace process gains, which had taken off in November 2006. An inclusive constitution had been one of the demands of the Janajati/Adivasi or 'ethnic minorities' and later by the Madhesis (inhabitants of the Terai region)—to bring to an end the centuries-old discriminations faced by them at multiple levels by the State and ruling elites.

After seven years of difficult deliberations, the new constitution was finally promulgated—not based on consensus but by majority voting—on 20 September 2015. Unfortunately, more than half the population in Nepal branded the new constitution as regressive and non-inclusive and protested against it. The anti-constitution protests, especially in the southern Terai plains, started on 09 August 2015. The protestors felt that their demands had not been addressed in the constitution despite commitments by different governments since 2006.

Since then, Nepal has witnessed many protests against the new constitution both in the hills and in Madhesh. Over a hundred people were killed, which included civilians and security personnel, in the popular agitation. More than a hundred were injured in clashes between security forces and protesters. The situation worsened when the protestors imposed a defacto blockade along all the major trading points between Nepal and India and choked supply lines to Kathmandu.

Many parts of Nepal witnessed a shortage of essential commodities due to prolonged protests and roadblocks by the Samyukta Loktantrik Madhesi Morcha (SLMM), Tharus, and various ethnic minority groups. The blockade was lifted in February 2016 after the government and leaders of major political parties assured the agitating groups that they would make necessary modifications/amendments to the constitution after a healthy dialogue with them.

The agitating groups have rejected several attempts to initiate dialogues. They have insisted that the government failed to create a conducive environment for negotiation and implementing their demands. The marginalised groups of Nepal feel that the 2015 Constitution could not accommodate their long-pending demands.

These demands include the demarcation of provincial boundaries on ethnic lines, the formation of two Madhes provinces in the Terai region, proportional representation in the State agencies and parliament, equal political rights to all citizens, the introduction of changes in the laws on citizenship and implementation of previous agreements between them and the State. The SLMM also demanded the withdrawal of the Nepali Army (NA) from the Terai region as one of the pre-conditions for negotiation between the State and agitating groups. Even after the promulgation of the constitution with 85 percent of votes by the CA, the agitating groups have continued their protests.

Although the Janajatis and Madhesis have been demanding that the new constitution accommodate their demands to make it inclusive, the ruling establishment implemented the constitution after its promulgation. This has vitiated the atmosphere of trust between the people living in the plains and the ruling *Pahadi* (hill) elites. Rather than fostering unity in Nepal, the new constitution appears to have, in practice, contributed to divisions along ethnic and geographical lines within the Himalayan nation.

The Constitution sets ambitious values that guide the nation toward an inclusive future. However, despite these noble goals, specific actions or frameworks have been lacking to turn these principles into reality. For example, Article 42 (1) states:

Economically, socially, or educationally backward women, Dalits, Indigenous nationalities, Madhesi, Tharu, Muslims, backward classes, minorities, marginalised communities, persons with disabilities, gender and sexual minorities, farmers, labourers, oppressed or citizens of backward regions, and indigent Khas Arya shall have the right to participate in State bodies based on the principle of proportional inclusion.[12]

The minorities feel that the term 'principle of inclusion' is vague and does not give any constitutional guarantee for marginalised groups' representation in government jobs according to their population. This clause of the Constitution is, in reality, a derogation from the principles spelled out in the Interim Constitution 2007, which guaranteed proportional representation of marginalised groups in government jobs.[13]

Ever since the new constitution of Nepal was promulgated, its procedures, contents, and spirit have been challenged by different marginalised groups. These groups have expressed their dissatisfaction with the implementation of inclusive provisions pertaining to them. This has been reflected both at the State and political party levels.

The marginalised groups challenged the decision of the then Nepal Communist Party (NCP), which finalised its merger process on April 30, 2019, by appointing district committees of the party. Of the 77 chairpersons appointed for district committees—chiefs and secretaries—only three were women, two were from the Dalit community, and 19 were from indigenous nationalities.

The representatives of these marginalised groups in the party expressed concern over the negligible representation of women, Dalits, and Janajatis in the party committees, arguing that the top leadership failed to abide by the party statute. The party's interim statute states that all the committees will have at least one-third women representation.

Sashi Shrestha, a central committee member of the Janamorcha Nepal (Amik Sherchan faction), who has advocated for inclusivity within the party, stated, "Once again, the leaders have failed to demonstrate honesty. They did not implement the existing provisions in the party statute that ensure one-third women representation in all committees."[14]

The problem, however, is not only in the district committees. With only 75 women in the Central Committee, many had questioned the legality of the Nepal Communist Party, saying the Election Commission requires 33 percent women representation for any party to register with it. Clause 15(4) of the Act on Political Parties-2073 states that at least one-third of the party's members must be represented in all its committees.

For the registration of a political party, Article 269(4c) of the Constitution clearly states that there must be a provision for such inclusive representation in its executive committees at various levels reflecting the diversity of Nepal. The 441-strong Central Committee had 21 Dalit members. The Dalit community accounts for 13.2 percent of Nepal's total population. The 45-member Standing Committee had only one Dalit member—Chhabilal Biswokarma. Only two women had made it to the Standing Committee—Asta Laxmi Shakya and Pampha Bhusal. No women or Dalit representation was in the nine-member Secretariat—the party's highest body. It had only two members from the indigenous nationalities.

The country has earned accolades for ensuring 33 percent representation of women in parliament. But many say this provision is being followed only because the constitution demands it. Reluctance to follow the principle of inclusivity, however, is rampant across the board, as none of the parties have ensured proper representation of women, Dalits, and Janajatis. The 2017 parliamentary election was a glaring example. Only six women were elected to the 165-member parliament (a mere 3.64 percent) under the direct election system.[15]

Despite criticisms from civil society and foreign media regarding the major political parties, constitutional bodies, and ruling elites for failing to ensure an inclusive Parliament in the 2017 elections, a similar pattern persisted in the 2022 Parliamentary elections. The parties again could not nominate more candidates from marginalised groups under the First-Past-the-Post (FPTP) system, resulting in a limited representation of these groups in Parliament. Only one Dalit candidate won under the FPTP system. [16] One scholar noted Dalits, who constitute 13.12 percent of the population (according to the 2011 census), held only 5.81 percent of the 275-member federal lower house. In 2017, three Dalits were directly elected, while 16 entered through the proportional representation system. Similarly, Janajatis comprised 24 percent of the total representation despite constituting 38 percent of the national population.[17]

Women were sent to the parliament under the proportional representation system, as the constitution made it mandatory. The Nepal Communist Party, which claims to be a progressive party, however, failed to include women, Dalits, and Janajatis in its committees as per the prescribed norms. While responding to a media interview, Pasang Sherpa, a central committee member in the party and former chair of the Nepal Federation of Indigenous Nationalities, said, 'We will press the leadership to ensure inclusiveness. All sections of society should have a fair representation in new committees.'[18]

While the leaders have failed to implement constitutional provisions, they promise that the constitution could be amended and revised. One of the chairpersons of the then Nepal Communist Party (NCP), Pushpa Kamal Dahal 'Prachanda,' had said that the constitution could be amended and revised per the needs and demands of the people as it is a living and dynamic document.' He made this remark while welcoming leaders and cadres of the Madhesh Tarai Forum from Province 2 (renamed as Madhesh Pradesh in February 2022) into the NCP. He claimed that he took the initiative to amend the constitution to ensure maximum rights to the people by discussing the same with Prime Minister Khadga Prasad Sharma Oli.[19]

However, the NCP coped earlier with the marginalised and inclusive issues. The same issues perhaps prompted the merger of the Baburam Bhattarai-led Naya Shakti Party (NSP) and Federal Socialist Forum Nepal (FSFN) in early May 2019. The NSP and the FSFN officially announced their unification on May 6, 2019, to create a new political force—Samajbadi Party Nepal (SPN). The SPN leaders argued that the new party would launch a struggle to amend the constitution, consolidate federalism, form a 10+1 province model, and a directly elected presidential system.[20] The Bhattarai-led party demanded that FSFN accept a directly elected executive of the country and a fully proportional representation category election system for parliament.[21] The top leaders of the SPN called on the Rastriya Janata Party-Nepal (RJPN)—a regional party with a strong base in the southern plains—to join hands to launch a collective fight to protect and promote the cause of the poor, the marginalised and the oppressed. RJPN could not join the unification between FSFN and NSPN since the FSFN did not concede the demand to first pull out of the Oli government. Since FSFN did not meet RJPN's condition, unification negotiations could not proceed.[22]

Although the constitution was adopted nine years ago, the struggles of various marginalised groups for identity and rights highlight either slow progress in implementing the constitution or a lack of political willpower by major political parties, predominantly led by Bràhmins and Chhetris, to address the grievances of Indigenous communities. For instance, major indigenous groups in eastern Nepal, such as the Limbu, Kirat, and Rai, have protested against renaming Province 1 as Koshi, arguing that 'Koshi' is a Hindu name. The Kirat-Limbuwan Sangharsh Committee has staged protests in Biratnagar since March 2023, opposing the province's new name. Other ethnic organisations, including the Federal Kirat Rai Yaokkha, Kirat Yakthung Chumlung, and Sherpa Sangh, also called for a general strike. These indigenous groups believe the province should be named based on the region's socio-cultural identity, advocating for names like Kirat Limbuwan or Limbuwan Kirat. On the other hand, the major political parties, such as the Nepali Congress, CPN-UML, Maoist Centre, and Rashtriya Prajatantra Party (RPP), supported naming the province based on its geographical features. Although these parties collectively endorsed the new name on 01 March 2023, the Maoist Centre reversed its stance.[23]

Similarly, the Madhesi community has remained dissatisfied with the constitution. The formation of the Rashtriya Mukti Kranti (National Liberation Revolution) Party on 17 September 2024 by Rajendra Mahato suggested that despite addressing many of the significant demands of Madhesis' in the new constitution, discrimination from Kathmandu towards the Terai region persists. This new party seeks to establish a "Multi-nation State" in Nepal. It is committed to addressing the rights and identity issues of those who remain unrecognised even within a democratic framework. The party's central committee includes indigenous members from various communities, including Newar, Tamang, and Sherpa, and its mission is to fight for the rights of oppressed groups across the country.[24]

However, the historical unity between Janajati and Madhesi groups against the ruling classes in Nepal has often been unsuccessful. The Bahuns and Chhetris have marginalised both the Madhesi and Janajati communities. Individual interests and opportunism have primarily driven the unity. While they may share a common goal of challenging the oppressive structures in Nepali society, the Janajatis tend to feel more at ease with the dominant hill-based classes than the Madhesi. The recent split within the Janata Samajbadi Party (JSP) Nepal, led by Upendra Yadav, on 05 May 2024, and the formation of a new party under Ashok Rai's leadership reveal fractures in the Madhesi-Janajati alliance in eastern Nepal. The JSP was a pioneering political experiment aimed at uniting Madhesis and Janajatis to jointly address issues concerning marginalised groups and challenge the Kathmandu-based ruling elites. However, this experiment has now unravelled, casting doubt on the future of such alliances.

The slow progress in implementing the new constitution and the growing disenchantment of the minority groups have allowed some Maoist factions to consolidate in Nepal. In response to a series of bomb blasts and the kidnapping of a member of the legislative assembly in Bajhang district. The Nepal government, on March 12, 2019, proscribed the Netra Bikram Chand-led Communist Party of Nepal (CPN) by branding it as a criminal group. The government took the decision based on reports by security agencies, which found that the CPN had stepped up its activities and moved beyond its 'donation drive.' In November 2018, the CPN's top leaders rejected the dialogue offer of the High-Level Political Talks team formed under lawmaker Som Prasad Pandey.

Despite implementing a new constitution, Nepal's ongoing socio-political tensions could potentially disrupt the country's peace and stability. While the ruling classes of Nepal claim the constitution is the most advanced and inclusive in South Asia, resolving these tensions could require continuous dialogue between the ruling parties and marginalised groups. Periodic amendments reflecting socio-economic changes and the sincere implementation of constitutional provisions could ease tensions. Given Nepal's relatively recent transition to multiparty democracy under a republican system, a consensus-driven approach, possibly supported by the international community, may be necessary to strengthen its democratic process further.

## Significance of the Study

The book identifies and analyses trends in the anti-constitution movements led by Madhesis, Janajatis, and other marginalised groups in Nepal. It explores the complex relationship between the various actors in these movements. The study also examines the State's failure to produce an inclusive constitution despite recurring protests and how the resulting political instability could impact peace and development in Nepal, as well as India's strategic interests—particularly in security and economic matters—and its bilateral relationship with Nepal.

The book also explores the crucial support base, both internal and external, of these movements, the leadership behaviour, and responses of the external powers in the anti-constitution movement in Nepal in the post-2015.

## Research Gap

Many articles, research papers, and books have been written on Nepal's Janajati/ Adibasi and Madhesi movements. However, most of the research on this issue was done before the promulgation of the 2015 Constitution of Nepal. Moreover, none of these studies explored the implications of such movements for Nepal's contemporary internal political dynamic and India-Nepal relations.

Further, there are several scholarly works on the Janajati movements in Nepal after the 2015 Constitution. Although the book *From the Margins to the Mainstream: Institutionalising Minorities in South Asia*[25] was published in 2016, its chapters cover mainly pre-constitutional debates about the Janajati movements in Nepal.

This study fills this research gap by undertaking a detailed assessment of the state of movements organised by all the marginalised groups of Nepal. It also studies their impact on the internal political dynamics in Nepal in the post-Constitution period.

The Janajatis and Madhesis have tried to ally to intensify their anti-Constitution agitation in a new political context. At the same time, the indigenous groups have been trying to readjust the movement to the contemporary situation. From the street-level movement earlier, it has now reached the community level. It is, therefore, relevant to revisit and re-examine movements organised by Nepal's marginalised groups and assess their impact on peace and stability in Nepal on the one hand and India-Nepal bilateral relations on the other.

The book argues that:

1. The movements have galvanised the marginalised groups and whetted their political aspirations so that any government reconciliation effort without empathetic consideration of their demands will prolong the agitation and lead to chronic political instability.
2. Hill elites, who have dominated the political scenario for centuries, will try to perpetuate their control over the levers of power and avoid conceding as much political space to the marginalised groups as the latter hope for.
3. Given Nepal's ethnic diversity and geopolitics, ethnic identity-based federalism could potentially lead to the emergence of newly marginalised groups that claim autonomy, further complicating the issue of inclusion.
4. Internal divisions within marginalised ethnic groups—be it within Madhesis or Janajatis—will weaken the movement. Without a coherent

and unified movement, the ruling political elite will easily ignore the demands and proceed with token and cosmetic changes.

5. The India-Nepal relationship will continue to be under strain, as India will find it challenging to insulate itself from the political instability in Nepal, given its deep links with Nepalese society and polity.

## Clarification of Terms and Historical Context

The 2015 Constitution of Nepal mentions "Indigenous people" and "Indigenous nationalities" as separate entities. It is important to note that the terms are not used interchangeably. Therefore, in academic contexts, particularly within the scope of this discussion, the terms "Janajati," "Indigenous populations/communities," and "ethnic groups" are utilised to denote "Adivasi Janajati," which corresponds to the concept of Indigenous nationalities.

The book also refers to the historical context in Nepal, where specific groups such as the Janajati (Indigenous nationalities), Dalit (those considered lower caste), and Madhesi (people of the Terai who use the Indian languages as their mother tongue) have been labelled as "Marginalised." The term "marginalised" here signifies these groups have been systematically disadvantaged and discriminated against by the ruling classes in Nepal since 1769. This marginalisation excluded social, economic, and political aspects from mainstream development and decision-making processes.

## Methodology

The topic was identified after diligent monitoring of political developments in Nepal over a considerable time. The study is based on both primary and secondary sources of data. Constitutions of Nepal and other policy documents related to indigenous nationalities, statements of senior political leaders, interviews during field visits with leaders of the movements, scholars, officials, and former officials or during their visits to India, reports. Publication of government thinks tanks, Parliament/Assembly debates on Janajati and Madhesi-related issues, NEFIN, AJRA, Federal Alliance press releases, and interviews have been used as primary sources. A research trip was undertaken during the elections in November 2013. Secondary research inputs involve constant monitoring of day-to-day developments and events from open sources. Books, articles, commentaries, private research institutes' reports and relevant websites have been utilised.

Certain sections of this book are taken from my earlier publications. I have improved and updated them according to the contemporary internal political developments in Nepal.

**Chapter 1** focuses on Nepal's broad ethno-regional canvas in the present context. The data and information are from the 2011 Census and a new constitution. The chapter argues that despite attempts to make an inclusive constitution, the two dominant castes—Chhetri and Bahun (also known as Bahun-Hill)—continue to dominate the Nepali polity and governance system. Poor coordination between Janajati and Madhesi and intra-organisation factionalism have contributed to the emergence of these groups as an unsuccessful political force in Nepal.

**Chapter 2** investigates the evolution and progress of the Janajati/Adivasi movement since 1769. This chapter also discusses extensively the role of Janajatis in the constitution-making process and their demands. It argues that despite their combined demographic strength of over 35 percent (minus Muslims and Madhesi) of the total Nepali population and the formation of the Nepal Federation of Indigenous Nationalities (NEFIN) in the early 1990s, Janajatis have been struggling to emerge as a powerful political force in Nepal. This is due to their scattered geographical spread, poor leadership, an affiliation of NEFIN with major upper-caste political parties, and over-dependence on Western NGOs.

**Chapter 3** seeks to study different narratives on the 'Madhes' identity, situate this discourse in the ethnolinguistic mosaic of the Terai region and within the larger Nepali political scenario, and isolate the reasons for their increasing assertion in politics. The chapter argues that a sense of cultural discrimination played an essential role in the consolidation of the Madhesi identity. While the mainstream Madhesi parties took a soft stand on the issue, the armed groups have demanded outright 'independence.' Since 2008, the Madhesi movement has lost public support because of differences among various Madhesi groups (over their objectives and methods). The fragmentation of the movement has also dragged India into controversy. *Pahadi* (the inhabitants of hill regions) and Madhesi groups are critical of India's role in the Madhesi issue.

**Chapter 4** discusses the linkages between the grievances of ethnic minority groups and the Maoist movement in Nepal. It argues that the Maoists hijacked the political and social agenda of the Janajatis to expand their support base for political and military purposes. The Maoists included the demands of the Janajatis in their 40-point demands, which were presented before the then-government in 1996. The Maoists also assured us they would address all these demands upon forming a Maoist government in Kathmandu instead of Janajatis' support of the movement. In the post-conflict period, the Janajatis felt that the Maoist party had deviated from its earlier commitments and failed to address their demands.

**Chapter 5** examines the first Constituent Assembly (CA)'s failure to deliver a constitution on time and debates over the minority demands in the first CA. Since the first CA failed to draft the constitution, even with four extensions, the Supreme Court ordered its dissolution and held fresh elections for a new CA-cum-Parliament. The elections were a significant barometer of popular aspirations for democracy and change.

In the wake of the elections, a brief study of the contents in the Nepalese media and writings on the state of Nepalese politics indicated that the people as a whole looked quite sad about the way the political parties conducted themselves and felt quite disillusioned with the process of democracy in Nepal. Against this backdrop, a field trip was undertaken to Nepal on the eve of the second CA elections to enable extensive interaction among people from all walks of life across different geographical and ethnic terrains.

**Chapter 6** deals with external influence on the internal political dynamics of Nepal. It is found that Western countries, especially some EU members and Nordic countries, encouraged Janajatis to demand a single ethnic-based province and an inclusive constitution. Since the Janajatis failed to put pressure on Kathmandu in this regard, the demand was later picked up by the Madhesis during the constitution drafting process. Madhesi's demands for a single Madhesh Pradesh, by including all the 22 Nepali districts sharing borders with India, generated suspicion amongst the ruling classes of Kathmandu about India's role. This perception created resentment against India across the hill population. Further, the federalism issue became complicated by China's reservations against ethnic-based federalism, especially the carving of a separate province for the Sherpa minority group, which shares geo-cultural linkages with Tibet.

The conclusion focuses on the dissenting voices on the new constitution and its implications on future Nepali policy and India-Nepal relations. Although the peace process in Nepal has been partially successful so far, it has failed to address some of the pertinent issues agreed to in the Comprehensive Peace Agreement (CPA). Of the four major components—elections to the CA, reintegration of former Maoist combatants, providing justice to war victims, and writing an inclusive constitution, the last two components have remained elusive.

The major stakeholders in the peace process (PP) or the CPA deviated from their commitment to either acquiring or continuing in power. That left the core demands of the PP either unaddressed or diluted by the traditional power holders. A new set of dissenting groups has emerged in the post-constitution period. This might plunge Nepal into another round of political conflict because the failure of moderate parties to bring about changes in the constitution and implement the CPA could create a space for radical groups to start a new movement against the state.

## NOTES

1 Conflict means any activities or actions of a group or association that affect day to day functioning and create a public order issue in a society/state. These activities and actions could have emerged due to disagreements, differences of opinion on certain issues between the state and people. Conflict is not necessarily always characterised as violence. Even a low level conflict in a society might affect peace and stability.

2 Nepal promulgated its seventh Constitution on 20 September 2015.

3 The Article 306 of the 2015-Cosntituoin defines, "marginalised" means communities that are made politically, economically and socially backward, are unable to enjoy services and facilities because of discrimination and oppression and of geographical remoteness or deprived thereof and are in lower status than the human development standards mentioned in Federal law, and includes highly marginalised groups and groups on the verge of extinction". As per the article 42 (1), these groups "shall have the right to participate in the State bodies on the basis of inclusive principle" (The Constitution of Nepal, 2015, Ministry of Law, Justice, and Parliamentary Affairs, Government of Nepal).

4 The World Bank, *Conflict, Security, and Development, World Development Report, 2011*, p. 92.

5 Madhesi, the inhabitants of Nepal's Terai region, primarily communicate in their mother tongues, such as Hindi, Awadhi, Bhojpuri, and Maithili.

6 "NEFIN warns of agitation", *The Kathmandu Post*, 23 February 2017.

7 In a press conference in Kathmandu on 10 May 2017, The Nepal Federation of Indigenous Nationalities (NEFIN), the Indigenous Nationalities Joint Struggle Committee (INJSC), the Nepal Federation of Indigenous Nationalities Students (NEFINS), the National Indigenous Nationalities Women Federation (NINWF) and the Nepal Indigenous Nationalities Youth Association, jointly announced their struggle programmes. *The Himalayan Times*, 11 May 2017.

8 Jasmine-Kim Westendorf, "Why Peace Processes Fail: Negotiating Insecurity After Civil War", Boulder, Lynne Rienner Publishers, 2015, p.1.

9 Barbara F. Walter, "Conflict relapse and the sustainability of post-conflict peace," Background Paper, *World Development Report 2011*, 13 September 2010, p. 1.

10 The World Bank, *Conflict, Security, and Development, World Development Report, 2011*, pp. 57-58.

11 Havard Hegre and Havard Mokleiv Nygard, "Governance and Conflict Relapse", *Journal of Conflict Resolution*, 2015, 59(6) 984-1016.

12 The Constitution of Nepal, Ministry of Law, Justice and Parliamentary Affairs, Government of Nepal, September 2016, pp.24-25.

13 Authors interactions with some members of the marginalised groups in Kathmandu in July 2019.

14 "Leadership failed to follow principle of inclusivity, ruling party leaders say," *The Kathmandu Post*, 24 April 2019 (accessed on 23 September 2021).

15 "Nepal: Few women elected to parliament under FPTP" *AGORA*, 18 January 2018, http://old.agora-parl.org/news/nepal-few-women-elected-parliament-under-fptp (accessed on 11 April 2022). AGORA (www.agora-parl.org) is the leading global knowledge platform on parliamentary development.

16 "Exclusionary parliament," Editorial, *The Kathmandu Post*, 01 December 2022, https://kathmandupost.com/editorial/2022/12/01/exclusionary-parliament (accessed on 04 October 2024).

17 Nishan Khatiwada, "November polls fail to ensure fair representation of Dalits", *The Kathmandu Post*, 13 December 2022, https://kathmandupost.com/politics/2022/12/13/november-polls-fail-to-ensure-fair-representation-of-dalits (accessed on 04 October 2024).

18 "Leadership failed to follow principle of inclusivity, ruling party leaders say," *The Kathmandu Post*, 24 April 2019.

19 "Constitution will be amended and revised as per people's need: NCP Chair Dahal", *Online Radio Nepal*, 30 April 2019, accessed 24 September 2021. Also see https://osnepal.tv/734998 (accessed 24 September 2021). For further details, https://www.nepal24hours.com/nepals-constitution-will-be-amended-and-revised-ncp-chair-dahal/ (accessed on 24 September 2021).

20 "Bhattarai, Yadav launch Samajbadi Party Nepal in bid to create an alternative force", *The Kathmandu Post*, 07 May 2019 (accessed on 24 September 2021).

21 "FSFN-NSP merger deal stalled as Bhattarai demands Yadav quit govt", *myRepublica*, 02 May 2019 (accessed on 24 September 2021).

22 "FSFN and Naya Shakti unify as Samajbadi Party Nepal", *myRepublica*, 07 May 2019, https://myrepublica.nagariknetwork.com/news/fsfn-and-naya-shakti-unify-as-samajbadi-party-nepal/ (accessed on 24 September 2021).

23 "Protests staged against the naming of Koshi Province", *The Kathmandu Post*, 03 March 2023, https://kathmandupost.com/province-no-1/2023/03/03/protests-staged-against-the-naming-of-koshi-province (accessed on 04 October 2024).

24 "Rajendra Mahato announces new political party", *Khabarhub.com*, Kathmandu, 17 September 2024, https://english.khabarhub.com/2024/17/398219/ (accessed on 04 October 2024).

25 Hugo Gorringe, Roger Jeffery, Suryakant Waghmore (eds), "From the Margins to the Mainstream: Institutionalizing Minorities in South Asia," New Delhi, Sage Publications, 2016.

## *Chapter One*

# *The Ethno-cultural Structure and State Discrimination*

Nepal is a sovereign nation characterised by its diverse ethnic, linguistic, and religious composition, situated in the central Himalayas. Its unique topography and geographical location have significantly contributed to its present pluralistic ethnological framework, accommodating over 126 caste and ethnic groups within an area of 147,181 square kilometres. Despite the considerable presence of various ethnic and cultural communities, it is noteworthy that no single group possesses an overwhelming majority within the society, differentiating it from other South Asian countries.

The Nepali society is profoundly stratified along the lines of caste, culture, region, and ethnic identity. The Bahuns and Chhetris, comprising 16.6 percent and 12.2 percent of the total population respectively, dominate Nepal's administrative, political, security, and economic structures. This dominance can be attributed to two primary factors. Firstly, the Shah dynasty, which unified Nepal in 1769, is associated with the Chhetri clan.[1] Secondly, the indigenous nationalities and cultural groups have experienced fragmentation, largely due to the social and geographic barriers presented by the mountainous terrain, which has hindered effective communication. Furthermore, numerous ethnic and cultural groups have historically migrated to the central Himalayan region at various points,[2] resulting in a lack of coordination and cohesive resistance against the Chhetri leadership—both during the Shah dynasty and later under the Ranas—who strategically integrated Bahuns as spiritual advisors within the palace and subsequently in the state administrative framework.

Although early ruling classes did enlist some indigenous nationalities in the Gorkhali armed forces (later known as the Nepali Army), many of these groups vehemently opposed the alterations to land tenure systems and the introduction of the civil code in 1854, which was subsequently replaced by a new code in 1963.

The initial opposition was not rooted in religious considerations, a misconception perpetuated by Western anthropologists and subsequently appropriated by the leftist (Communist) factions in Nepal. The conflict between the monarchy and indigenous nationalities was fundamentally territorial, exacerbated by the palace's failure to uphold Prithvi Narayan Shah's policy of cultural accommodation amid internal power struggles. Following the conquest of Kathmandu and other regions of Nepal, Prithvi Narayan Shah indeed demonstrated respect for the diverse local cultures of the indigenous populations. For instance, he endorsed the Kumari tradition of the Newar community and ensured that Magar priests continued to perform rituals at the Manakamana temple. Moreover, the rights and dignity of the Limbus were safeguarded during the monarchical period[3] against the Gurkhali culture.

The ethnic and cultural identity in Nepal is multifaceted, shaped by language, identity issues, and the preservation of indigenous cultures and rights. This complexity has transboundary implications, as the interconnectedness of these cultural and ethnic groups can contribute to irritants in bilateral relations. For instance, Nepalese authorities often perceive India's suggestions for crafting an inclusive constitution that accommodates the demands of minority groups, particularly those of the Madhesi, as an unwarranted intervention in internal affairs. Similarly, the constitution drafting process experienced delays due to Chinese opposition to ethnic-based federalism, which exacerbated existing ethnic fault lines within Nepal. Concurrently, both India and China harbour suspicions—albeit independently—regarding the influence of Western-funded international non-governmental organisations (INGOs) in exacerbating identity politics in the region. In this context, this chapter examines the ethno-cultural structure to elucidate the dynamics of identity politics in Nepal.

## Topography

Geography has profoundly influenced the ethno-cultural frameworks and internal political dynamics of Nepal. Geographically, the country is broadly classified into four primary landscapes: the upper Himalayas, the mid-Himalayas, the Siwalik range, and the Terai plains. The upper Himalayan region predominantly features snow-capped areas, where agricultural opportunities are severely limited. Consequently, this region experiences sparse population density, and it has been dependent on other regions for food and other basic amenities. The administrative districts within these areas are primarily inhabited by indigenous nationalities.

The mid-Himalayan region, encompassing the Mahabharat range with an elevation of 4,877 meters, constitutes approximately 64 percent of the total land area. To the south, the lower Churia or Siwalik range extends from an altitude of 610 meters to 1,524 meters. This area is predominantly inhabited by various indigenous hill communities, as well as numerous upper-caste groups residing in the hills.

The Terai region, characterised by a width of approximately 26 to 32 kilometers and a maximum altitude of 305 meters, constitutes about 17 percent of the total land area of Nepal. Kechanakawal, the lowest point in the country, situated at an altitude of 70 meters, is located in the Jhapa district of the eastern Terai.[4] According to the 2011 census, over 51 percent of Nepal's total population resides in this region, which encompasses 20 southern districts. In contrast to the upper and mid-Himalayan regions, the Terai is densely populated and offers numerous livelihood opportunities. Besides the Tharu and other agrarian cultural groups[5]—commonly referred to as Madhesis by the hill Nepalis—a significant proportion of the population comprises migrants from the hill and mountain regions, driven by various factors, including political decisions, rehabilitation of victims of natural disasters, and economic opportunities.

## The Intermingling of Ethnic Groups

Nepal represents a confluence of diverse castes and ethnic groups affiliated with the Tibeto-Burman and Indo-Aryan linguistic families. This diversity reflects the historical waves of migration that have transpired over the past 2,000 years from both northern and southern regions.[6] Despite the intermingling that has occurred among the various groups, they exhibit considerable variation in terms of cultural adaptations, having synthesised elements of Animism, Buddhism, and Hinduism acquired through historical cultural exchanges.

Furthermore, the resettlement of hill and mountain communities in the Terai region since the 1960s has introduced a new dimension to the social landscape, resulting in an extraordinarily heterogeneous and complex population in the Terai. Additionally, a porous border to the south has historically facilitated the free movement of populations between Nepal and India. Consequently, small geographical distances have engendered significant disparities in social contexts—whereas certain areas may exhibit relatively homogeneous populations aligned with a specific ethnic group, thereby creating local majorities that constitute national minorities, other regions may display a pronounced heterogeneity in their demographic composition.[7]

## Structure of Ethnic Groups

The topography of Nepal significantly influences the distribution of its cultural and ethnic groups, as well as their associated customs and practices. According to the 2011 census, the population of Nepal is approximately 28 million, with a growth rate of 1.35 per annum. The highest population density is observed in the Kathmandu district, with 4,416 individuals per square kilometer. In contrast, the Manang district has the lowest density, at just 3 individuals per square kilometer. The national average population density stands at 180 individuals per square kilometer, an increase from 157 in 2001.[8]

According to the 2011 census, there were 1,265 distinct castes and ethnic groups identified. The Chhetri group is the most populous, comprising 16.6 percent (4,398,053) of the total population, followed by the Brahman-Hill at 12.2 percent (3,226,903), Magar at 7.1 percent (1,887,733), Tharu at 6.6 percent (1,737,470), Tamang at 5.8 percent (1,539,830), and Newar at 5 percent (1,321,933). All other castes and ethnic groups collectively account for less than five percent of the total population individually. This demographic composition reflects Nepal's complex societal fabric where no single group holds a dominant majority.[9]

As Nepal is a multi-linguistic state, there are 123 languages spoken as mother tongues and 90 percent of these languages are spoken by indigenous nationalities. Nepali is spoken as mother tongue by 44.6 percent (11,826,953) of the total population followed by Maithili (11.7 percent 3,092,530), Bhojpuri (6.0 percent; 1,584,958), Tharu (5.8 percent; 1,529,875), Tamang (5.1 percent; 1,353,311), etc. Despite this, Nepali has been declared as the only official language. Under the 2015 Constitution, the Language Commission on 06 September 2021, recommended 11 different languages[10] to be used as official languages apart from Nepali.[11] Similarly, there are ten types of religion reported in the census. Hinduism is followed by 81.3 percent (21,551,492) of the population while Buddhism by 9 percent (2,396,099) and Islam by 4.4 percent (1,162,370).[12]

East Asian mixed individuals, alongside Indo-Aryans, predominantly inhabit the mountainous and hilly regions of the country, while Tibetans reside in the central and western areas of Nepal. The Chhetris and Brahmins, collectively referred to as Khas Arya or upper caste groups, constitute approximately 29-30 percent of the total population. These caste groups have historically been the most influential within the Nepali state structure, including in the realms of bureaucracy, the military, and political parties. Primarily residing in mid-hill urban areas, these groups are dispersed largely throughout the central mid-hill regions. Given the diverse ethnic, caste, and linguistic groups that are interspersed across the country, no single caste, linguistic, or religious group monopolises a specific geographic area.[13]

The Madhesi, recognised as a significant cultural identity, constitutes approximately 19 to 21 percent of the total population in the Terai region. However, this group is not homogeneous; it is fragmented along various caste and sub-caste lines. The Tharu community represents the largest ethnic group in the Terai, accounting for 6.6 percent of the overall Nepali population dispersed throughout the region. Furthermore, indigenous nationalities comprise a majority in 27 out of the 75 districts of Nepal.[14]

## *Ethnic Composition*

The ethnic composition of Nepal can be delineated into three principal overlapping categories: (i) hierarchical caste-structured groups (jats) and egalitarian ethnic groups (Janjatis); (ii) high caste or ritually 'pure' castes versus low, ritually 'impure untouchable' castes (Dalits); and (iii) Pahadis and Madhesis. Significant cultural disparities exist not only between caste and ethnic groups but also between Pahadis (hill dwellers) and Madhesis.[15]

An ADB study noted that the caste groups, referred to as Jats, are predominantly of Caucasoid descent and communicate in various Indo-European languages, including Nepali, Maithili, and Bhojpuri. In contrast, the ethnic groups are primarily of Mongoloid heritage, utilising various Tibeto-Burman languages such as Tamang, Gurung, Newar, and Magar, and adhere to a range of religious beliefs, including Buddhism, Animism, and Kirant, alongside Hinduism.[16]

The aforementioned study also identified a hierarchical structure among castes in terms of ritual purity. With the exception of the Newars, other ethnic groups in Nepal exhibit an egalitarian social organisation. Within caste-structured groups, a fundamental division exists between 'pure' castes, including Brahmin, Chhetri, and Vaisya, and the 'untouchable' castes, such as Kami, Sarki, Chyame/Chamars, and Damai, collectively referred to as Dalits. Notably, under the influence of the Hindu caste system, certain ethnic groups perceive Dalits as 'untouchables.'[17] This observation suggests two significant points: Firstly, the ethnic groups in Nepal have not entirely repudiated Hinduism, contrary to interpretations by some Western scholars. Secondly, both Janajatis and the so-called upper-caste Hindus engage in nature worship, albeit with some ritualistic variations at the local level.

The division between Dalits and all other groups, including 'upper' castes and ethnic communities, is as fundamental as the dichotomy between caste-structured Hindus and various ethnic groups. The Pahadis encompass a diverse range of populations, including the Nepali-speaking Parbatiya castes, as well as ethnic groups such as Tamang, Magar, and Rai, each possessing distinct languages and cultural practices. Additionally, there are five indigenous groups originating from the hills, including those from the high mountainous regions that maintain close cultural and social affinities with populations from the Tibet Autonomous Region (TAR) of China.[18]

Figure 1 illustrates that no ethnic or caste group in Nepal possesses an absolute majority, either geographically or in terms of population size. The dominant groups, which exhibit both extensive geographical distribution and significant numerical strength, overshadow the minority groups, which tend to be dispersed throughout the country. Consequently, the former has emerged as the predominant community.

**Figure 1: 20 Major Ethnic Groups in Nepal by Population (2011)**

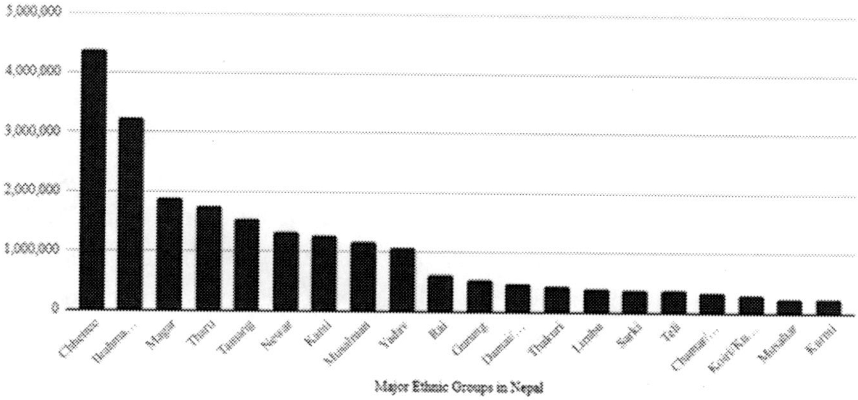


*Source: Madhesi Youth*[19]

While the aggregate population of indigenous nationalities, cultural groups, and other ethnic minorities may exceed that of the two predominant upper caste groups, the former has not succeeded in coalescing into a unified force. This is largely due to their dispersed geographical distribution, inter- and intra-ethnic group divisions, and the prevailing sentiments of superiority among Janajatis toward the Madhesi. Consequently, the indigenous nationalities and other minority groups have struggled to effectively oppose the dominant ruling classes and to present themselves as a cohesive political entity thus far.

Conversely, the Madhesis, who initiated their movement in the 1950s, managed to present themselves as a cohesive political entity due to their concentration within a specific geographical region. The Madhesi organisations and groups that engaged in the identity movement against the State subsequently transitioned into political parties within the region. In the post-constitutional era, two Madhesi-based parties—the Rastriya Janata Party-Nepal (RJP-N) and the Samajwadi Party Nepal—emerged as governing entities in the Madhes Pradesh province. This development was facilitated by the Madhesis' dominance in both limited geographical scope and numerical representation within the province, particularly in the Terai.

Additionally, a nuanced analysis of the demographic composition across the seven provinces would be instrumental in evaluating the influence of marginalised groups on the future of Nepali polity. This exploration could also address their outstanding demands, whether through amendments to the new constitution or through organised street protests.

## Ethnographic Representation at the Provincial Level

At both the national and provincial levels, the ethnographic configuration favours Chhetris and hill Bahuns, followed by indigenous nationalities such as Rai, Limbu, Tamang, Magar, Tharu, Newar, Muslims, and Kami. Chhetris constitute the ethnic majority in Province One. Consequently, the unity of Chhetri and Brahman populations will likely secure a majority in this region, unless the Rai, Limbu, Tamang, and Magar communities collaborate to achieve a majority on social and political matters. The intricate social structure within the province has contributed to the protracted process of renaming the province. In the post-constitutional period, the position of Chief Minister (CM) was predominantly held by minority groups, even though upper caste groups were prevalent within the province. Although the influence of caste has historically played a diminished role in the internal political dynamics, this trend has shifted in the post-constitutional era due to the implementation of inclusivity and proportional representation systems. Caste and ethnicity have become pivotal criteria in the formation of government within this province.

The Yadav community has emerged as the predominant caste in Madhesh Pradesh, with Muslims constituting the second most influential group. Smaller communities, such as the Tharus, are geographically dispersed and fragmented. The existing tensions rooted in geography, regional disparities, and community identities between the Madhesis and the Hill populations have led the lesser Madhes-based caste groups to align with the Yadav-led political coalition. In contrast, as Muslims typically do not identify as Madhesi, their support tends to be heterogeneous, oscillating between parties from both the Hill and Madhes regions.

Although the Yadav community constitutes the predominant caste group in this province, both Muslims and Brahmins have gained advantages by securing pivotal political positions, attributed to the fragmentation among Yadav leaders. The provincial government formed in 2017 was primarily dominated by the Yadavs. In a strategic move to maintain their dominance in provincial politics while marginalising upper-caste leaders, Yadav leaders appointed a Muslim as Chief Minister.

Besides that, certain Madhesi leaders are engaging with indigenous nationalities to establish a united front aimed at sustaining their protests against the Kathmandu elites. Their goal is to address unresolved demands by advocating for amendments to the Constitution.

Bagmati Province, formerly known as Province No. 3, is predominantly inhabited by the Tamang, Hill-Bahun-Hill, Chhetri, and Newar ethnic groups. The Chhetris and Brahmins, as representatives of the upper caste, often assert their influence and resist the predominance of other groups within this province. Their identification as upper caste positions them to prevent the ascendancy of alternative forces, thereby facilitating a Chhetri-Brahmin alliance that prevails in the region. The Newar community also constitutes a significant demographic in this province, although they do not represent a clear majority. Notably, Newars have historically maintained closer ties with the ruling classes of Kathmandu compared to other ethnic groups.[20] Despite the numerical superiority of minority communities in the province, a lack of cohesion and fragmentation among these ethnic groups has enabled upper-caste groups to dominate provincial politics. Furthermore, in certain instances, other indigenous groups do not regard the Newars as a marginalised ethnic group due to their historical affiliations with the ruling elite.

In Province 4, Hill-Bahun constitutes the largest caste group. Similar to other provinces, Chhetris and Brahmins function collectively, exhibiting a disproportionately higher representation in the upper echelons of state services. While the Magar and Gurung communities are significantly represented in this province, the ruling class has frequently sought to divide them by providing lucrative positions.[21]

In light of the significant dominance of Tharus in province number 5, now designated as Lumbini Province, there has been a concerted demand for the establishment of a Tharuhat autonomous state. The Tharu community perceives marginalisation by the state and exploitation by the Chhetri, Magar, and Bahun groups within this region. The Magar, another prominent ethnic group, lacks a clear majority and is dispersed throughout the mid-hill districts. Due to the existing inter-community tensions between the Tharus and Magars, coupled with ineffective leadership, Chhetris and Brahmans have come to dominate the state's governance framework. Several ethnic groups in this region have historically been categorised as "untouchables," particularly the Tharus.

In response to dissatisfaction with the Constitution and the persistent exploitation faced by the Tharus, Resham Chaudhary established the Nagarik Unmukti Party in January 2022.[22]

Chhetri and Bahun exhibit pronounced dominance in the Karnali and Sudurpaschim provinces. The Tharus maintain a notable presence in Sudurpaschim province; however, they have yet to secure a majority in the provincial assembly, primarily due to the upper caste's demographic advantage and elevated levels of political consciousness. Other ethnic groups are often perceived as marginal or minority populations due to their dispersed distribution throughout the region. Moreover, within these predominant areas, the upper-caste hill elites have adeptly exploited inter- and intra-ethnic divisions to further their interests.

Consequently, it has been observed that in seven states, the combination of Bahun and Chhetri groups has been predominant in both state and political structures, with the exception of Madhesh Pradesh. This trend is likely to persist in the future despite the introduction of the new constitution. Although ethnic groups possess a significant presence in provinces 3, 4, 5, and 7, the Bahun and Chhetri coalition is expected to surpass them in governance matters. Furthermore, the Bahun and Chhetri communities are poised to maintain dominance within the state apparatus despite being numerically inferior in certain provinces.

## Minorities and Major Political Parties

The leadership of the two predominant political parties in Nepal—the Nepali Congress and the CPN-UML—is predominantly composed of individuals from the Bahun and Chhetri castes. Additionally, organisations representing indigenous peoples are both directly and indirectly linked to the major front organisations of these parties. For instance, the Nepal Federation of Indigenous Nationalities (NEFIN), which is spearheaded by leaders from indigenous communities, has affiliations with both the Nepali Congress and the CPN-UML. A similar dynamic is observed with the newly established Adivasi Janajati Rastriya Andolan (AJRA).[23] The Maoist party exhibits analogous trends, with its leadership predominantly comprising upper-caste individuals. The Rastriya Swatantra Party (RSP), formed in 2022, have a similar structure.

Furthermore, the Rashtriya Prajatantra Party (RPP) has historically been led by upper-caste leaders. A notable instance illustrating this trend is the perception in Nepal regarding the resignation of former party chairperson Kamal Thapa in February 2022; it was widely believed that he stepped down to avoid being led by Rajendra Prasad Lingden, a Janajati leader. This reflects a new pattern within Nepali politics where upper-caste-dominated parties are headed by leaders from Janajati backgrounds.

## Poor Coordination between Janajati and Madhesi

The Khas Arya have predominantly influenced Nepali politics in the post-constitution era, primarily due to inadequate coordination and unity among marginalised groups such as Janajatis/Adibasis and Madhesis. Despite both groups being victims of systemic discrimination by the Khas Arya-controlled State, they have infrequently united in opposition to the State. The underlying reasons for this phenomenon may include the following:

1. Both groups are victims of cultural, caste, and class discrimination; however, the intensity of discrimination experienced by the Madhesis is significantly greater. This disparity may be attributed to the Terai region, where the Madhesis predominantly reside, sharing both a border and cultural ties with India. The sociocultural differences between the Hill communities and those in the Terai region have played a crucial role in this dynamic.
2. Indigenous communities have historically been integrated into state structures, such as the Nepali Army, bureaucracy, and law enforcement, albeit at a proportionally lower rate compared to their overall population and, notably, in contrast to the Khas Aryas. Consequently, the Khas Aryas' attitude of contempt towards indigenous peoples was less pronounced than towards the Madhesi community. Crucially, the monarchy engaged influential indigenous leaders and conferred special privileges upon certain Janajati figures within state institutions. This approach mitigated the initial resentment among indigenous peoples towards the monarchy, a phenomenon that has not been observed with the Madhesis.
3. There exists a pronounced perception of the racial distinction between the indigenous populations and the Madhesis, largely attributable to

variations in skin colour. Politically, indigenous nationalities often perceive Madhesis as akin to Indians, particularly due to their advocacy for Hindi as an official language and historical linkages between Janakpur and Ayodhya of India. Both places are popular Hindu pilgrimages. Notably, at the community level, there is a prevailing animosity of indigenous nationalities towards the hill upper castes, indicating a complex interplay of identity and perception within the region.[24]

4. Most significantly, the severity of state discrimination was somewhat mitigated by addressing certain grievances of the Janajatis in the 1990 Constitution. Nevertheless, the Madhesis persist as the most marginalised community.
5. Nepali nationalism frequently articulates a critical stance toward India. This phenomenon is evident across the hill regions of Nepal, transcending caste and ethnic divisions. Long-standing state discrimination has compelled the Madhesi community to seek assistance from India in addressing cultural and regional marginalisation. However, indigenous nationalities often perceive the Madhesis as a pro-Indian constituency. This sentiment is predominantly manifested at the leadership level, particularly among individuals leading the front organisations of the CPN-UML.
6. One of the significant contributions of the Madhesi movement in 2007 was its successful resistance to the longstanding practice of co-opting Madhesi leaders by mainstream political parties. In contrast, the Janajatis have struggled to overcome this trend of co-optation, despite possessing a robust organisation such as the Nepal Federation of Indigenous Nationalities (NEFIN) and engaging in multiple resistance movements against the state since 1769. Regrettably, similar to the Khas Aryas, there is a prevailing perception that Madhesis are merely supported by India, rather than acknowledging the underlying factors contributing to the emergence of Madhesis as a crucial stakeholder in Nepali politics.[25]

## State Discrimination

The marginalisation of indigenous nationalities commenced in 1769 with the unification of tribal leaders under Prithvi Narayan Shah. The indigenous communities vehemently protested when the Shah, followed by the Rana rulers, instituted a new system of landholding, revenue collection, and civil code in 1854. This issue was eventually addressed through the incorporation of indigenous nationalities into state administration, the military, and through the assimilation of Hindu cultural norms with indigenous traditions. Notably, some indigenous groups were permitted to maintain their cultural practices and landholding customs.[26]

In the post-Prithvi Narayan Shah period, the dynamics of discrimination shifted significantly. During the Rana regime, this discrimination intensified as the state struggled to exert control over local administrations amidst political rivalries within the palace. Additionally, the persistent demands for separate and independent ethnic states by certain indigenous groups in eastern Nepal may also have contributed to the evolving situation.[27]

The state's discrimination against indigenous peoples and other cultural groups became evident during the Panchayat regime. Constitutionally, Nepal became a Hindu Kingdom under the Panchayat regime in 1962, further marginalising Indigenous communities. Article 20 described the king as an 'Adherent of Aryan Culture and Hindu Religion'. Moreover, despite enacting the New Legal Code (Naya Muluki Ain) in 1963, the pro-established castes, including Newars, dominated society and state organs. The people's resistance to the 1963 Act reflected the continuation of discriminatory proactive during the Panchayat regime.[28]

Broadly, two distinct forms of discrimination were perpetuated through the targeting of cultural and regional issues. During this period, a series of reforms, including cultural initiatives, were introduced to address the regime's insecurity in response to the burgeoning pro-democratic movement in Nepal and India's support for it. The authorities were particularly concerned with the establishment of the Nepal Tarai Congress (NTC) in 1951, led by Bedanand Jha, who advocated for various initiatives, including the designation of Hindi as a state language. Additionally, given the contentious relationship with India, King Mahendra harbored suspicions regarding India's rising influence and its ethno-cultural connections across the border. Consequently, King Mahendra promoted the ideology of *Ek Raja, Ek Bhesh, Ek Bhasa, Ek Desh* (One King, One Dress, One Language, One Nation). Both Madhesi and indigenous groups were adversely affected by this policy, as they were compelled to adopt new attire, a new language—Khas Kura/Nepali—and new festivals.[29]

Another approach involved the denial of citizenship and economic opportunities within state institutions by characterising the Madhesi as pro-Indian and as illegal immigrants from India. During the Panchayat period, the authorities actively sought to implement demographic alterations by encouraging higher-caste individuals from the Hill region to resettle in the Terai area, in a bid to undermine the citizenship claims of the Madhesis.

The discriminatory policies implemented by the monarchy were met with vigorous resistance from the affected communities, who organised street protests, rallies, and sought support from democratic forces both domestically and internationally. Unfortunately, despite both indigenous nationalities and Madhesis being victims of the same policies, they engaged in separate struggles. The impacted groups established ethno-cultural associations and coalitions to express their solidarity and unity. As public protests intensified in the late 1980s advocating for a new constitution, these communities extended their support and engaged in negotiations with democratic forces to ensure that their concerns were addressed within the new constitutional framework.

The state implemented a divide-and-rule strategy by addressing certain demands of the indigenous nationalities while mainly neglecting the language-related concerns of the Madhesi community. Furthermore, it fostered an atmosphere where indigenous groups were encouraged to be critical of the Madhesis.

## Conclusion

Despite the increasing involvement of the state against the interests of ethno-cultural groups, Nepal did not experience ethnic conflict at the community level until the adoption of the 1990 Constitution. Initially, conflicts were primarily confined to narrative construction.[30] The Maoists repudiated the 1990 Constitution and effectively polarised society along caste, religious, and ethnic lines to garner support from marginalised groups for their insurrection against the state. This escalation culminated in the onset of ethnic conflict, marked by targeted attacks on upper-caste individuals who occupied administrative positions. From 1996 to 2006, thousands of civilians and security personnel were victimised, being labelled as 'class enemies'.

The marginalised groups achieved success by integrating their demands following a decade of support for the Maoists. The 2008 Interim Constitution addressed nearly all the requests of these marginalised groups. However, it was subsequently rejected by the major political parties that had backed them throughout the 1990s.

In the post-peace process era, certain political factions endeavoured to exacerbate divisions between the Tharus and Madhesis in the Terai region during the anti-constitution agitation of 2015. These same groups also sought to provoke the Muslim community to advocate for a distinct non-Madhesi identity. This behaviour underscores the persistent ethno-cultural discrimination entrenched within society and the mindsets of the ruling elites, who appear reluctant to share power with marginalised groups.

## NOTES

1 The Shahs' of Nepal identify them as Thakuri. The Thakuris', although belong to the Chhetri clan, consider themselves as the rulers or superior than other Chhetris.

2 Gerard Toffin, "The Janajati/Adivasi Movement in Nepal: Myths and Realities of Indigeneity," *Sociological Bulletin*, Vol. 58, No.1, January-April 2009.

3 Author's discussion with Yubaraj Ghimire, a Kathmandu based senior journalist and political analyst, over phone on 24 September 2021.

4 Nepal Profile, Ministry of Foreign Affairs, Nepal, https://mofa.gov.np/about-nepal/nepal-profile/, accessed on 24 September 2021. Also see https://www.himalayastrek.com/information/informationgeography-of-nepal/, (accessed on 24 September 2021).

5 Both the Tharus and plain-caste groups also known as Madhesi (Yadav, Kurmi, Brahmin, Bania, etc.) claim themselves as the autochthony. Madhesi is a political identity of the cultural groups-Awadhi, Bhojpuri, Maithili, and Hindi language speaking people-who live in the Terai regions of Nepal. This identity was formed by these groups over a period of time (mostly in 1950s onwards) to fight against the systematic State policies to impose hill-upper caste cultures on these groups and depriving them from preserve and protect their culture.

6 Gerard Toffin, no. 2, p. 35.

7 Rajendra Pradhan and Ava Shrestha, "Ethnic and Caste Diversity: Implications for Development," Working Paper Series No. 4, Nepal Resident Mission, ADB, June 2005.

8 Census 2011, Government of Nepal.

9 Gehanath Poudel, "Relation between Caste and Household Level Decision of Gender," *The International Journal Of Humanities & Social Studies*, Vol 3, Issue 1, January 2015, p. 126.

10 Maithili and Limbu for Province 1; Bhojpuri, Maithili and Bajjika for Province 2; Tamang and Nepal Bhasa for Bagmati; Magar, Gurung and Bhojpuri for Gandaki; Tharu and Awadhi for Lumbini; Magar for Karnali; and Dotyali and Tharu for Sudur Paschim.

11 "Adoption of official languages recommended for provinces challenging, experts say", *The Kathmandu Post*, 18 September 2021.

12 Central Bureau of Statistics, National Planning Commission, Government of Nepal, http://cbs.gov.np/image/data/Population/National%20Report/National%20Report.pdf, pp. 1-8, (accessed on 24 September 2021).

13 Ibid.

14 Lai Ming Lam, "Land, Livelihood and Rana Tharu Identity Transformations in Far-Western Nepal", Vol.31, No.1, 2012.

15 E. Cedamon, I. Nuberg & K. K. Shrestha, "How understanding of rural households' diversity can inform agroforestry and community forestry programs in Nepal" *Australian Forestry*, Vol. 80, No. 3, 2017, p. 153.

16 Rajendra Pradhan and Ava Shrestha, "Ethnic and Caste Diversity: Implications for Development", Working Paper Series No. 4, ADB, Nepal Resident Mission June 2005, p.3.

17 Ibid.

18 Ibid.

19 Madhesi Youth is a digital platform for young Nepalis to express themselves. It offers fact-based, data-driven and independent analysis on issues that affects Nepalis in general and marginalized groups in particular. For further information visit, http://www.madhesiyouth.com. The website claims that it has used data from Nepal's Central Bureau of Statistics (accessed on 26 March 2021). For details see https://www.madhesiyouth.com/data/federal-states-in-nepal/ethnic-groups-in-nepal/(accessed on 11 April 2022).

20 Krishana Hachhethu, "State Building in Nepal: Creating a Functional State", Enabling State Programme, 2009, p. 86.

21 "Ethnic Groups in Nepal," *Madhesi Youth*. Other details about the website is not available. For details visit http://www.madhesiyouth.com/data/federal-states-in-nepal/ethnic-groups-in-nepal/state-6/, (accessed on 24 September 2021).

22 Ibid.

23 AJRA was formed in 2013 under the leadership of former civil society activist Padmaratna Tuladhar.

24 The author's interview with Jay Nishant in Kathmandu in September 2023. Mr. Nishant is a political activist and researcher based in Terai.

25 Author's telephonic and personal interactions with Janajatis and Madhesis in New Delhi and Kathmandu.

26 Mahendra Lawoti, "Contentious Politics in Democratizing Nepal", in *Contentious Politics and Democratization in Nepal*, Mahendra Lawoti (ed.), Sage Publications, New Delhi, 2007, p. 24. Also see Susan Hangen, "Creating a "New Nepal": The Ethnic Dimension", Policy Studies 34, West-West Center, Washington, 2007, p. 08.

27 Susan Hangen, "Creating a "New Nepal": The Ethnic Dimension", Policy Studies 34, West-West Center, Washington, 2007, p. 15.

28 Hari P. Bhattarai, "Making and Inclusive Constitution in Plural State: Issues of Identity and Representation", in *Democratic Constitution Making*, Hari P. Bhattrai and Jhalak Subedi (eds.), Nepal South Asia Center, Kathmandu, 2007, p. 58-59.

29 Manjeet Mishra, "Recognizing diversity" Opinion, *myRepublica*, 2018, https://myrepublica.nagariknetwork.com/news/recognizing-diversity/ (accessed on 20 October 2024). Also see Pranab Kharel & Gaurab KC, "Reassessing Panchayat", Opinion, *myRepublica*, 2019, https://myrepublica.nagariknetwork.com/news/reassessing-panchayat/ (accessed on 20 October 2024). Dipendra Jha, "Federal Nepal: Trials and Tribulations", AAKAR Books, Delhi, 2018.

30 Author's interactions over phone with some Madhes based political analysts, who requested to remain anonymous.

# *Chapter Two*

## *The Janajati Movement: A Struggle for Land, Identify and Proportional Representation*

The Janajati Movement in Nepal represents a significant socio-political and economic mobilisation driven by indigenous groups rooted in their quest for land rights, cultural identity, and proportional representation within the state's governance structures. This movement has emerged as a response to the deeply entrenched historical patterns of systemic exclusion and socio-economic marginalisation that have long affected Janajati communities since the formation of Nepal under the Shah dynasty. It signifies a distinct rights movement within the framework of identity politics and post-colonial theories, which critique historical injustices and state-imposed inequities.[1]

The movement's emphasis on land rights goes beyond just economic concerns, viewing land as essential to the cultural survival and heritage of indigenous peoples. This perspective connects land with identity and autonomy, framing the struggle as one for both material resources and cultural rights. Thus, the movement is embedded in a discourse that links territorial rights to the preservation of indigenous existence, challenging the state's historical erasure of these communities.

Despite experiencing seven constitutions over the past 70 years in Nepal's modern political landscape, a significant portion of the population continues to face political and cultural marginalisation, as well as economic impoverishment. Approximately 21 percent of the populace resides below the poverty line, with a per capita income of merely US$240. The pervasive poverty, coupled with entrenched discrimination based on gender, ethnicity, region, and caste, has engendered heightened frustration and disillusionment among these communities. The protests against state oppression and systemic injustices perpetrated against indigenous nationalities can be traced back to 1769.

Three primary factors have been identified as contributing to the country's ethnic diversity, structured hierarchy, and socio-economic inequality. These include: (i) the migration of various groups into Nepal, (ii) the political unification of these groups into a cohesive nation-state by the Nepali-speaking populations historically referred to as Khas Arya and currently known as Parbatiyas, and (iii) the implementation of state laws and policies.[2]

Modern-day Nepal has been shaped by the migration of various ethnic groups over the past 2000 years. Ethnic communities such as the Gurung, Limbu, and Sherpa, who speak Tibeto-Burman languages, migrated at different intervals from regions across the Himalayas. The Newars, another Tibeto-Burman-speaking ethnic group, have resided in the Kathmandu Valley for over two millennia and practice both Hinduism and Buddhism. Additionally, the Nepali-speaking Parbatiya migrated into Nepal from the western and southern regions over several centuries.[3]

In the Terai plains, diverse caste and cultural groups, such as the Tharu and Madhesi, have inhabited the region for over two millennia. The Madhesi community is often perceived as illegal immigrants from India, despite their historical presence predating the demarcation of political boundaries between India and Nepal. These distinct groups, each characterised by unique languages, religions, and cultures, settled in various regions of Nepal, establishing separate yet fluid political units, primarily consisting of small chiefdoms and principalities. Additionally, larger political entities such as the Lichhavi and, later, the Malla kingdoms based in the Kathmandu Valley, the Khas kingdom in the west, and various confederations of ethnic groups, including the Magars and Gurungs in central Nepal, along with the Limbus in the east, also emerged.[4]

## Political Unification and its Implications

In the latter half of the 18th century, Prithvi Narayan Shah, the sovereign of the small principality of Gorkha, along with his immediate successors, galvanised support from Brahmins, Chhetris, and the Magar and Gurung communities to conquer and politically consolidate various small political entities into the Gorkha kingdom, which is now recognised as Nepal.[5] This political unification of the numerous Janajati principalities and the subsequent nation-building process had significant implications for the diverse groups involved, including the 'Nepalisation' of the region, transformations in social relations, and alterations in access to and control over economic and political resources, particularly concerning land and administration.[6]

During this period, Nepalese society was characterised by legally sanctioned hierarchical structures, resulting in the social exclusion of 'lower' castes, women, ethnic communities, and non-Nepali speaking linguistic groups from state administration and land rights. Hindu religious law, along with increasingly prevalent customary law, further perpetuated these inequities and exclusions. Most fertile land and other economic resources were primarily controlled by the upper-caste *Parbatiyas* (hill-upper castes), with notable exceptions such as the communal land (kipat) managed by the Limbus in eastern Nepal, and the trans-Himalayan trade overseen by the Thakalis.[7]

The ethnic groups and lower castes constituted the majority of the labour force and services, frequently under compulsion, serving as tenants and cultivators, artisans, porters, and general labourers. Conversely, the 'upper' castes, as governing entities, exerted control over the political and administrative frameworks, albeit with some exceptions at the local level among ethnic groups, such as the *subbas* within the Limbus.[8] Krishna Bhattachana observed that "In the last 230 years one caste (Bahun-Chhetri), one religion (Hindu), one culture (Hindu), one language (Khas Nepali) and one sex (male) has been dominant in a multi-caste and ethnic, multi-religious, multi-cultural and multi-lingual society...tribal or indigenous peoples are marginalised, displaced and suppressed by the ruling, dominant group for the last two and half centuries."[9]

## Origin of the Janajati Movement

The Janajati movement in Nepal represents a significant protest against the state's abrogation of the traditional land-holding system of Janajatis (Kipat) and the imposition of Gorkhali culture on these communities following the political unification of 1769. This movement emerged in response to a series of discriminatory and exploitative policies enacted by the state, which marginalised the Janajatis and undermined their cultural heritage.[10] The ethnic and caste groups exhibited strong opposition to the encroachment of their traditional systems by new cultural and political forces. The initial instance of ethnic resistance against the state was documented in 1770 at Pallo Kirat in the eastern region of Nepal, led by the Limbus. This was subsequently followed by the Majh Kirnat rebellion in 1773 in the Dudhkosi Arun area of eastern Nepal, which persisted until 1781. In total, there were over 18 significant rebellions by various ethnic groups in Nepal against Gurkha cultural hegemony up until 1950.[11]

Between 1950 and 1990, the resistance of ethnic groups against the Gurkhali culture and political system manifested through a network of clandestine ethnic associations. During this period, more than a dozen protest movements were initiated by various organisations, including peasant, student, and professional groups. Additionally, individual activists engaged in significant efforts to evade state repression. Notably, there was a lack of coordinated initiatives aimed at protesting the state during this timeframe.

### *Organised Movements*

Nepal Federation of Indigenous Nationalities (NEFIN) was established following Nepal's adoption of a multi-party democratic system under the 1990 Constitution. Since its inception, NEFIN has played a pivotal role in various ethno-political initiatives. In 1996, NEFIN compiled a comprehensive list of 61 'nationalities' encompassing all ethnic minorities in Nepal. This list was later revised to 59 and received governmental recognition in 2002.[12] The movement transitioned into a systematic and organised entity under the NEFIN. This platform provided the previously marginalized and voiceless Jajajatis with an avenue to articulate their concerns in a democratic manner. Furthermore, NEFIN served to engender a political identity and foster unity among the marginalized ethnic groups.

Consequently, it indicates that Nepali indigenous communities opposed the state for broadly three reasons. First, the imposition of Bahun and Chhetri culture, religion, and language upon them. Second, the hegemony of Bahuns and Chhetris over minority groups by exerting control over the state apparatus, which led to perceptions of political and administrative marginalisation. Third, the state displaced them from their traditional living areas, forests, and ancestral lands, severely impacting their livelihoods. The indigenous tribes experienced dispossession and displacement from their forests and communally held lands. Prior to the territorial "unification" initiated by King Prithvi Narayan Shah, indigenous peoples maintained their own autonomous "principalities" with landholding arrangements tailored to local conditions. The adoption of the Birta and Jagir land tenure systems enabled rulers to possess or reallocate land at their discretion.[13] Nevertheless, some indigenous groups continue to depend significantly on forest resources for their livelihoods, while others have become Sukumbasis (landless), relocating to urban areas or India in search of labour opportunities.[14] Although the new constitution has addressed political and administrative marginalisation to a certain extent, the other two factors remain largely unaddressed. According to Mukta S. Lama-Tamang, "In Jana Andolan II (JA-II or People's Movement II), the Nepali people expressed their aspirations to end all forms of autocracy and to establish democracy."[15] The indigenous nationalities played a pivotal role in JA-II.

Despite strong organisational support and external assistance, particularly from European Union member states and NGOs, NEFIN struggled to exert pressure on Kathmandu to adopt an inclusive constitution. Tewa Dolpo noted that "The Janajati movement comprises several leaders who were also affiliated with mainstream parties, even while occupying significant positions within NEFIN."[16] Notably, NEFIN experienced internal divisions due to its engagement with upper-caste-dominated political entities. Consequently, the Janajati movement, and NEFIN specifically, diminished in relevance as the Maoists initiated a people's armed revolution against the state in 1996, incorporating all the demands of Janajatis in their 40-point agenda presented to the government. The Maoists also established both cultural and political fronts for marginalised groups.

## Janajati Organisations

### *Nepal Federation of Indigenous Nationalities*

Nepal Federation of indigenous Nationalities (NEFIN) was established in 1991 with the primary objective of advocating for the rights and identity of indigenous peoples. The organisation seeks to contribute to the establishment of an equal, equitable, and democratic society. NEFIN operates autonomously and serves as the sole representative umbrella organisation for the 59 indigenous nationalities recognised by the government of Nepal. Comprising 56 distinct indigenous member organisations distributed throughout Nepal, NEFIN features a federal council where both a woman and a man represent their respective organisations. The structure of NEFIN includes 21 portfolios within the secretariat of the federal council (the board), ensuring a minimum of 33 percent representation of women through an electoral process conducted every three years.[17]

The organisation maintains both national and international chapters or networks. It comprises Province Coordination Councils (PCCs), District Coordination Councils (DDCs), Local Coordination Councils (LCCs), as well as entities such as Metropolitan Cities (Mahanagarpalika), Sub-Metropolitan Cities (Upa-Mahanagarpalika), Municipalities (Nagarpalika), Village Executives or Rural Municipalities (Gaunpalika), and Ward Coordination Councils (WCCs). It is aligned with eight distinct indigenous federations, which include sectors such as journalism, youth, student bodies, women's groups, lawyers, filmmakers, individuals with disabilities, and labour organisations. Additionally, the organisation has established 23 international chapters across various countries.[18]

NEFIN acquires funding from both domestic and international sources. The organisation's reputation as an apolitical entity has frequently been scrutinised, particularly given that several of its senior officials have had affiliations with prominent political parties in Nepal. Additionally, some former leaders of the organisation have participated in electoral contests.

## *Challenges before the NEFIN*

This indicates a notable overlap between political engagement and leadership within NEFIN, raising questions regarding the organisation's dedication to Janajati issues. Furthermore, the involvement of certain former high-ranking NEFIN leaders in electoral politics complicates the organisation's claim of being an autonomous advocacy entity. Due to these leaders' associations with major political parties, NEFIN's agenda is often seen as influenced by the priorities of these parties.

Another challenge has been the country's perennial dependence on foreign funding. That again raises questions about its autonomy in its function, operational activities, and agenda settings. For example, NEFIN could not organise any programs in 2012 and 2013 because the Department for International Development (DFID) and other donors abruptly stopped funding it.

NEFIN has also been grappling with other challenges, such as the lack of cohesion in articulating a unified vision, institutional resistance to adopting inclusive policies, and coping with the emergence of rival ethnic organisations such as AJRA.

## *Adivasi Janajati Rastriya Andolan*

Similar to NEIFN, the Adivasi Janajati Rastriya Andolan (AJRA) constituted a coalition of diverse Janajati groups. Established in late 2013, it was spearheaded by former civil society activist Padma Ratna Tuladhar. AJRA functioned as a loose coalition of Janajati leaders, intellectuals, and rights advocates. It broadened its support base by incorporating other marginalised and excluded communities, including Khas, Madhesi, Muslims, and Dalits. AJRA advocated for the establishment of a single ethnic-based federal government comprising at least ten provinces just prior to the promulgation of the constitution. The coalition organised numerous street protests in Kathmandu and other urban areas of Nepal, seeking to foster an alliance between Janajatis and Madhesis.

The establishment of the AJRA during the constitutional drafting process highlighted significant divisions within the NEFIN along ideological, political, and regional lines. Given that NEFIN leaders predominantly aligned with the CPN-UML, which had opposed ethnic-based federalism under the leadership of K P Sharma Oli, it is reported that AJRA was formed with the backing of Pushpa Kamal Dahal to counter the influence of the CPN-UML.

As a politician and human rights activist, Padma Ratna Tuladhar was recognised for his vocal advocacy for an inclusive constitution. Despite his involvement, the AJRA struggled to garner significant support for ethnic-based federalism. Several factors may have contributed to this. Firstly, despite being a former minister, Tuladhar faced opposition from NEFIN leaders who disseminated the notion that a non-political figure should not spearhead a Janajati front. In a media interview, Raj Kumar Lekhi, former chairman of NEFIN, stated, "Tuladhar lacks 'appeal, ability, and honesty' to lead the movement that encompasses various Janajati communities...he turned out to be more like a 'puppet' of UCPN (Maoist) Chairman Pushpa Kamal Dahal. The movement he leads has been benefiting some select political parties, instead of Janajati people."[19] Secondly, given that NEFIN favoured geography and economically based federalism, as proposed by the CPN-UML and the Nepali Congress (NC), this stance was in stark contradiction to AJRA's position on federalism. Thirdly, similar to NEFIN, AJRA's demands and agendas were Janajati-centric, which resulted in minimal appeal or support from the Madhesh-based parties. Consequently, it failed to emerge as a pan-Nepal organisation.

### *Madhesi's Perception of AJRA*

Nepal's Madhesi and Janajati communities exhibit two distinct classifications. The Janajatis residing in urban areas, who are integrated into the administrative and security frameworks, experience relatively less discrimination, and the ruling elite tend to be more comfortable in their presence. For instance, ethnic groups such as the Gurung, Tamang, Rai, Limbu, and Newar have long been engaged in the state apparatus. In contrast, discrimination is notably more pronounced among Janajatis in rural settings, particularly those who lack connection to the ruling establishment. Consequently, the degree of discrimination varies within the same ethnic group, influenced by both geographical location and socio-economic status. A comparable categorisation is applicable to Madhesis and Tharus; however, the level of discrimination remains consistent across these groups.[20]

In this context, the AJRA failed to foster cohesion between intra-ethnic divisions and the sentiments of Janajatis towards the Madhesis. Urban Janajatis, a significant demographic, displayed indifference towards Padma Ratna Tualadhar's campaigns, highlighting a notable disconnect. This apathy can be ascribed to a perceived lack of relevance or direct benefit from Tualadhar's initiatives, which aimed to advocate for local issues and rights. Furthermore, the effort to unite Madhesis and Janajatis under a common cause encountered both practical and psychological barriers. Despite Mr. Tualadhar's commendable reputation as a civil activist and his advocacy for local languages, the proposed alliance between Madhesis and Janajatis did not effectively materialise. This was partly due to entrenched biases and preferences among the hill elites, who exhibited a clear inclination to support Janajatis over Madhesis.[21]

## *Lawyers' Association for Human Rights of Nepalese Indigenous Peoples*

Lawyers' Association for Human Rights of Nepalese Indigenous Peoples (LAHURNIP) is a human rights organisation engaged in advocacy, legal support to the indigenous nationalities and human rights monitoring activities in Nepal. It was established in 1995 by professional Indigenous lawyers.

It generates knowledge on indigenous peoples' rights through evidence-based research, decolonising methodologies, documentation, critical policy analysis, and high-level policy dialogues. This knowledge is disseminated to a broader audience to foster public discourse and advocate for policy reforms aligned with the principles of the UN Declaration on the Rights of Indigenous Peoples (UNDRIP) and International Labour Organisation (ILO) Convention No. 169.[22]

### *Vision*

It envisions a scenario in which the indigenous peoples of Nepal fully exercise their collective rights, including the right to self-determination, ownership and control over their lands, territories, and resources, as well as the preservation of their customary rights and justice systems, and self-determined development. In this envisioned state, Indigenous Peoples are liberated from all forms of colonisation, discrimination, racism, and hegemony, and actively participate in decision-making processes at all levels of governance through representatives of their own choosing. They are empowered to realise their full potential, enjoying equal rights, dignity, and a robust democratic environment.[23]

However, during the constitution-drafting process, LAHURNIP expanded its geographical and community outreach programs beyond ethnic groups. LAHURNIP monitored the situation of human rights in hills, and Terai-Madhes as well. It extended support to the marginalised caste groups of Terai. For example, it monitored the situation of human rights during the Terai-Madhes movement and aftermath of the Tikapur incident in Kailali district. The incident had attracted global media and human rights organisations. Around nine people—eight police officers and a toddler—were killed in a faceoff between Tharu protestors and the police in Tikapur, Kailali district, on 24 August 2015. Media reports said Police had filed cases against 58 people for their involvement in the Tikapur incident. The police arrested 27 of them, while 31 others were on the run. The arrested persons were reportedly tortured and were forced to admit their involvement.[24]

The incident occurred during a session of the Constituent Assembly-II, where federalism was under discussion. Protests had escalated across the Tarai plains and the hills following the Assembly's decision to establish a federal structure based on geographical and economic criteria rather than ethnic considerations. The Tharu community expressed dissatisfaction with this resolution, as they have long demanded the establishment of a separate Tharuhat province in southwestern Nepal. Their concerns focused on the potential erosion of political representation and failure to free from historical exploitations, underscoring the necessity for the establishment of a separate Tharuhat province.

A counter-movement emerged in response to the proposal for a separate Tharuhat province, primarily opposed by the Pahadis, the inhabitants of the hilly regions. They advocated for the establishment of Akhanda Sudurpaschim, or an undivided Far-West province, based on geographical considerations. Notable political figures, including Sher Bahadur Deuba from the Nepali Congress, Bhim Rawal of the CPN-UML, and Lekhraj Bhatta from the Communist Party of Nepal (Maoist Centre), either tacitly or overtly endorsed the Akhanda Sudurpaschim concept, as all were representatives from the region.

In a similar vein, it has observed the state of human rights concerning police brutality in Sindhuli and the inequitable distribution of relief materials in earthquake-affected regions. To promote, protect, and defend human rights, LAHURNIP has actively participated in advocacy activities spanning local to international levels.[25]

### *National Indigenous Women's Federation*

The National Indigenous Women's Federation (NIWF) is a Kathmandu-based pan-Nepal umbrella organisation representing Indigenous Nationalities, with a specific focus on women. These women assume multifaceted roles in the preservation, promotion, and maintenance of the unique identities of indigenous peoples. Their linguistic and cultural competencies, alongside their traditional knowledge of community and resource management, are distinctive. Nonetheless, their contributions and roles are inadequately recognised by the state. Existing laws, policies, and practices marginalise, exclude, deprive, and discriminate against indigenous women.

In 1999, women leaders from various indigenous organisations established the National Indigenous Women's Federation as a federation, subsequently registering it in 2000. The primary objective of the NIWF is to ensure the participation of indigenous women in all state structures while representing their unique identities. Currently, there are 31 indigenous women's organisations affiliated with this overarching entity.

In Nepal, Adivasi Janajati women have encountered significant challenges stemming from patriarchal and political structures. Social exclusion based on ethnicity poses a critical issue within the country. Indigenous nationalities women experience marginalisation not only due to their gender but also because of their ethnic identity. Women constitute 50.4 percent of the Nepali population, with Adivasi Janajati women representing 37.5 percent of this group. Adivasi Janajati women face a tripartite form of discrimination: first, as women; second, as Adivasi Janajati; and third, as Adivasi Janajati women.[26]

## *The Indigenous Women's Legal Awareness Group*

The Indigenous Women's Legal Awareness Group (INWOLAG) is a non-profit, non-governmental, and non-political international organisation established in 2000. It operates globally, with branches in various countries, including Nepal. INWOLAG consists of indigenous women who are legal experts and professionals committed to advancing the human rights of indigenous women. Its mission is to safeguard and enhance the dignity and well-being of indigenous women by eradicating all forms of discrimination and violence against them and their children.

The United Kingdom endorsed women's empowerment and the advocacy of rights through a Para Legal Committee (PLC) programme from March 2010 to August 2013. PLCs, initially established in 1999, have evolved into a significant component within villages and communities throughout Nepal, aimed at preventing and addressing violence against women.[27]

## *National Indigenous Women Forum*

The National Indigenous Women Forum (NIWF) is a local non-governmental organisation (NGO) founded and chaired by Stella Tamang, who is also a co-founder of the South Asia Indigenous Women's Network. Tamang presided over the Indigenous Women Caucus at the United Nations Permanent Forum on Indigenous Issues in 2003 and 2004, where she effectively advocated for the third session's focus on the challenges faced by indigenous women. NIWF primarily engages in initiatives aimed at women's empowerment, advocacy, and providing legal support to women who experience injustices. In light of the strong yet fragmented women's rights movement in Nepal, NIWF has sought to unify activists by establishing a women's federation.[28]

### *Indigenous People's Mega Front*

The Adivasi/Janajati Vrihat Morcha, also referred to as the Indigenous Peoples' Mega Front (IPMF) Nepal, was established on November 21, 2009. It serves as a coalition of volunteer human rights advocates representing indigenous communities dedicated to empowering these groups in Nepal to assert their rights and safeguard their lands and cultural identities. The primary objective of this organisation is to initiate a robust campaign aimed at ensuring the immediate implementation of the agreements reached between the State and indigenous organisations concerning the rights of indigenous peoples in the new constitution.[29]

The text ensures that the political and social issues articulated in the constitution are grounded in historical, ethnic, linguistic, and regional contexts, as outlined in documents such as the United Nations Declaration on the Rights of Indigenous Peoples and the International Labour Organisation Convention No. 169, to which Nepal is a state party. It supports communities in their advocacy efforts by educating them about their rights, enhancing their advocacy capabilities, facilitating their lobbying at both national and international levels, and disseminating pertinent information through various media channels.[30]

### *Federation of Nepalese Indigenous Nationalities*

The Federation of Nepalese Indigenous Nationalities (FONIN) functions as an umbrella organisation for non-governmental organisations (NGOs) representing over 60 indigenous nationalities. It actively engages in establishing networks with NGOs focused on the integration of indigenous peoples, ensuring their rights and enhancing their participation in the overall development process. FONIN assists marginalised indigenous communities by promoting their involvement in development initiatives through organisation and awareness-raising efforts. The organisation collaborates with both national and international partners, including ActionAid, Danish International Development Agency (DANIDA), the Asian Development Bank (ADB), the United Nations Development Programme (UNDP), and Danida Human Rights and Good Governance Advisory Units (HUGOU). With over one hundred member organisations operating at the community level throughout Nepal, FONIN has undertaken a diverse array of capacity-building activities, as documented in Danida-HUGOU's reports, particularly in the post-peace agreement era. Furthermore, FONIN's advocacy efforts have led to the introduction of an inclusion bill that addresses the rights of indigenous peoples and establishes quotas within civil service and security forces.[31]

## Minimal Impact of NGOs

Despite the presence of numerous non-governmental organisations (NGOs) in Nepal that have dedicated several decades to empowering indigenous groups, these communities have been unable to significantly impact the constitutional drafting process, which could have addressed the discrimination faced by minority groups. Furthermore, some NGOs have functioned merely as a safety valve, mitigating the anger and frustration of indigenous groups towards the state rather than effecting meaningful structural change.

Significant political interference in the operations of NGOs might have contributed to the absence of a distinct political party representing indigenous groups, such as the Madhesis in the Terai region. As the Madhesis have successfully transformed their movement into a political force by establishing political parties, they find themselves in a position where negotiation with mainstream parties for their interests is more feasible. This has allowed them to enhance their status as influential political actors within the competitive political landscape of Nepal. In contrast, indigenous groups remain largely confined to NGOs and small collectives in more remote areas, primarily reliant on three mainstream political parties: the Nepali Congress (NC), the Communist Party of Nepal (UML), and the Communist Party of Nepal (Maoist Center).

## New Ethno-Cultural Fronts

In the post-constitution era, the ethno-cultural movements aimed at addressing the outstanding demands of marginalised groups seem to have lost direction due to several factors: The 2015 Constitution and its subsequent amendments address a substantial number of demands from marginalised groups, prompting renewed debates among ethnic communities regarding the continuation of their movements. Some advocate for sustained activism, emphasising both the implementation of existing policies and the need to address longstanding issues. Furthermore, several marginalised ethnic groups have expressed diminishing confidence in organisations such as NEFIN and AJRA, opting instead for community-based organisations that facilitate direct negotiations with the state. For instance, the Tharu community lost faith in both NEFIN and Madhesi organisations in the post-constitutional period, leading to the establishment of the Tharuhat Tharuwan Rastriya Morcha (TTRM) in 2018. Notably, the Madhesi people are not affiliated with NEFIN. In light of the state's neglect of outstanding demands, indigenous nationalities and Madhesi political parties are negotiating to form a broader democratic alliance to exert pressure on the government. Additionally, there exists a competitive dynamic among NEFIN, emerging community-based organisations, and the affiliated organisations of various political parties, all vying for leadership on contemporary issues, particularly the threats to ethnic cultures posed by ongoing infrastructure and development projects. In the Tarai region, numerous culture-based organisations have united to establish political parties. Although new entities such as the Tarai Madhes Cultural Council (TMCC) have emerged since 2015, there remains significant public confusion regarding their capacity to effectively represent and advocate for their community's demands before the state.

### *Brihat Nagarik Andolan*

In the absence of a credible ethnic front that could serve as both a unifying force and mobilising agent, similar to the role previously played by the CPN-Maoist, certain civil society organisations have established a loose alliance known as the Brihat Nagarik Andolan (BNA) to sustain the movement for rights in Nepal. Since 2015, the BNA has been at the forefront of advocating for constitutional amendments, arguing that the current constitution fails to adequately address the concerns of marginalised individuals and communities. The BNA represents a contemporary iteration of the movement by marginalised groups opposing the new constitution. Several academicians and intellectuals, such as columnist CK Lal, author Khagendra Sangraula, political analyst and civil society advocate Rajendra Maharjan, former member of the National Human Rights Commission Mohan Ansari, and representatives from various marginalised communities, including Madhesi, Tharu, Muslim, and indigenous groups, have actively participated in BNA initiatives.[32]

In the post-constitutional period, a new coalition has been established, spearheaded by leaders of several Madhesi-based political parties and Janajati groups. The Sanghiya Gathbandhan, or the Federal Alliance, has resolved to organise protests against the constitution. This coalition consists of approximately 30 parties, including numerous ethnic organisations representing Janajatis, Dalits, women, and members of the United Democratic Madhesi Front.[33]

## *Tharuhat Tharuwan Rashtriya Morcha*

The Tharuhat Tharuwan Rashtriya Morcha (TTRM) was established in 2018 with the aim of initiating negotiations with the State regarding prior agreements and securing the release of Tharu protesters and leaders who were detained following the Tikapur incident in August 2015. Additionally, the TTMR advocates for the preservation of Tharu culture, the cessation of bonded labour in the region, the recognition of the Tharu language, and the establishment of a distinct Tharuwan province in western Nepal.

Laxam Tharu was the coordinator of the TTRM. Other notable leaders of the TTRM were Bhanu Ram Tharu, who served as an adviser to the TTRM, Resham Chaudhary, and Shrawan Tharu, who is currently acting as the coordinator of the Morcha.

An additional factor contributing to the formation of the TTRM may be the consolidation of the Tharus under a unified organisation. Although a coordinated movement commenced in 2009 aimed at safeguarding cultural heritage and ethnic identity and ensuring proportional representation within state mechanisms, this movement has largely remained fragmented. This fragmentation can be attributed to the co-optation of leadership by hill-based political parties, the quest for a distinct identity within the Terai sub-region separate from Madhesi-based parties, and intra-leadership conflicts.[34]

As of April 2022, there were four prominent Tharu-based organisations: Banu Tharu's Nepal Democratic Party, Ranjita Shrestha (Chaudhary)'s Nagarik Unmukti Party (Citizen Liberation Party), Rukmini Tharu's Federal Democratic National Forum (Tharuhat), and the TTRM. Notably, among these organisations, only the TTRM explicitly incorporates the Tharu designation in its title. The other entities lack a clear Tharu identity and have predominantly operated to serve individual interests rather than effectively representing the broader community.

On January 23, 2020, the TTRM organised a protest program, presenting a 14-point agenda. The organisation issued a warning that it would mobilise public demonstrations if its demands were not addressed promptly. Additionally, the party has advocated for the official recognition of the Tharu language in all governmental offices within the Tharuhat region.

On March 27, 2021, a six-member delegation was established under the chairmanship of Laxman Tharu to engage in discussions with the government concerning the families of the individuals convicted and accused in relation to the 2015 Tikapur incident. The team comprised Ram Prasad Tharu, Chuniram Tharu, Bina Chaudhary, Yamuna Chaudhary, and Resham Chaudhary. All members have been convicted by the court in connection with the Tikapur incident, which resulted in the fatalities of nine individuals during a violent confrontation.[35]

On the commemoration of the sixth anniversary of the Tikapur incident, the TTRM initiated a renewed protest in Kathmandu on August 18, 2021, advocating for the government's adherence to previous agreements. The primary demand of the protestors was for the release of individuals incarcerated in connection with the incident. Notably, significant pressure was exerted for the release of Resham Chaudhary, who is regarded as a prominent activist within the movement.

As a prominent Tharuhat organisation, the TTRM is an integral component of the Brihat Nagarik Aandolan BNA. Ultimately, the TTRM's participation in the BNA underscores its commitment to advancing the cause of the Tharu people while contributing to a larger vision of a just and inclusive society in Nepal.[36]

## The Future of Indigenous People's Movement

Despite articulating dissatisfaction with the new constitution, the indigenous people's (IPs) movement in Nepal finds itself at a crossroads. It appears to lack a coherent strategy for sustaining its protests moving forward, particularly given the absence of robust support from the international community, the dominance of major political parties within its ranks, and insufficient coordination with other minority groups such as the Madhesi and Muslims. In the post-constitution period, the Nepal Federation of Indigenous Nationalities has not organised any significant street protests.

The most significant political initiative undertaken by NEFIN occurred on September 11, 2016, when it presented a memorandum to Prime Minister Pushpa Kamal Dahal, articulating eleven amendments to the constitution aimed at addressing the grievances of indigenous populations. Key demands included the 'establishment of identity as a fundamental criterion for state restructuring, the designation of provinces and local entities based on the historical, linguistic, and cultural identities of the ethnic groups residing therein, the allocation of 60 percent of parliamentary seats to facilitate a proportional representation system, and the formal recognition of the one-horned rhinoceros as the national animal'.[37]

Similarly, the AJRA has not organised any street protests or articulated new demands to the government in the post-constitution period. The viability of AJRA has been called into question following the passing of its founding member, Padma Ratna Tuladhar, in November 2018. Notably, the ideological differences between AJRA and NEFIN have diminished significantly since the merger of the former UCPN (Maoist) and the CPN-UML in May 2018. It is worth noting that Prachanda has refrained from commenting on single ethnic-based federalism since assuming the position of vice-chairperson of the newly established Nepali Communist Party (NCP), which was subsequently disbanded due to a ruling by the Supreme Court.

Despite the passage of over seven years since the promulgation of the new constitution, a significant number of provisions remain unimplemented, often due to deliberate inaction. Federalism is a prime example of this stagnation. A scholar has observed that "while provincial governments resist heteronomy, the federal parliament continues to propose bills that perpetuate anti-federalist features."[38] Furthermore, it is important to note that discrimination against indigenous populations persists in remote areas.

A report released by Nepal's Indigenous Peoples for Voluntary National Review under the UN High-Level Political Forum on Sustainable Development reveals that 'the 11 articles of the 2015 Constitution are inconsistent with the rights of indigenous peoples, 23 articles exhibit discriminatory practices against IPs, 49 articles are exclusionary in nature, and 5 articles appear to prioritise the supremacy of dominant caste groups.'[39]

It is widely posited that the issue of identities and political positions could undergo a significant transformation with the establishment of the Samajwadi Party-Nepal, following the amalgamation of the Naya Shakti Party-Nepal, led by former Maoist leaders and Prime Minister Baburam Bhattarai, with the Federal Socialist Front Forum-Nepal in May 2019. The Samajwadi Party-Nepal has committed to the institutionalisation of a federal democratic republic, asserting that its political ideology will be "Prosperous Federal Socialism."[40] The Samajwadi Party-Nepal has also engaged with Rastriya Janata Party Nepal (RJP-Nepal), a Madhesh-based political entity, to explore the possibility of a merger. This initiative aims to consolidate their efforts in order to exert pressure on the government to address the concerns of Madhesis, Janajatis, and other marginalised communities and groups.[41]

Over five years have elapsed since the establishment of the Sanghiya Gathabandhan (Federal Alliance), a coalition of Madhesi and Janajati forces. This alliance has not exerted any significant pressure on successive governments to amend the constitution in order to address issues related to secularism, identity-based proportional representation, and the federal democratic republic. Instead, in a public statement made in July 2019, the alliance suggested a potential willingness to join the government, indicating that their demands could be negotiated at a later date.

## NOTES

1 Gayatri Chakravorty Spivak, "Can the Subaltern Speak?" Use the link for accessing the PDF, https://jan.ucc.nau.edu/~sj6/Spivak%20CanTheSubalternSpeak.pdf. Also see Edward W. Said, "Orientalism", Vintage Bok, New York, 1979.

2 Rajendra Pradhan and Ava Shrestha, "Ethnic and Caste Diversity: Implications for Development", Working Paper Series No. 4, ADB, Nepal Resident Mission June 2005, p.4

3 Ibid. Also see Gerard Toffin, "The Janajti/Adivasi Movement in Nepal: Myths and Realities of Indigeneity", *Sociological Bulletin*, 58 (1), January-April 2009.

4 Rajendra Pradhan and Ava Shrestha, no. 2, p.4.

5 Rajendra Pradhan, *Ethnicity, Caste and a pluralistic society*, in Kanak Mani Dixit and Shastri Ramachandran (eds.), "State of Nepal," Lalitpur, Nepal, Himal books, 2002.

6 Udhav P. Pyakurel, "Maoist Movement in Nepal: A Sociological Perspective, New Delhi: Adroit Publishers, 2007.

7 Rajendra Pradhan and Ava Shrestha, no. 2, p. 6.

8 Ibid. Also see Ram Kumar Ghimire, "Abolition of 'Kipat' land tenure system: The Context and consequences", Tribhuvan University Journal, 27(1-2), 113–120. Available online at https://www.nepjol.info/index.php/TUJ/article/view/26394 (accessed on 22 April 2022).

9 Krishna Bhattachan, "Dominant Groups Have Right to Live?" This article available online as it was presented at a Working Session on "Sustainable Livelihood" in a South Asia Conference on Legacy of Mahbub ul Haq-Human Development organized in May 19-23, 2000 by the Institute of Social Sciences in New Delhi, India. For details visit https://www.nefin.org.np/wp-content/uploads/2017/09/Dominant-Groups-Have-Rights-to-Live_Krishna-B.-Bhattachan.pdf, (accessed on 24 September 2021).

10 Ram Kumar Ghimire, "Abolition of 'Kipat' land tenure system: The Context and consequences", Tribhuvan University Journal, 27(1-2), 113–120. Available online at https://www.nepjol.info/index.php/TUJ/article/view/26394 (accessed on 22 April 2022). Also see Binayak Sundas, "The Gurkha Empire", *myRepublica*, 09 August 2017.

11 Mahendra Lawoti, "Contentious Politics in Deocratizing Nepal", in Mahendra Lawati (ed.) *Contentious Politics and Democratization in Nepal*, Sage Publications, new Delhi, 2007, pp.32-33.

12 Gerard Toffin, "The Janajati/Adivasi Movement in Nepal: Myths and Realities of Indigeneity", *Sociological Bulletin*, 58 (1), January-April 2009, pp. 25-42.

13 Krishna Bhattachan, no. 9, p. 4.

14 Ibid.

15 Mukata S. Lama-tamang, "Adivasi Janajati Exclusion: Status and Trend Update" June 2005-April 2009, this is a NEFIN publication.

16 Tashi Tewa Dolpo, "Internal Divide," *The Kathmandu Post*, 25 November2014, https://kathmandupost.com/opinion/2014/11/25/internal-divide (accessed on 13 April 2022).

17 NEFIN, http://www.nefin.org.np/en/indroduction/ (accessed on 13 April 2022).

18 Ibid.

19 "Against odds, Ajra still sees a fighting chance", *The Kathmandu Post*, 01 April 2015, https://kathmandupost.com/valley/2015/04/01/against-odds-ajra-still-sees-a-fighting-chance (accessed on 27 April 2022).

20 The author's interview with Jay Nishant in Kathmandu in September 2023. Mr. Nishant is a political activist and researcher based in Terai.

21 The author's interview with Chandra Kishore took place in December 2023 in New Delhi. Mr Kishore is a senior freelance journalist based in Terai.

22 https://www.lahurnip.org/what-we-do (accessed on 30 October 2024).

23 Ibid.

24 "Six years after Tikapur incident, Tharus still wait for justice", *The Kathmandu Post*, 27 August 2021.

25 LAHURNIP, Kathmandu, *Annual Report*, 2015-2016 and 2016-2017.

26 NIWF, Nepal, Forest Peoples Programme, England, for details visit https://www.forestpeoples.org/en/partner/national-indigenous-womens-federation-niwf-nepal (24 September 2021).

27 Namati, Washington, DC 20036, USA, https://namati.org/search/?swpquery=Nepal. For direct access https://grassrootsjusticenetwork.org/resources/annual-review-of-integrated-development-

programme-of-women-cooperatives-to-reduce-gender-based-violence-in-nepal/ (accessed on 24 March 2021).

28 "Inspiring Indigenous Women and Girls to Rise: Stella Tamang" Cultural Survival Quarterly Magazine, December 2014, at https://www.culturalsurvival.org/publications/cultural-survival-quarterly/inspiring-indigenous-women-and-girls-rise-stella-tamang (accessed on 13 April 2022).

29 Christina Nilsson and Sille Stidsen, "Constitutional Politics and Indigenous Peoples in Nepal", May 2014, https://www.iwgia.org/images/publications/0686_Constitutional_ Politics_ and_ Indigenous_Peoples_in_Nepal.pdf (accessed on 30 October 2024).

30 Press Communique, Adivasi/Janajati Vrihat Morcha (Indigenous Peoples' Mega Front), Nepal, 17 January 2011. http://nepalindigenousissues.blogspot.com/2011/01/adivasijanajati-vrihat-morcha.html (accessed on 13 April 2022).

31 Cecilia Magnusson Ljungman and Mohan Mardan Thapa, "Evaluation of Danish Support to Civil Society Annex G: Nepal Country Study", April 2013, (accessed on 30 October 2024).

32 "Civic group marches in Kathmandu to demand amendments to constitution", 18 September 2021, *Nepal Monitor*, https://nepalmonitor.org/reports/view/36188 (accessed on 27 Aril 2022).

33 Smita Sharma, "Nepal set for round 2 of protests against Constitution: Here's all you need to know", *Indian Today*, 15 May 20216, https://www.indiatoday.in/world/neighbours/story/nepal-on-the-boil-again-beyond-the-headlines-323620-2016-05-15 (accessed on 27 Aril 2022).

34 Krishna Pandey, "Politicising Ethnicity: Tharu Contestation of Madhesi identity in Nepal's Tarai", The South Asianist, Vol.5, no. 1, p.313.

35 "Nepal: A team formed for talks with the government over the Tikapur incident", *The Orient News*, 27 March 2021, https://theorientnews.com/index.php/latest-news/item/4119-nepal-a-team-formed-for-talks-with-the-government-over-the-tikapur-incident (accessed on 27 April 2022).

36 "Tharu Morcha in protest, pressuring government to implement past agreements", *The Kathmandu Post*, 18 August 2021, https://kathmandupost.com/national/2021/08/18/tharu-morcha-in-protest-pressuring-government-to-implement-past-agreements (accessed on 27 April 2022).

37 "Indigenous nationalities demand 11 amendments to Constitution," *The Himalayan*, 11 September 2016, https://thehimalayantimes.com/kathmandu/indigenous-nationalities-demand-11-amendments-constitution/ (accessed on 24 September 2021).

38 Rai, "Nepal's pseudo-federalism", *The Kathmandu Post*, 25 April 2019, https://kathmandu post.com/opinion/2019/04/25/nepals-pseudo-federalism (accessed on 24 September 2021).

39 "Report of Nepal's Indigenous Peoples for Voluntary National Review of Nepal Under the UN High-Level Political Forum on Sustainable Development," 10-19 July 2017, Prepared by Indigenous Peoples' Network for SDGs, Nepal Kathmandu, Nepal, June 2017, https://www.indigenouspeoples-sdg.org/index.php/english/all-resources/resource-materials2/reports-and-publications/57-report-of-nepal-s-indigenous-peoples-for-voluntary-national-review-of-nepal-under-the-un-high-level-political-forum-on-sustainable-development/file (accessed on 24 September 2021).

40 "Nepal Deputy PM's Madhesi party merges with former PM's party to form new political outfit", *The New Indian Express*, 07 May 2019, https://www.newindianexpress.com/world/2019/may/07/nepal-deputy-pms-madhesi-party-merges-with-former-pms-party-to-form-new-political-outfit-1973883.html, (accessed on 24 September 2021).

41 "RJP-N, SP-N intensify merger talks," *The Himalayan*, 07 July 2019, https://thehimalayantimes.com/nepal/rjp-n-sp-n-intensify-merger-talks/ (accessed on 24 September 2021).

# *Chapter Three*

# *The Madhesi Movement: A Struggle for Cultural and Political Inclusion*

The historical context of social discrimination and marginalisation in Nepal dates back to the nation's formative period. Numerous anti-state movements aimed at addressing social inequities and advocating for the preservation of ethnic identities, particularly among ethnic groups in the Terai region, have largely culminated without satisfactory outcomes. Even armed insurgencies led by the Limbus have failed to exert sufficient pressure on the State to incorporate special provisions in the constitution aimed at safeguarding the rights of minority groups. A variety of factors contributed to the ineffectiveness of these organised movements against the state, as discussed in the preceding chapter. A pivotal factor, however, was the co-opting of leaders from indigenous nationalities and the Madhesi[1] movement by the State and the dominant political parties, primarily influenced by the hill Brahmin elite.

The Madhesi movement of January 2007, which occurred just prior to the promulgation of the interim constitution, was spearheaded by the Madhesi Janadhikar Forum (MJF) and constituted a pivotal event in the struggle against the State to address the grievances of marginalised groups in Nepal. The MJF advocated for autonomy, comprehensive proportional representation, and the establishment of a democratic republic. The organisation orchestrated strikes and large-scale demonstrations throughout the eastern Terai districts.

The protests subsequently disseminated to other regions of Terai and areas predominantly inhabited by indigenous nationalities. Approximately 20 Madhesi individuals lost their lives during the eight-month-long anti-state demonstrations. The MJF suspended its protests following the signing of an agreement (Appendices I and II) in August 2007 with the government, which acquiesced to augment the number of electoral seats allocated to the Terai region in the Constituent Assembly elections. The repercussions of the Madhesi movement exerted pressure on the state to address the demands of indigenous groups and to pre-empt joint protests. In this context, the government entered into a separate agreement with the indigenous nationalities (Appendix III) while negotiations with the Madhesi representatives continued.

During the constitutional drafting process, political parties engaged in earnest deliberations regarding the prioritisation of issues, ultimately debating whether to conclude the peace process or promulgate the constitution first. Among the key issues vigorously contested was the concept of federalism. The political party with the most substantial representation in parliament at that time (2008), the Unified Communist Party of Nepal (UCPN-Maoist), advocated for an ethnic-based federalism, while the other two major liberal democratic parties—the Nepali Congress (NC) and the CPN-UML—supported a federal structure grounded in geographic and economic considerations. The protracted delay in the promulgation of the constitution and the absence of consensus on the federal framework led to the resurgence of ethnic and identity-based movements in Nepal, particularly in the eastern region and the Terai.

The Terai-based political parties, in the interests of Madhesh, have proposed the establishment of a single autonomous province within the new constitution. The Maoist party was comparatively more inclined towards the notion of creating two Madhesh provinces. However, other political factions expressed apprehension that granting autonomous status to these provinces could potentially lead to demands for separate states in the future. Consequently, the Madhesi parties found themselves in a predicament: by endorsing the Maoists, they risked compromising their political autonomy in exchange for the prospect of autonomy, whereas supporting the liberal democrats could hinder their aspirations for Madhesh to be recognised as a separate province.

If the new constitution had not adequately addressed the rights of minorities, the Madhesi issue could have resurfaced as a significant internal challenge for future governments in Nepal. The international community has been closely monitoring political developments in the region since the protests initiated by Madhesh groups in January 2007. The involvement of international agencies in the Madhesi situation posed challenges for India, which has a vested interest in the political unrest in the Terai region due to its open border and cultural ties. India was particularly concerned that persistent tensions in the Terai could lead to a humanitarian migration (for the purpose of taking shelter to avoid harassment by the security forces) into bordering Indian states and potentially result in a law and order crisis fuelled by anti-India elements.

## What is Madhesh?

As discussed earlier, Nepal has four topographic regions: The upper Himalayas, the middle Himalayas, the Hills (the Shiwalik[2]/Chure range) and the Terai[3] plains or Madhes (also known as the southern plains). Among the different narratives about the origins of the word Madhesh, the most accepted version is that it stands for 'Madhya-desh', a region between the Siwalik and the Ganges. There is a view in Nepal that 'Madhesh' is not only a geographical term, but it also has cultural connotations. According to some Madhesi intellectuals, the word 'Madhesh' is a political identity of some cultural minorities of Terai who speak Awadhi, Bhojpuri, Maithili and Hindi. This cultural identity was turned into a political identity issue due to the failure of the state to address their grievances.[4]

The aspiration of the Madhesi communities in this region to establish a distinct identity encompassing language, cuisine, attire, and cultural celebrations within Nepal has prompted them to self-identify as 'Madhesi.' The Terai region comprises 20 districts that share a border with India. Existing literature indicates that much of the Terai was historically dominated by dense tropical forests. At that time, the area was largely uninhabitable due to the high incidence of malaria, the presence of wild animals, and a hot, humid climate.

The original inhabitants of Madhesh were many caste groups and the Tharu tribe of Nepal. The caste groups were determined based on traditional occupation and the Hindu *Varna* system. Historical evidence suggests that the Buffalo-herder dynasty had replaced the Cowherd dynasty in the ancient geographical region of present Nepal. The Buffalo dynasty came from "the country between Simraungarh and Janakpur in the Terai."[5] In contemporary Nepal, Yadav is a dominant community in the Madhesh Pradesh. Moreover, anthropological studies found that the Tharus migrated from Rajasthan in India during the Mughal invasion of India in the sixteenth and seventeenth centuries. Most historical evidence indicates that the Tharus were first located in the western Terai region before other castes or tribes settled there.[6]

## The Ethno-cultural Fabric of Terai

Like any other region of Nepal, the demography of Terai was tampered with from time to time broadly under two circumstances like: administrative and strategic purposes by the rulers and the demarcation of the new boundary under the influence of geo-political developments in the region. In contemporary Nepal, three major communities comprise the Terai population. These are (i) Janajatis (Tharus); (ii) some minor cultural and religious communities who speak Awadhi, Bhojpuri, Maithili, Marwari and Urdu (Musalman) and maintain cultural linkages with Uttar Pradesh and Bihar of India; (iii) and the people who migrated from the hills and the mountains in search of better livelihood and on account of state-sponsored migrations during the 1960s and 1970s—called *Pahadi Madhesi*.

Like the Hindu caste groups of the hill region, Madhesis have strong social, cultural and ethnic linkages across the border. One report suggests that, in 1954, the Teraian accounted for 35 percent of the population of Nepal; by 1979, the population rose to 52 percent; the 2001 census, which is the latest figure available, shows it to be 57 percent.[7] Some other reports suggested that over 51 percent of the total Nepali population lives in Terai. However, according to the 2001 census, hill caste/ethnic groups in Terai (Madhesh) constitute 31.70 percent of the total population.[8]

Madhesi includes different castes and ethnic groups: Tharu, Yadav, Muslim, Teli, Chamar, Koyar, Brahman, Bhumihar, Amat, Mali, Tatma, Kanu, Rauniyar, Rajdhobi, Tamoli, Kathaoniya, Hajam, Sonar, Lohar, Tajpuriya, Bantar, Jhangar, Dhanuk, Rajbanshi, Meche, Satar, Dhimal, Mushar, Dom, Dushad, etc. (see Appendix V). Madhesis are divided linguistically into Maithili, Bhojpuri and Abadhi (MBA) in the eastern, central and western regions. Maithili is the second largest language in Nepal (11 percent); Bhojpuri is spoken by 8 percent and Abadhi by 4 percent. The Tharus, in the mid-western and far-western regions, speak three different dialects. Hindi is the lingua franca in the region.[9]

## The Discrimination and Identity Problem

The Madhesi community experiences a profound sense of discrimination and resultant deprivation. Ethnic groups and Madhesi individuals perceive themselves as being exploited and marginalised by the predominant upper-caste Pahadi migrant populations. Furthermore, the Madhesi people contend that they have been systematically discriminated against by the state apparatus. While both indigenous nationalities and Madhesis endure state-sponsored discrimination, they frequently engage in separate struggles, with indigenous groups conflating Madhesis with Indian identity, particularly due to the Madhesi demand for Hindi to be recognised as an official language in the Terai region. Since 2009, within the Terai region, the Tharu and Muslim communities have distanced themselves from the Madhesi populace.[10]

### *Citizenship*

Citizenship represents a pivotal issue in the Terai region. The Madhesi community has been advocating for citizenship rights since 1964. The Citizenship Act of 1964 and the Constitution of 1990 stipulate that citizenship is to be determined based on 'descent' and proficiency in the Nepali language. In the absence of legitimate documentation confirming Nepali heritage, such as birth certificates and land ownership documents, Madhesi individuals are excluded from obtaining citizenship certificates. This lack of citizenship documentation precludes them from securing land titles and accessing government benefits, thereby perpetuating their marginalisation.

These policies were adopted by the rulers, thereby targeting the Madhesis even though they knew that many of them did not have land-holding records and could not speak the Nepali language. The Terai forest was mainly used as a hunting ground during the Rana regime. Given the emerging geo-political situation, in the 1950s, Kathmandu elites conspired to displace Terai residents and thus deprived them of land holdings. The Nepal Resettlement Company was established in 1964, and it distributed forest land in Terai among those loyal to the palace. One scholar observed, "In the 1970s, around 1,414 hectares of land were distributed among 696 politicians in the Terai. A large number of logging permits were used to finance the Panchayat campaign in 1980."[11] The land was also distributed among the hilly migrant population partly by clearing the forest and uprooting many indigenous people. That deprived the Madhesis of acquiring citizenship certificates without land-holding records.

A government commission in 1994 reported that almost 3.5 million Nepalese did not have citizenship certificates.[12] In November 2006, the Citizenship Law was amended, making anyone born in Nepal before 1990 and permanent resident eligible for citizenship.[13] Many Madhesis and Dalits, however, were deprived of citizenship certificates even then. According to UNHCR, 'about 800,000 citizens remained de facto stateless after a largely successful Government campaign during which about 2.6 million citizenship certificates were distributed in 2007.'[14]

### *Language and Culture*

The Madhesis faced systemic discrimination due to their cultural ties with neighbouring regions. In 1954, the National Planning Commission advocated for the implementation of Nepali as the mandatory language for official communication and educational instruction. Although the first elected Prime Minister, B.P. Koirala, integrated Hindi into the curriculum in the Madhes region in 1959, King Mahendra subsequently annulled this decision. In 1962, he promulgated the slogan, "*Hamro Bhasa, Hamro Bhesh, Pran Bhanda Pyaro Chha*" (our language and attire are dearer to us than life itself), reinforcing the significance of cultural identity.[15]

Analysing the writings of Indian-born British novelist and essayist George Orwell and Nepali novelist and statesman Bishweshwar Prasad Koirala about the relationship between totalitarianism and language use, Abhi Subedi observed that "language is used to create a culture of control and totality. Using language that includes writing creates grounds for a dictatorial state of order to prevail."[16] The interpretation fits into the Nepal case. For example, King Mahendra's policy on the language and culture of marginalised groups was targeted to minimise democratic space in Nepal.

Even during the multiparty system after the popular movement, the parliamentarians were bound to wear *Daura Surwal* (Nepali costume), and *Nepali Topi* was mandatory in government offices.[17] King Mahendra and his successors did not recognise the existence of Madhesh and Madhesi. They had identified the southern part of Nepal as Terai.[18] This policy of King Mahendra has been firmly embedded in Nepali psychology even today. "At present, not all Nepalis are accepting the Terai part of Nepal as Madhesh. Terai / Madhes is not a synonym."[19] That could be a strong reason behind the failure of

Indigenous groups and the Madhesis to come together despite being marginalised by the Nepali upper-caste nationalism.

### *Under-representation*

Table 1 reflects that the share of the Madhesi, Muslims, Janajatis, Dalits and others at the level of gazetted employees was merely less than 5 percent when they constitute nearly one-third of the country's population. On the other hand, the Brahmins and Chhetris account for 87.89 percent of gazetted employees, followed by the Newar (7.14 percent). These figures suggest a disproportionate representation of the ethnic and caste groups in the top jobs in Nepal. The Bahuns, Chhetris and Newars, despite having less population in comparison to the marginalised group, occupied a substantial portion of top government jobs, and that helped to protect their interest by influencing the state policies in their favour and, directly and indirectly, affected the progress of the marginalised groups.

**Table 1: Caste/Ethnic Representation of Special and Gazetted Level Employees in Nepal**

*(All figures in percent)*

| *No.* | *Caste/Ethnicity* | *Population* | *Representation in the Civil Services* |
|---|---|---|---|
| 1. | Bahuns | 12.74 | 72.00 |
| 2. | Chhetris | 15.80 | 15.89 |
| 3. | Newar Janajatis | 5.48 | 7.14 |
| 4. | Non-Newar Janajatis | 30.83 | 1.64 |
| 5. | Madhesi | 12.32 | 1.17 |
| 6. | Dalit's | 14.99 | 0.67 |
| 7. | Muslims | 4.27 | 0.1 |
| 8. | Others | 3.57 | 1.39 |
| | Total | 100 | 100 |

*Source:* Ministry of General Administration. Cited by Baburam Bhul.[20] It appears that the data was used first in 2016.

After the January 2007 Madhes movement and the eight-point agreement between the government and Madhes-based parties, the government has tried to bridge these gaps in different sectors through affirmative action. The reservation policy for civil services in Nepal was established in 2007 under the interim constitution as a pivotal element of the state's restructuring efforts.

Significantly, the Civil Service Act allocated 45 percent of available positions to marginalised groups, while the remaining 55 percent were designated for open competition.[21]

Interestingly, over the past 17 years, there has been an increase in the representation of marginalised groups in the state structure. Madhesi representation in civil services increased from less than 2 percent in 2006 to 8 percent in 2016.[22] However, this increase has not been proportional to the total population of these groups. Quoting the Public Service Commission report, a media report said that although the percentage of Khas Arya in civil services has decreased from 80.60 percent to 70 percent as of 2024, they still hold the largest share in the civil service. Of that total of 85,520 civil service employees in Nepal, 68.6 percent have entered through direct competition, 7.4 percent of civil service workers are women, 5.4 percent are from indigenous communities, 4.1 percent are Madhesi, 1.6 percent are Dalit, 0.8 percent are people with disabilities, and 0.7 percent are from backward areas.[23]

Despite the existence of a standing provision, discrimination persists within the judiciary. An investigation into judicial appointments revealed a failure to implement this provision both in letter and spirit. A media report indicated that, although the constitution guarantees proportional representation of all marginalised groups in state institutions, the judiciary has not upheld this commitment. Among the 19 Supreme Court judges appointed between August 2016 and December 7, 2019, only one was selected from the Madhesi community. Similarly, the Judicial Council recommended 80 High Court judges in 2017, of whom merely three were Madhesi, and one identified as belonging to the Dalit category. Furthermore, the principle of proportional inclusion was not adhered to in the appointment of judges from other marginalized groups.[24]

### *Economic Exploitation*

Although the Terai region is endowed with mineral wealth and possesses fertile land, a significant portion of the Madhesi population experiences socio-economic deprivation. Madhesh accounts for 70 percent of Nepal's agricultural output and nearly 65 percent of its Gross Domestic Product (GDP). Furthermore, 76 percent of the nation's total revenue is generated from this region. The economy of Nepal is also bolstered by large-scale industries and key trading points between Nepal and India. Ironically, despite these contributions, the region lacks adequate educational institutions, infrastructure, and healthcare facilities.[25]

Madhesis have poorer education and health indicators than Pahadis (see Table 2). Some Madhesi activists argue that this is an inevitable result of Kathmandu's stranglehold on decision-making: even when significant revenues are generated locally, they are disbursed on the whims of capital-centric bureaucrats.[26] During the monarchy period, in the guise of land reform, the land of the Madhesis was given away to Pahadis. The King also used to give land to Pahadis as Birta—'a royal gift'.

**Table 2: Per-capita Income and Unemployment Rate in Nepal**

| *Region* | *Per capita in Rs (1995-96)* | *Unemployment Rate* |
|---|---|---|
| Himalayan | 5938 | 2.1 |
| Hilly | 8433 | 3.7 |
| Terai | 7322 | 6.5 |

*Source*: Nepal Living Standard Survey Report, 1996.

## *The Penalisation of Terai*

Large-scale migration of Pahadis to the Terai started in the 1950s and 1960s with malaria eradication. Madehsis believed that in 1951, "Nepalese rulers conspired to displace Terai residents to control Terai land in the name of population distribution."[27] The Nepal Resettlement Company was established in 1964. King Mahendra utilised the resettlement program to relocate the hill population, deemed more loyal to the Panchayat governance system, in an effort to counterbalance the predominant demographic of individuals perceived as Indian immigrants in the Terai region. By 1974, approximately fifty percent of the original land grantees had divested their properties, while others had chosen to relocate.[28]

Land was distributed among the hilly migrant population partly by clearing the forest in the Terai districts and partly by uprooting many indigenous people, including the Tharus, Satars and Rajbanshis. The Tharus in the far western region were the most brutal hit. For generations, they have had no option but to live as bonded labourers.[29] Being a Janajati, Harkha Bahadur Gurung, a staunch supporter of the Terai resettlement program in the 1980s, said that "people from Terai are a conquered people ... conquered people have got no rights because they are second-class citizens or non-citizens, for that matter."[30]

## Historical Development of the Madhesi Movement

Apart from the language factor and proximity to the Indian border, the Terai was the hub of the pro-democratic movement during the 1950s and 1960s. The ruling elites perceived India as anti-establishment and the Madhesis as India's agents. The ruling elites of Nepal have given the impression that Madhesi are mostly people of Indian origin and speak Hindi.[31] Fearing an influx of Indian immigrants into the Terai, which might prompt India to claim the Terai as Indian territory, the Nepali elite adopted stringent policies to curb the Madhesis' activism as discussed earlier.

This led to the emergence of identity-based movements in Nepal with the formation of the Nepal Terai Congress under Vedanada Jha in 1951[32] and Madheshi Mukti Andolan by Raghunath Thakur in 1956. Both the organisations raised their voices against discrimination and exploitation of the Madhesis by the ruling elite. Autonomy of the Terai region and equal representation of Madhesis in the state apparatus was demanded under Article 73 of the UN Charter.[33]

Thakur travelled to India to solicit support for the movement. During his visit, he engaged with prominent figures, including then-President Sarvepalli Radhakrishnan and Prime Minister Indira Gandhi, among others. Indian leaders articulated their apprehensions regarding the injustices faced by the Madhesis and the potential repercussions of these issues. Notably, on June 29, 1971, the Indian Parliament deliberated on the anti-India riots occurring in southern Nepal.

Members from northern Indian states bordering Nepal expressed apprehensions regarding the assaults on Madhesis. Nevertheless, the Indian government characterised the situation as an internal affair of Nepal, asserting that Madhesis were citizens of Nepal. Furthermore, India contended that the identification of the Madhesis with India could potentially incite Nepali suspicion; therefore, the Madhesis should endeavour to become "full citizens of Nepal."[34]

The first phase of the movement could not be sustained for an extended period. Nevertheless, it effectively planted the seeds of an identity movement in Nepal. The subsequent phase of the Madhesi movement, spearheaded by Gajendra Narayan Singh, emerged as a resistance initiative against both royalists and democrats. In 1983, he resigned from the Nepali National Congress (NNC) to establish a cultural organisation known as the Nepal Sadbhavana Parishad (NSP).

He distanced himself from the NNC when he felt that B.P. Koirala and others continued to discriminate against the Madhesis. The NSP was converted into a regional political party in the post-1990 multiparty system.[35] The NSP advocated for citizenship rights for the Madhesi population, recognition of Hindi as an official language, adequate Madhesi representation within state structures, and the establishment of a federal system. However, the party's credibility diminished due to its alliances with political groups primarily based in the hills. The Madhesi movement weakened as a result of its association with major political parties, compounded by the co-optation of its leaders by the monarchy. Additionally, there were recurrent efforts by the monarchy 'to foster a homogeneous hill-based identity'.[36]

## Madhesi and Jana Andolan-II

During the Maoist conflict, the CPN-Maoist established the Madhesi Rashtriya Mukti Morcha (MRMM) in 2000 under the leadership of Jai Krishna Goit to enhance Maoist influence in the Terai region. The Maoists endorsed the Madhesi's demand for autonomy. The CPN-Maoists promised a 'federal state in Madhesh, rights of self-determination and many other assurances during their decade-long revolution against the monarchy and the state.'[37]

The Jana Andolan II in 2006 heightened the aspirations for an inclusive democracy in Nepal, leading the Madhesi community to anticipate the establishment of Madhesh as an autonomous region. Consequently, they offered their unequivocal support to the movement opposing the state.

Following the success of the Jana Andolan II in April 2006 and the subsequent peace agreement between the Maoists and the government in November of the same year, marginalised groups in Nepal, including the Madhesis, anticipated the establishment of an inclusive political system defined by equality and justice within a democratic framework.

Nevertheless, the Maoists marginalised the Madhesi community following their inclusion in the interim government, where they appointed five cabinet ministers in December 2007 under the 23-point agreement. The Interim Constitution, enacted on January 15, 2007, also failed to adequately address the grievances of the Madhesi. Consequently, the Madhesi felt a sense of betrayal upon discovering that their demands were not incorporated into the 2007 interim constitution.

The Madhesi community advocated for full proportional representation, while the Nepali Congress proposed an electoral system comprising 50 percent proportional representation (PR) and 50 percent first-past-the-post (FPP) voting. The CPN-UML suggested a distribution of 60 percent PR and 40 percent FPP, whereas the Maoist Party favoured an 80-20 split in favour of PR. The political landscape was further complicated by the historical antagonism between the Pahadi and Madhesi populations. In an effort to highlight Madhesi grievances, the Madhesi Janadhikar Forum declared a shutdown of the Madhesh region on January 16, 2007. Gradually, these peaceful demonstrations escalated into widespread violent protests, strikes, and bandhs (general shutdowns). Following 23 days of unrest, the government extended an invitation for peace talks with the MJF. Concurrently, the Maoists expressed concerns about the potential involvement of certain cultural groups in India, whom they suspected of inciting separatist movements in the Terai and attempting to undermine the Constituent Assembly elections scheduled for April 2007.[38] The Maoists also tried to suppress the protests by engaging the MRMM, a front organisation of the party, which led to large-scale violence in the Terai.

After prolonged negotiations, the MJF agreed to a 22-point[39] deal with the government on August 30, 2007. However, the deal soon fell through. The MJF stated that the government had failed to fulfil its part of the agreement and declared a fresh round of protests in November 2007. The Madhesi groups formed a united platform called the United Democratic Madhesi Front (UDMF) comprising MJF, SP and Terai Madhesh Loktantrik Party (TMLP) to push forward their demand for a Madhesh autonomous state.

Their under-representation in the interim government headed by G.P. Koirala was another concern for Madhesh-based political parties and other groups. This feeling of betrayal was not confined to the Madhesis alone. The indigenous nationalities also felt the same way.[40] One Madhesi scholar observed that 'the Madheshis expected, at least, the fulfilment of promises (federalism and participation in all sphere of institutions) from all power players and policymakers' after the Jana Andolan II.[41] As a result, the movement took a militant form, which was reflected in 2007. Perhaps this led to the radicalisation of certain sections of the Madhes population and led to the establishment of some of the Madhes armed groups during this period.

The UDMF announced protests on February 11, 2008. The second phase of the Madhesi movement ended with an eight-point agreement[42] between the government and the UDMF with the guarantee of an autonomous Madhesi state under a multiparty federal state structure. In the Constituent Assembly elections of 2008, the Madhesi parties rallied around the slogan of 'Ek Madhes, Ek Pradesh', collectively gaining 11.3 percent of the nationwide vote and 85 of the 601 seats.[43]

## Madhesi and Maoist Differences

The differences between the Maoists and Madhesis also widened since the 2008 elections. The Maoists had declared in their election manifesto that they would divide Madhesh into five autonomous regions—Tharuwan, Awadh, Bhojpura, Mithila and Kochila—based on ethnicity, language and culture. In contrast, the Madhesis had asked for a single autonomous region.[44] In 2009, the Maoists changed tack and promoted the idea of two Madhesi provinces—Tharuwan and Madhesh. The Madhesis were unhappy with the Maoist vacillation over their demands.

However, the Madhesi groups failed to capitalise on their electoral success and splintered. The UDMF became defunct. Three different types of groups fought for the Madhesi cause: Madhes-based political parties, alliances between these parties, and armed outfits.[45] According to a 2007 report by the Nepalese Home Ministry, more than a hundred disgruntled groups had taken up arms or announced their intention to unleash violence to secure their interests.[46]

Many scholars have argued that the eight-point agreement was just a tactic of the major political parties. Jason Miklian notes that 'SPA leaders are pragmatic about "One Madhes", choosing to ignore the most inflammatory rhetoric while simultaneously signing multiple agreements with the UDMF in a conciliatory short-term attempt to diminish violence.'[47]

There are reports of 'internal tensions and lack of clarity on immediate demands and long-term strategy'[48] of Madhesi groups. While the Madhesh-based parties adopted a conciliatory stance on the issue, the armed groups demanded nothing short of sovereignty. Furthermore, the Madhesi political parties faced a dilemma regarding their alignment with the dominant political factions. Supporting a liberal democratic government in Kathmandu would jeopardise their pursuit of autonomy. Conversely, endorsing a Maoist-led administration in Kathmandu raised concerns about the potential erosion of the multiparty democratic system in Nepal.

Some armed groups, meanwhile, were involved in kidnapping, killing and extortion, targeting businessmen and upper-caste Pahadis. Most Madhesis dismissed the armed groups as criminals.[49] In this scenario of diffused leadership and objectives, the future of the Madhesh cause remains uncertain. There is a general feeling that 'some leaders might return to their parent parties or support a new Madheshwadi political party.'[50] The new party could be liberal, democratic, secular and all-inclusive.

## Intra-Madhesi Division

In the wake of significant political advancements in 2007 and the increasing prominence of the Madhesi issue within the region, several cultural organisations, such as the Madhesi Janadhikar Forum, transitioned to political parties. Although Madhesi groups had previously established political parties, they had not garnered comparable levels of public support or international attention as the MJF. The primary objective behind the formation of this new political entity may have been to ensure that the Madhesi community had direct representation in Parliament, stemming from a lack of trust in Pahadi leaders. Additionally, the adoption of a proportional representation (PR) system by the interim constitution may have served as a further motivating factor.

However, the MJF and other political parties based in the Madhesh region experienced several divisions within a relatively brief period. By the time of the 2008 Constituent Assembly elections, seven distinct political parties emerged from the Madhesh region. The momentum of the movement diminished due to the absence of cohesion among the various political entities and non-state actors, who operated in a fragmented manner. Some of the notable political parties engaged in advocating for Madhesi rights included the Nepal Sadbhawana Party (NSP)-Anandi Devi, NSP-Mahato, Madhesi Janadhikar Forum (MJF), Terai Madhesh Loktantrik Party (TMLP) under the leadership of Mahanta Thakur, and the Madhesi Janadhikar Forum (Loktantrik).

Among these political entities, the most significant has been the MJF, which emerged as the largest regional party, securing 51 seats in the 2008 Constituent Assembly election. The MJF was founded in 1997 as a cross-party intellectual forum with the aim of deliberating on and advocating for Madhesi issues while fostering awareness among the populace.[51]

The MJF played a pivotal role in the January 2007 protests against the Interim Constitution due to its failure to address the demands of the Madhesi community. In April 2007, the MJF was officially registered as a political party with the Election Commission, under the leadership of Upendra Yadav. Prior to the Constituent Assembly elections, the MJF presented a ten-point charter outlining its objectives and demands:

- Long live the Federal Democratic Republic.
- Constituent Assembly (CA) election with a proportional electorate system.
- One autonomy to the entire Madhes region.
- Long live the unity of all Madhesi nationalities/ethnicities and Dalits.
- End the internal colonisation of Madhesis.
- Provide a citizenship certificate to all Madhesis without discrimination.
- Establish a regional autonomous governance system, including the right to self-determination.
- Guarantee rights on the land, natural resources and biological diversity to Madhesis.
- End racial and regional discrimination.
- Stop the conspiracy to displace Madhesis.[52]

As indicated in Table 3, a total of 85 representatives from seven Madhesi political parties participated in the Constituent Assembly in 2008. A schism emerged within the MJF in September 2007 when vice-chairmen Bhagyanath Gupta, Kishor Kumar Bishwash, Ram Kumar Sharma, and Jitendra Sonal opposed Upendra Yadav's 22-point agreement with the government. The MJF experienced further fragmentation in June 2009 when a faction led by Bijaya

Kumar Gachhadar established a new party, the Madheshi Janadhikar Forum-Loktantrik, which was subsequently registered with the Election Commission.

**Table 3: Terai-based Political Parties' Position in the 2008 Constituent Assembly**

| *Sl. No.* | *Madhesi political parties* | *Seats* |
|---|---|---|
| 1 | MJF-Nepal (Upendra Yadav) | 25 |
| 2 | MJF-Loktantrik (Gachhadar) | 28 |
| 3 | Terai Madhes Democratic Party (Thakur) | 11 |
| 4 | Terai Madhes Democratic Party-Nepal (Mahendra) | 09 |
| 5 | Madhesi Janadhikar Forum-Madhesh (Bhagyanath) | 00 |
| 6 | Nepal Sadhvawana Party (Mahato) | 09 |
| 7 | Nepal Sadhvawana Party-A (Sarita Giri) | 03 |
| | Total | 85 |

*Sources: Constituent Assembly of Nepal and media reports.* *CA members elected from the Terai region under other political parties are not included.

By December 2010, the number of political parties had increased to seven from three in 2007. This proliferation was primarily attributable to personality conflicts, ambitions for power, and the nepotistic distribution of party nominations during electoral processes, among other political factors. Given that most of these parties originated from the major Kathmandu-centric political organisations, such as the Nepali Congress and the Communist Party of Nepal-Unified Marxist-Leninist, the leaders who defected tended to maintain their allegiance to their former parties. For instance, the Madhesi Jana Adhikar Forum-Nepal (MJF-Nepal) demonstrated loyalty towards the Unified Communist Party of Nepal-Maoist (UCPN-Maoist), while the Tarai Madhes Democratic Party (TMDP), under the leadership of Thakur, expressed solidarity with the Nepali Congress.

Other minor political parties were also amenable to establishing opportunistic coalitions with the three major parties. Notably, the MJF, which emerged as the pivotal force in the 2008 Constituent Assembly elections, has diminished in influence due to the fragmentation within the Madhesi movement.

By the 2013 Constituent Assembly elections, as indicated in Table 4, Madhesi-based parties had fragmented into nine distinct political entities. This fragmentation primarily occurred due to personal rivalries rather than ideological differences. Furthermore, the motivations of these leaders appeared to be largely driven by the proportional representation arrangements established in the interim constitution, prioritising personal ambition over the advancement of the Madhesi cause.

**Table 4: Terai-based Political Parties' Positions in CA Election Results 2013 under the FPTP and PR**

| *Sl. No.* | *Political parties* | *Leaders* | *FPTP* | *PR* | *Total* |
|---|---|---|---|---|---|
| 1. | Madheshi Jana Adhikar Forum, Nepal (Loktantrik) | Bijaya K. Gachhadar | 4 | 10 | 14 |
| 2. | Terai-Madhesh Loktantrik Party | Mahantha Thakur | 4 | 7 | 11 |
| 3. | Madheshi Jana Adhikari Forum, Nepal | Upendra Yadav | 2 | 8 | 10 |
| 4. | Sadbhavana Party | Rajendra Mahato | 1 | 5 | 6 |
| 5. | Terai-Madhesh Sadbhavana Party | Mahendra Raya Yadav | 0 | 3 | 3 |
| 6. | Rastriya Madhesh Samajbadi Party | Sarat Singh Bhandari | 0 | 3 | 3 |
| 7. | Madhesh Janaadhikar Forum Ganatantrik | Raj Kishor Yadav | 0 | 1 | 1 |
| 8. | Sanghiya Sadbhavana | Anil Jha | 0 | 1 | 1 |
| 9. | Madhesh Samata Party-Nepal | Meghraj Sahani | 0 | 1 | 1 |

*Source:* Constituent Assembly Elections 2013, Nepal, Report of the Election Observation Mission, Asian Network for Free Elections, Thailand.

## Madhesi Leadership

An analysis of the current leadership composition of these parties reveals that their members originate from diverse socio-economic backgrounds and hold a range of ideological perspectives. This diversity has significantly contributed to the fragmentation and lack of cohesion among them. For instance, Upendra Yadav of the MJF-Nepal aligned himself with the Maoist revolution and subsequently assumed district leadership, only to later depart from the party. In 2004, he encountered allegations related to providing intelligence to Indian security agencies regarding Matrika Yadav and Suresh Ale Magar, individuals associated with the Maoist politburo.

Following the dissolution of the MJF, Yadav's influence diminished; however, he continues to be regarded as one of Nepal's most prominent Madhesi leaders. He has fostered amicable relationships with the Maoists and is perceived as 'pro-Maoist' among Madhesi leaders. Yadav possesses a substantial support base in eastern Nepal. His party emerged as the predominant political force in

Terai (ranking fourth nationally) during the 2008 Constituent Assembly elections, and he served as the Minister of Foreign Affairs in the government led by the Maoists.

Mahanta Thakur, a prominent Madhesi leader, initially aligned with the Nepali Congress before establishing the Terai Madhes Democratic Party (TMDP) in 2007. Thakur has held various ministerial positions, including Minister of Agriculture and Cooperative, Minister of Information and Communication, and Minister of Forest and Soil Conservation within successive Nepali Congress-led administrations. Additionally, he served as the Deputy Speaker of the House of Representatives from 1991 to 1994. Although he is highly esteemed among the Madhesi community, he is perceived as lacking decisiveness. Thakur maintains strong connections and amicable relations with leaders of the Nepali Congress and is widely regarded as having favourable relations with India within the context of Nepal.

Bijay Kumar Gachhadar (MJF-Loktantrik), similar to Mahanta Thakur, was originally affiliated with the Nepali Congress. In the 2008 election, he transitioned to Upendra Yadav's MJF-Nepal after not receiving a ticket to compete under the Nepali Congress. He secured victory in the election from Sunsari-3 and possesses considerable influence among the populace in the southeastern Terai region. Gachhadar has served as a minister multiple times. Due to his Tharu ethnic background, he is frequently perceived as a Pahadi among the Madhesi community.

Rajendra Mahato won the 1994 and 1999 elections from Nepal Sadhvawana Party (NSP) and later split away from it and formed his own faction of NSP.[53] He is a senior Madhesi politician who won the Constituent Assembly election in 2008. He served as Deputy Prime Minister and held ministerial positions several times within various coalition governments. However, his popularity as a Madhesi leader is limited, largely due to his frequent shifts between political parties. Upendra Yadav and Mahanta Thakur have significantly overshadowed his contributions to advocating for Madhesi issues in different forums. In September 2044, he established a new political party called Rashtriya Mukti Kranti Nepal (RMKN), which aims to address the unresolved issues of marginalised groups through constitutional amendments.

Sarita Giri of the Nepal Sadhvawana Party (Anandi Devi) cultivated a favourable reputation among the Madhesi community due to her gender and educational background. Although her party lacked significant strength, her endeavours were widely recognised and appreciated by the Madhesi populace. She was acknowledged for her advocacy of the Madhesi cause. In 2015, she departed from the Nepal Sadbhawana Party in response to the party's decision to participate in elections conducted under the 2015 Constitution, which the party had previously rejected.

Mahendra Raya Yadav established the Terai Madhes Loktantrik Party-Nepal following a schism with nine other leaders from the Terai Madhes Loktantrik Party led by Mahant Thakur in December 2010. He exhibits a pronounced affinity for left-wing politics, with particular regard for Maoist ideologies.

## Madhesh-based Major Armed Groups

In addition to the established political parties, various armed groups from the Terai region assert that they are the legitimate representatives of the Madhesi populace and have been advocating for a separate sovereign nation since 2007. These groups contend that the mainstream Madhesi political entities have inadequately represented their interests at the national level. They argue that the Madhesh political leadership has failed to effectively engage with the interim government, resulting in a decline in popularity for numerous political parties, including the MJF, since 2007.[54]

According to a 2009 report by Nepal's Ministry of Home Affairs, approximately 109 armed entities were active in Nepal, with 58 of these located in the Terai region. The majority of these groups incorporated the terms 'Terai' or 'Madhesi' in their designations, with some utilising both terms. There may be additional groups whose names do not reflect words such as Terai, Madhesh, or Tharu, yet still operate within the region. The second most prevalent term associated with these organisations is 'Mukti' (liberation).[55]

These armed groups are characterised by intense inter-and intra-group rivalries, which have resulted in numerous breakaway factions. For instance, the Janatantrik Tarai Mukti Morcha comprises eight factions (Ranavir, Himmat, Pawan, Tufan, Jwala Singh, Rajan, Prithivi, and Bisfot). Notably, the majority of these groups are splinter factions of the former CPN-Maoist. The objectives and motives of many of these entities remain ambiguous. Nearly all of them engage in extortion and criminal activities, often justifying their actions in the name of a struggle for "independence."[56] The most prominent of these organisations are enumerated below.

### *JTMM*

The Janatantrik Terai Mukti Morcha (JTMM) was established in 2004 following a break from the CPN-Maoist. The organisation advocated for the creation of an autonomous Terai region. The JTMM subsequently fragmented into two factions: one led by Jai Krishna Goit and another by Jwala Singh, also known as Nagendra Paswana, as well as a separate group identified as the Janatantric Terai Mukti Morcha (Bisphot Singh).[57] The aforementioned groups opposed the 2006 peace process in Nepal. The members of these three factions, along with Maoist cadres, frequently participated in violent confrontations against one another, as well as directed their hostility towards the Pahadi community.

### *Terai Cobra*

The outfit has vowed to launch an armed separatist struggle for a sovereign Terai state. The party's strategy was to oppose the presence of Pahadis in the area. The outfit has a presence in the Bara, Parsa, Rautahat, and Sarlahi districts, and it claims that its headquarters is in the southern town of Birgunj. The outfit came to the limelight for the first time by killing a truck driver in the Madhuwan area of Sarlahi district in February 2007.[58]

## Janatantrik Tarai Mukti Morcha (Revolutionary) (JTMM-R)

The JTMM-R is a militant organisation led by Jaya Krishna Goit, operating primarily in the eastern Terai region of Nepal. This group represents a more extreme faction of the JTMM, which previously entered into a peace agreement with the Nepalese government. The JTMM-R was implicated in a bomb explosion at a government office in Lahan, located in the Siraha district of south-eastern Nepal, in March 2021.

Eight government employees were injured in the incident. Releasing a press statement hours after the incident, Goit stated that the blast was a part of his group's 'campaign against corruption'.[59] The organisation has warned of implementing stringent measures should corruption persist, holding both the Government of Nepal and the Provincial Government accountable. It is alleged that Goit has engaged in peace agreements with the government on multiple occasions. Subsequent to each agreement, he modified the name of his political party and operated with relative impunity, primarily for extortion endeavours. Consequently, he has altered his party's name nine times up until 2020.

## Terai Mukti Morcha

Vinod Kumar Yadav spearheaded the All Nepal Janatantrik Terai Mukti Morcha (Vivek group), an underground organisation that initiated armed activities in the Terai region. On December 14, 2018, he renounced violence in favour of engaging in peaceful political discourse. Following a split from the Jayakrishna Goit-led Janatantrik Terai Mukti Morcha in 2010, the group operated independently in the plains; however, it has remained largely dormant in recent times.

Four members of the group submitted their firearms at the District Administration Office of Morang. An automatic pistol and two additional pistols were presented to the coordinator of the government-formed negotiations team, Som Prasad Pande. With the surrender of weapons, the organisation's Chairperson, Bivek Yadav (Binod Kumar Yadav), along with central members Ramanandan Kumar Kamait (Ramu), Binaya Kumar Yadav (Chandrashekhar), and Jaya Prakash Lichpuriya (JP), publicly identified themselves in the presence of human rights advocates, journalists, and representatives of the administration. The organisation declared to the media that 'after talks with the government, we decided to submit our arms wishing to join peaceful politics.' The team has requested an extension to collect and submit all remaining weapons, indicating that some are still unaccounted for.[60]

## Alliance for Independent Madhes

The Janamat Party (JP) was established on March 17, 2019. The party is led by C.K. Raut, who previously founded the Alliance for Independent Madhes (AIM) and subsequently rebranded it as JP, thereby relinquishing its foundational objective of advocating for a separate Madhesh state. The AIM had sought the delineation of a distinct Madhesh region from Nepal. Initially, the AIM was predominantly involved in secessionist activities; however, there are no documented indications of the organisation possessing any armed factions.

The AIM publicly unveiled its manifesto and programs during a press conference held in Kathmandu on May 21, 2012. Its political objective was to attain the independence of Madhesh through peaceful and non-violent methods. The organisation advocated for the cessation of Nepal's colonial practices in the Madhesh region and calls for an end to the racism, oppression, and discrimination faced by individuals of Madhesi origin within the country.

The AIM altered the name and flag of the party following a two-day national council meeting held in Lahan, situated in the Siraha district. The party is duly registered with the Election Commission of Nepal. The Janamat Party comprises a 35-member central committee. Prior to the establishment of the party, the AIM had engaged in mainstream politics by entering into an 11-point agreement with the State/Government on March 8, 2019.

As per the agreement, the AIM withdrew its campaign for independent Madhesh and accepted Nepal's territorial integrity and the constitution.[61] There were allegations of Raut's connections with certain Western nations; however, the precise nature of these affiliations remains ambiguous. Notably, despite his secessionist inclinations, the Unrepresented Nations and Peoples Organization (UNPO) called for the immediate release of Raut following his arrest on October 8, 2018.[62]

## Anti-Constitution Agitation

After seven years of deliberation and negotiation aimed at reconciling the divergent perspectives of various political factions, Nepal's Constituent Assembly promulgated the new Constitution on September 19, 2015. Following the president's endorsement of the draft, a significant celebration ensued in and around Kathmandu. However, a substantial portion of the population, particularly among the Janajatis, individuals residing in the Terai region, Dalits, and women's rights organisations, expressed opposition to the new Constitution.

The Terai region experienced significant civil unrest following the promulgation of the Constitution. Protests escalated from August 9, 2015, resulting in the fatalities of over 46 individuals, including ten security personnel, during various incidents. Some media reports indicated that certain Madhesi activists and their families were contemplating seeking political asylum in the Indian states of Bihar and Uttar Pradesh due to concerns regarding potential reprisals from Nepali security forces. To suppress the protests, the Nepal Armed Police reportedly engaged in excessive use of force. There were concerns that some individuals might resort to underground activities if the Constitution failed to adequately address their demands.

## *Madhesi Demands*

Everyday life in Nepal was significantly disrupted, and various regions experienced shortages of essential goods due to prolonged protests and roadblocks organised by the Samyukt Loktantrik Madhesi Morcha (SLMM), the Tharu community, and Janajati groups. As a component of their protests, some elected representatives from the Terai region either resigned from the Constituent Assembly or boycotted the constitution-making process. The marginalised groups contended that the constitution promulgated by the CA failed to address their longstanding grievances. These grievances included the demarcation of provincial boundaries along ethnic lines, the establishment of two Madhesh provinces, proportional representation of ethnic groups within state agencies and the parliament, equal political rights for individuals to acquire citizenship through naturalisation, and the implementation of prior agreements between the State and the Janajati and Madhesi communities. Subsequently, the SLMM also demanded the withdrawal of the Army from the Terai region as a precondition for negotiations.

The government of Nepal responded to the Madhesi protests at the border, characterising them as an undeclared border blockade enforced by India. In a televised address, Prime Minister K. P. Sharma Oli articulated this perspective. "Nepal is passing through a serious humanitarian crisis that should not happen even during wars. The blockade imposed by our southern neighbour has underestimated the feelings of the Nepali and Indian people. Imposing a blockade on a landlocked nation is a breach of international treaties, norms, and values."[63]

Earlier, the Indian government had cited the safety and security of the Indian truckers in Nepal and the technical reasons behind the disruption of the supply of fuel and essential commodities to Nepal. India issued its third note on Nepal on 21 September 2015, which said: 'We are deeply concerned over the incidents of violence.... Our freight companies and transporters have also voiced complaints about the difficulties they are facing in movement within Nepal....'[64] The aforementioned note instigated apprehensions in Nepal regarding the possibility of India implementing an economic blockade similar to that of 1988-89. Groups opposed to India capitalised on the increasing anxiety over potential Indian repercussions in Nepal. Notably, India was taken aback by the emergence of anti-India sentiments across Nepalese print, electronic, and social media platforms.

## Contentious Provisions in the Constitution

The draft constitution did not unify Nepal but instead exacerbated divisions among its populace, categorising individuals into two significantly polarised groups: the so-called Pahadis and the non-Pahadis, which include the Madhesi, Tharus, and Janajatis. Despite the demands for greater representation from the Janajati and Madhesi communities in the formulation of an inclusive constitution, the ruling authorities proceeded with the promulgation of the constitution without addressing these appeals. This decision undermined the trust between the inhabitants of the plains and the dominant Pahadi elites. Rather than fostering national cohesion, the new constitution further fragmented the country along ethnic and geographical lines.

According to the Madhesi interpretation, Article 42 (1) stipulates that socially disadvantaged women, Dalits, Adibasi, Janajati, Madhesi, Tharu, minority groups, persons with disabilities, marginalised communities, Muslims, backward classes, gender and sexually diverse groups, youths, peasants, labourers, the oppressed, citizens from underprivileged regions, and economically disadvantaged Khas Arya shall possess the right to employment in state structures based on the 'principle of inclusion.' However, the phrase 'principle of inclusion' has been perceived as ambiguous and fails to provide any constitutional assurance of adequate representation for marginalised groups in governmental positions in accordance with their demographic proportions. Consequently, this Article has been regarded as a regression or dilution compared to the Interim Constitution of 2007, which assured proportional representation of marginalised groups in government employment.[65]

Article 84 (1) stipulates that the House of Representatives shall comprise two hundred and seventy-five members, distributed as follows: (a) One hundred and sixty-five members are elected through a first-past-the-post electoral system, with one member representing each of the one hundred and sixty-five electoral constituencies established by partitioning Nepal based on geographical and population considerations. Madhesi stakeholders interpret this provision as detrimental to the equitable representation of marginalised groups within the lower house. The dual criteria for delineating electoral constituencies appear to contravene democratic principles. Furthermore, the constitution lacks clarity regarding the criteria for constituency delineation based on geography and population, thereby engendering insecurity among marginalised groups. Notably, the practice of determining electoral constituencies for the lower house based solely on geography and population is virtually unprecedented globally. The implementation of these provisions could potentially grant the hill regions an additional 35 seats on a geographic basis, as each district is likely to elect one representative. Additionally, based on population metrics, the hill regions could secure approximately 22 more seats than those allocated to the Terai region.[66]

Similarly, the Terai region may face inadequate representation in the National Assembly (NA). According to Article 86 (2) (a), eight members are to be elected from each province. As a result, the two Terai provinces would contribute 19 members based on the current provincial boundaries. This situation would lead to a dominance of representatives from the hill provinces, who would possess an additional 24 seats in the NA.[67]

Another contentious issue was the constitution discriminates against persons who have obtained citizenship through naturalisation. Article 11 (7) says, "Notwithstanding anything contained elsewhere in this Article, in the case of a person born from a woman who is a citizen of Nepal and married to a foreign citizen, the person may acquire the naturalised citizenship of Nepal under the Federal law if he or she has permanently resided in Nepal and has not acquired the citizenship of a foreign country."[68] Again, Article 289 (1) restricts the persons who obtain citizenship through the naturalisation process from getting top constitutional positions.

Moreover, while residents of the plains of Nepal have advocated for the establishment of two Madhesh Pradesh, the newly enacted constitution has partitioned the region into six provinces. With the exception of province number six, all other provinces maintain direct access to India. This has exacerbated the political and social vulnerabilities faced by the inhabitants of the Terai region. They perceive that the ruling elites from the hill regions are reluctant to share power with them.[69]

Among the four debated provisions in the new constitution, Articles 42, 84, and 86 are seen as notably significant. If these provisions are not amended, the Terai region may continue to experience violent protests. Although the government has established a three-member committee to facilitate negotiations with the agitating groups, and the cabinet has approved amendments to Articles 42 and 84, the protesters express scepticism regarding the government's sincerity. They believe that the government's initiative is merely a tactic to divert attention from the agitation. Furthermore, the government has yet to develop a comprehensive plan to address their demands. There is a prevailing concern that the amendment process may face significant obstacles due to profound ideological differences among the three leading political parties regarding the election of a consensus candidate for the Prime Minister's position. This discord among the principal political factions could potentially derail or prolong the amendment process, which necessitates a two-thirds majority for approval.

## New Demands under the New Constitution

In the post-constitution period, the Madhesi continued their agitation against the State to make amendments to the constitution to address the following issues:

1. Amendments in the constitution to create a more parliamentary constituency in the Terai regions based on population.
2. Amendments in the Citizenship Act.
3. Hindi as an official language of State no 2.
4. Withdrawal of criminal cases and the release of arrested Madhesi-based party leaders and cadres who had participated in the anti-constitution protests from September 2015 onwards.[70]

The Madhesi-based parties experienced a decline in their negotiating power with the new government in Kathmandu, largely due to intra-party factionalism. Certain Madhesi leaders compromised the region's fundamental political and social issues in pursuit of personal power and financial gain. In the 2017 local, provincial, and parliamentary elections, Madhesi parties participated as two distinct groups: the Upendra Yadav faction, known as the Federal Socialist Forum (FSF), and a coalition of six parties led by Mahanta Thakur, referred to as the Rastriya Janata Party (RJP-Nepal) or Thakur faction. Under exceptional circumstances, both entities amalgamated on April 23, 2020, to avert a potential dissipation of their influence, resulting in the formation of the Janata Samajwadi Party (JSP).

## International Community Responses

Despite divergent domestic reactions and occurrences of violence in the Terai region, Nepal garnered commendation from the international community for its adoption of the new constitution. China, the European Union, and Japan promptly extended their congratulations to Nepal. Subsequently, Norway, the United States, the United Kingdom, Russia, and the United Nations also expressed their approval.

India neither 'welcomed' nor 'congratulated' Nepal on this occasion. Instead, there was a press release with the title, 'Statement on the situation in Nepal', which stated:

> "We note the promulgation in Nepal today of a Constitution. We are concerned that the situation in several parts of the country bordering India continues to be violent ...We urge that issues on which there are differences should be resolved through dialogue in an atmosphere free from violence and intimidation, and institutionalised in a manner that would enable broad-based ownership and acceptance."[71]

In the interim, the Indian response prompted certain influential international actors to exercise caution. China, which initially endorsed and congratulated Nepal on the adoption of its new constitution, subsequently revised its stance and advised Nepalese leaders to adopt a more inclusive approach in order to incorporate the perspectives of marginalised groups.

A press briefing by the Chinese foreign office on September 21, 2015, stated: 'China sincerely hopes that all political parties in Nepal can bear in mind the fundamental interests of their country and the people, address the differences through dialogue and consultation, realise enduring development of the country and bring happiness to the people.'[72] The observation by the United States also followed similar lines.

Although India played a pivotal role in the 12-point agreement between the then Seven-Party Alliance (SPA) and the Maoists in 2005 and subsequently in the 2006 peace process, its proactive engagement diminished as the first CA failed to produce a constitution, leading to criticism from certain segments of the Nepali media and civil society regarding India's involvement. India subsequently adopted a 'hands-off' policy, conveying messages to refrain from interfering in the constitution drafting process and promoting a 'Nepali-grown model' to foster consensus, a process initiated in May 2010. However, in the immediate aftermath of the finalisation of Nepal's constitution, particularly with the escalation of violence and the anticipation of political asylum seekers entering Indian territory, India soon found itself entangled in Nepal's domestic affairs.

In addition, India perceived a sense of disregard as the Nepali political leadership dismissed its concerns and recommendations, which had been consistently communicated since Prime Minister Modi's visit to Nepal in August 2014. India expressed apprehension, recognising that a protracted conflict in Nepal would not serve its interests. Fearing a situation analogous to that of Sri Lanka along its northern border and genuinely concerned about the sustainability of a constitution already mired in controversy, India was apprehensive about Nepal's newly adopted constitution.

Moreover, India experienced a sense of disillusionment with the leadership in Nepal. Prominent Nepalese leaders—including K. P. Oli, former Prime Minister Sushil Koirala, Pushpa Kamal Dahal (Prachanda), and Sher Bahadur Deuba—had assured, during private engagements with Prime Minister Modi and other senior Indian officials, that the constitution would be promulgated with a foundation of consensus. India had consistently anticipated that Nepalese leaders would honour their commitments.

Furthermore, India expressed particular concern regarding the burgeoning 'united front' among the leftist political parties in Nepal—especially between the Maoists and the Communists—who were aligned against India, supported by external powers opposed to Indian influence in Nepal. India had already anticipated such a coalition of forces arrayed against it when it was kept uninformed about the 16-point agreement signed in June 2015 among Nepal's four principal political parties.[73] The Madhesi movement, which received minimal international attention until January 2007, abruptly emerged as a focal point for a new ethnic movement in South Asia. Certain media reports suggested that Paul Handley, an official from the United Nations Office for the Coordination of Humanitarian Affairs (OCHA), conducted a covert visit to Bihar in 2007 to engage with the Jwala Singh faction of the JTMM.[74]

Then UNMIN chief Ian Martin, in an interview, confirmed that 'both our own civil affairs officers and also the Office of the High Commissioner for Human Rights try to play a constructive role [in Terai] where there are local differences that threaten the peace in some way.'[75] Many Madhesi groups have also increasingly been paying attention to NGOs and INGOs. Reports show they also try to get funds from external sources to fight for their cause.

Conversely, the volatile political situation in Nepal, particularly in its border regions, affords significant opportunities for both China and Pakistan to bolster anti-India factions, facilitate arms and counterfeit currency trafficking, establish madrasas, and support terrorist organizations within Nepal. The MJF faction, led by Upendra Yadav, garnered controversy following the attendance of a high-level Chinese delegation at its General Convention in early 2009.

India instinctively perceived this development as a strategic challenge within its Himalayan sphere of influence. The nation's apprehensions were further corroborated when the alliance of three major political parties disregarded India's recommendations regarding the formulation of a comprehensive document that would accommodate the demands of marginalized groups. Even during Foreign Secretary Jaishankar's visit to Nepal on September 18, 2015, senior leaders dismissed India's proposals to postpone the constitution-making process by 10 to 15 days and to engage in dialogue with the protesting factions.

The deterioration of India-Nepal relations following the constitutional period could have been averted if Nepalese leaders had exercised caution and pragmatism. In light of the protracted protests, the leadership in Nepal ought to have sought to engage with dissenting voices, address mutual disparities, and implement necessary revisions to the constitution to address the concerns of groups feeling marginalised by its provisions.

On the Indian side, instead of abruptly transitioning from its policy of 'hands-off' to a state of 'panic reaction,' India should have proactively engaged all stakeholders and ensured that the new constitution was appropriately amended to address the demands of the marginalized groups in Nepal.

## India-Nepal Relations and Madhesh

Due to its inherent sensitivity, India has frequently implemented a prudent policy regarding the Madhesi issue. The country has regarded the Madhesi situation as an internal affair of Nepal. Furthermore, India has officially articulated the position that the dilemma can be addressed through the incorporation of minority rights in the new constitution.

Even so, Nepal's Pahadis believe India has been encouraging the 'One Madhes One Pradesh' demand. There was a suspicion amongst the Pahadis and major political leaders in Nepal that India was out to balkanise Nepal. Former Prime Minister G.P. Koirala, hinting at India's hand in the Terai crisis, had stated, "The ongoing Madhesh crisis can be solved within a minute if Nepal and India jointly work together for it."[76] The UCPN-Maoist Chairman Prachanda made a similar observation during the 2007 Madhesi protests against the Interim Constitution. If this perception gained further ground, it could cause more anti-Indianism in Nepal, giving more space to China and Pakistan to use Nepal as a hotbed for anti-India activities. This perception was further strengthened in the early 2000s when there was an effort to develop a new pro-India constituency in the Terai region.

Some leaders in Nepal contend that India has taken measures that address Madhesi grievances, thereby fostering political organisation among the Madhesi community. There may be ulterior motives at play, such as undermining the connections between the Maoists of Nepal and India. At that time, the Madhesis were collaborating closely with the Maoists; by distancing them from this alliance, India effectively weakened the Maoists in Nepal while simultaneously creating a buffer between the Maoist movements in both countries.[77]

As part of this initiative, the Nepal-India Friendship Association was reportedly established under India's active encouragement, and certain development projects financed by India were redirected to the Terai region to cultivate this constituency. The objective of this endeavour appears to be the establishment of long-term, dependable partners in Nepal and the influence of Nepali policies through these stakeholders.

The Madhesis, the other hand, believe India's policy towards Nepal has been more Kathmandu-centric. They accuse India of neglecting the Madhesi movement. In an interview, Upendra Yadav said, "India, especially South Block and the Indian Embassy, have been against the Madhesh and MJF. They created the TMLP to weaken us. One of the reasons the pre-election alliance did not happen was because India was trying to boost up TMLP."[78]

Another senior leader of the Sadbhavana Party remarked to this author that '80 percent of India's aid is being utilised in the hilly region.'[79] The Madhesis also accused India of having an engineering division in the MJF in June 2009. Keshav Mainali, the president of the Chure Bhawar Ekta Samaj (CBES), observed that 'it is only as and when India wants controversial issues to erupt, it shows up in Madhesh. India's stand on Nepali Madhesi issue has been self-contradictory.'[80]

In the Terai region, there is an ongoing debate suggesting that the Madhesi groups have not made any substantial decisions regarding their future. This impasse is attributed to India's support for liberal democratic parties that oppose ethnicity-based federalism.[81] One academic remarked that even the Madhesi political and insurgent leaders express discontent regarding Indian intervention, as such involvement may adversely affect the political prospects of their constituencies. Several of these leaders regard the Madhesh issue as exclusively an internal matter within Nepal, asserting that there are no elements present to transform it into a bilateral concern.[82]

## Madhesh and India's Economic and Security Interests in Nepal

A protracted crisis in the Terai region could adversely impact the overall bilateral relations between India and Nepal, particularly given the special arrangements that exist, such as the open border, the substantial diaspora in each country, over 27 trading points, the participation of Nepali citizens in the Indian Army, and robust people-to-people connections. These factors suggest that the anti-Indian sentiment arising from the Madhesh movement may undermine India's economic and security interests in Nepal. Frequent protests have previously disrupted trade and commercial relations between the two nations. Additionally, the prevailing anti-Indian sentiment could jeopardize India's hydroelectric projects and the operational viability of Indian investments in Nepal. Since the Terai region serves as a crucial link between India and northern Nepal, instability in this area could potentially disrupt all major highways and customs points.

India was blamed—both by the UCPN-Maoist party after Prachanda's resignation in May 2009 and by the ordinary people—for its perceived excessive intervention in the internal affairs of Nepal and encouraging encroachment of Nepalese territory along the borders. This anti-India feeling has affected India's economic relations with Nepal.

A survey by FICCI (Federation of Indian Chambers of Commerce and Industry) highlighted that Nepal's industries are badly hit by acute shortages of power and raw materials. Petrol and diesel supply have run out, and the labour unrest has struck at the heart of businesses.'[83] An Indian official has been quoted as saying, 'We view the developments in Nepal very disturbing as far as the Pancheshwar dam is concerned.'[84] India is, in fact, concerned about the delay in the implementation of hydroelectric projects like the proposed 6000 MW Pancheshwar dam.

India's engagement with Nepal is paramount for the preservation of long-term security interests, particularly in light of some anti-India elements assertive stance on a range of issues in relation to India.

A combination of rising anti-India feelings in recent years and the ongoing political instability have allowed anti-India forces in the region to step up their activities in Nepal. It needs to be reiterated that India shares a long open border with Nepal, which has been used by terrorists, smugglers and anti-India elements sponsored by Pakistan's Directorate of Inter-Services Intelligence (ISI). India's former Ambassador to Nepal, Rakesh Sood, said in an interview with the Nepalese media on April 29, 2010: 'Nearly 20 terrorists slipped into India from Nepal in 2009 using the open border between the two countries while fake Indian currency worth almost Rs 2 crore was seized in the country in what is a major security concern for India.'[85]

Some media reports reveal that radical Islamic groups operating within India (like Indian Mujahideen) are using Nepalese territory as a haven, especially after Bangladeshi security forces launched action against their bases in Bangladesh.[86] In June 2009, Mohammad Omar Madani, the alleged Lashkar-e-Taiba (LeT) head in Nepal, was arrested in Delhi. Madani had set up a madrasa in the jungles along the India-Nepal border from where newly trained militants could be sent to India. On April 4, 2010, Nepalese police arrested a LeT cadre who was instructed by his handlers to be part of the LeT's larger plan to carry out attacks on India's mainland.[87]

## Difficult Choices for India

Nepal's instability is poised to adversely affect India's political, economic, and security interests. At any given time, turmoil in the Terai region portends negative consequences for India. The Terai is characterised by a diverse population comprising multiple ethnic and caste groups, sharing cultural and religious affiliations with communities in India. Consequently, India confronts complex decisions. Any constructive efforts by India to ameliorate the situation in Terai through proactive engagement may be perceived as an unnecessary intervention in Nepal's internal affairs, potentially alienating the Pahadi population and the Nepalese Army. Conversely, a stance of passive indifference towards developments in Terai could be construed as a dereliction of responsibility by domestic observers and the Madhesi community.

India, in principle, opposes any form of discrimination against minority groups. The political challenges facing Nepal could be addressed by integrating minority perspectives into the new constitution and by institutionalising democratic norms and values. India firmly maintains that armed revolution, secessionist movements, and political violence are not viable solutions to discrimination and injustice. As a considerate neighbour, India values and respects Nepal's social and communal harmony. Consequently, an optimal approach for India regarding Nepal would be to act as a constructive facilitator in enhancing the capacity of various democratic institutions to alleviate social tensions in Nepal, particularly in the Terai region.

Considering the ethnic and caste diversity, social inequality, and historical animosity between the Pahadi and Terai populations, along with the political and economic significance of the Terai region in Nepal, the Madhesi issue is likely to remain complex in the future. Cultural and political identity constitutes only one facet of the problem. Within the Madhesi community, various minority and caste groups, such as the Tharus and the Chure Bhawar Ekta Samaj, are advocating for the establishment of separate provinces.

Furthermore, there exist caste divisions among individuals of Indian origin. The Madhesi movement has encountered a leadership crisis, with disparate factions lacking consensus regarding the movement's objectives. Given its significant influence in Nepal, India may assume a crucial role in facilitating dialogue among stakeholders to address these contentious issues. A timely resolution of the Madhesi issue would mitigate challenges along India's northern frontier.

## NOTES

1 Since the word 'Madhesi' is mentioned in the 2015 Constitution of Nepal, the same is used here. Madhes groups and scholars use 'Madhes (i)' and 'Madhesh (i) while expressing their identity. There is no mention of the word "Madhes or Madhesh" in the 2015-Cosntituion. Interestingly, on 17 January 2022, the Assembly of Province no -2, Nepal, renamed the province "Madhesh Pradesh" and Janakpurdham as its provincial capital. For details, see https://kathmandupost.com/province-no-2/2022/01/17/province-2-endorses-madhes-as-its-name-janakpurdham-designated-as-provincial-capital. Also, https://himalsanchar.com/in-the-madhesh-gazette-the-government-says-that-a-mistake-has-been-made-it-will-be-rectified/ (accessed on 14 April 2022).

2 Abhishek Kumar, et al, "Shivalik, Siwalik, Shiwalik or Sivalik: Which one is an appropriate term for the foothills of Himalayas?", *Journal of Scientific Research*, Volume 64, Issue 1, 2020, Institute of Science, Banaras Hindu University, Varanasi, India, https://www.bhu.ac.in/research_pub/jsr/Volumes/JSR_64_01_2020/1.pdf (accessed on 24 April 2022).

3 The word 'Terai' is mentioned in the schedule-2 of the 2015-Constituion. Therefore, Terai is used here onwards.

4 Author's interacting with Chandra Kishore in New Delhi in January 2022.

5 Rishikesh Shah, "Ancient and Medieval Nepal", *Kailash*. Further details are not available. A PDF link of the article is attached for details. https://www.repository.cam.ac.uk/bitstream/id/522659/kailash_14_0304_01.pdf/ (accessed on 14 April 2022).

6 Pitambar Sharma, "Unraveling the Mosaic: Spatial Aspects of Ethnicity in Nepal", Himal Books, Kathmandu, 2008, p.06.

7 Bishnu Pathak and Chitra Niraula, "Madhes Violence: Identity Clash in Nepal", *Conflict Study Center Report*1 February 2007. http://madhesi.wordpress.com/?s=Madhes+Violence%3A+Identity+Clash+in+Nepal&searchbutton=Go%21, (accessed on 24 September 2021).

8 Pitambar Sharma, no. 6, p. 11 (Table 2). The data does not include people from hills living in Terai.

9 Bishnu Pathak and Chitra Niraula, no. 7. Also see Harka Gurung, "Social Demography of Nepal: Census 2001", Himal Books, Kathmandu, 2005.

10 Krishna Pandey, "Politicising ethnicity: Tharu contestation of Madheshi identity in Nepal's Tarai", *The Southasianist*, Vol. 5, No.1, 2017, p. 306.

11 Deb Ranjan Sinha, "Betrayal or 'Business as Usual'? Access to Forest Resources in the Nepal Terai", *Environment and History*, Vol. 17, No. 3, August 2011, p.441.

12 "Nepal's Troubled Tarai Region," International Crisis Group, *Asia Report*, No 136, 9 July 2007, p. 4.

13 The Interim Constitution of Nepal 2007 mentioned, 'Any person born and living permanently

in Nepal before the end of mid April, 1990 shall acquire the citizenship of Nepal by birth in accordance with the existing law.'

14 Hugh Massey "Legal and protection policy research series, UNHCR and De Facto Statelessness" Division of International Protection, LPPR/2010/01, April 2010, http://www.unhcr.org/cgi-bin/texis/vtx/search?page=search&docid=4bc2ddeb9&query=Paul White Nepal (accessed on 25 September 2021).

15 "Who are Madhesis?" PDF file. Follow the link for details. https://indiamadhesi.wordpress.com/wp-content/uploads/2008/10/who-are-madhesis.pdf (accessed on 23 October 2024). Also see Nuru Lama, "Hope for a new Nepal", Commentary, *Nepali Times*, #45, 1 - 7 June 2001.

16 Abhi Subedi, "Politics and the Nepali language", Columns, *The Kathmandu Post*, 23 April 2022.

17 Bishnu Pathak and Chitra Niraula, no.7.

18 Author's interaction over phone with civil society leaders and senior journalists of Nepal in September 2021.

19 Mahesh Chaudhary, "Buddha was not born in Madhes", *Nagarik news*, July 23, 2075, https://nagariknews.nagariknetwork.com/others/153567-1530923460.html (accessed on 25 September 2021).

20 Baburam Bhul, "Representative Bureaucracy: The Nepalese Perspective", PRASHASAN, October 2021, Volume 52, Issue 1, No. 134, p. 198-216.

21 Hari Bansh Jha, "Continued Economic Backwardness of Terai: Its Reasons and Remedies", Centre for Economic and Technical Studies, Lalitpur, Nepal, 2010, p. 15.

22 Dipendra Jha, "Federal Nepal: Trials and Tribulations", AAKAR Books, Delhi, 2018, P.211.

23 Dhanu Bishwakarma, "Reaffirming affirmative action", *The Nepali Times*, a weekly new paper published from Kathmandu, 07 September 2024, https://nepalitimes.com/here-now/reaffirming-affirmative-action (accessed on 16 October 2024).

24 "Madhesi inclusion in judiciary still a far cry", *The Himalayan*, 08 December 2019, https://thehimalayantimes.com/nepal/madhesi-inclusion-in-judiciary-still-a-far-cry (accessed on 24 April 2022).

25 Jay Prakash Gupta, Madhesh Pradeshko Prastabana (Nepali), CPMHR, Kathmandu, 2007.

26 "Nepal's Troubled Tarai Region," ICG Report, Report 136 / ASIA, 09 July 2007.

27 J. K. Goait, "History of Terai in Nepal", 04 April 2007, http://madhesi.wordpress.com/2007/04/04/history-of-terai-in-nepal/.(accessed on 25 September 2021).

28 Deb Ranjan Sinha, "Betrayal or 'Business as Usual'? Access to Forest Resources in the Nepal Terai", *Environment and History* , August 2011, Vol. 17, No. 3, P.442.

29 Har Bansha Jha, *no.* 21. Also see Jay Prakash Gupta, Madhesh Vidhroh (Nepali), CPMHR, Kathmandu, 2008.

30 Sukhdev Shah, "Terai's Fate—Looking Within!" 31 January 2007, at http://demrepubnepal.blogspot.com/2007/02/sukhdev-shah-terais-fatelooking-within.html. (accessed on 25 September 2021).

31 Krishna Pandey, no.10.

32 "Nepal's Troubled Tarai Region," *ICG Report*, Asia Report No.136, 09 July 2007, p. 5.

33 http://madhesi.wordpress.com/2007/04/04/history-of-terai-in-nepal/.(accessed on 25 September 2021)

34 Lok Sabha debate on "Anti-Indian riots in South Nepal", 29 June 1971.

35 S. Chandrasekharan, "Terain leader Gajendra Narayan Singh passes away," *South Asia Analysis Group*, 18 February 2002.

36 "Nepal's Troubled Tarai Region," no. 32, p. 6.

37 Shree Govind Shah, “Peaceful Resolution of Ethno political Movement in Nepal Madhesh”, http://madhesh.org/articles/peaceful-resolution-of-ethnopolitical-movement-in-nepal-madhesh/(accessed on 25 September 2021).

38 UCPN-Maoist chief Prachanda's statement on 19 January on Madhesi uprising.

39 See Appendix I.

40 Shree Govind Shah, no. 37.

41 Ram Manohar Sah, “Madheshi Murmurings”, http://madhesh.org/articles/madheshi-murmurings/(accessed on 25 September 2021).

42 Appendix II.

43 Jason Miklian, “Nepal's Terai: Constructing an Ethnic Conflict”, South Asia Briefing Paper #1, PRIO Paper, Oslo, 2009, p. 5.

44 Pratibadhatta Patra (Nepali) 2008, Communist Party of Nepal-Maoist.

45 Appendix IV.

46 “More armed groups emerge in Nepal”, *reliefweb*, 18 September 2007.

47 Jason Miklian, no. 43, p. 7.

48 “Nepal's Troubled Tarai Region”, no. 32, p. 19.

49 Ibid., p. 16.

50 Author's interview with a senior leader from the Terai region in Patna in February 2010.

51 “Nepal's Troubled Tarai Region,” no. 32, p. 5.

52 J K Goait, “History of Terai in Nepal”, 04 April 2007, http://madhesi.wordpress.com/2007/04/04/history-of-terai-in-nepal (accessed on 25 September 2021).

53 The original Nepal Sadhavawana Party (NSP) is now headed by Anandi Devi, while another influential factions are led by Rajendra Mahato.

54 Shree Govind Shah, no. 37.

55 Other terms being used are ‘liberation’, ‘revolution’ and ‘republican’, ‘army’, ‘sena’, ‘force’, ‘ladaku dal’, and ‘military’.

56 Narayan Manandhar, “Nepal's armed groups”, *myRepublica*, Kathmandu, 29 August 2009, http://www.myrepublica.com/portal/index.php?action=news_details&news_id=9156 (accessed on 25 September 2021).

57 “Responses to Information Requests”, Immigration and Refugee Board of Canada, https://www.justice.gov/eoir/page/file/1045886/download (accessed on 25 September 2021).

58 “New armed groups sprout up in Nepal,” *The Asian Tribune*, 02 June 2007.

59 “Goit-led Janatantrik Tarai Mukti Morcha takes responsibility of Lahan blast”, *my Repuiblica*, 14 march 2021, https://myrepublica.nagariknetwork.com/news/goit-led-janatantrik-tarai-mukti-morcha-takes-responsibility-of-lahan-blast/ (accessed on 25 September 2021).

60 “Breakaway JTTM faction submits arms”, *The Himalayan*, 14 December 2021, https://thehimalayantimes.com/nepal/breakaway-janatantrik-tarai-mukti-morcha-faction-submits-arms (accessed on 25 September 2021).

61 “Secessionist CK Raut joins mainstream politics; signs 11-point agreement with government”, *Khabarhub*, Kathmandu, 08 March 2019. (accessed on 25 September 2021).

62 “UNPO Condemns Arrest of AIM Coordinator Dr CK Raut and Calls for Immediate Release”, 17 October 2018, https://unpo.org/article/21167 (accessed on 25 September 2021).

63 “Nepal PM Oli urges India to lift economic blockade, says it's causing a ‘humanitarian crisis”, *Firstpost*, 16 November 2015.

64 “Statement on the situation in Nepal,” 21 September 2015, Ministry of External Affairs, Government of India.

65 Dipendra Jha, “Federal Nepal: Trial and Tribulations”, AAKAR Book, Delhi, pp.59-64.

66 Ibid, pp. 179-189.
67 Ibid, pp. 62-63.
68 The Constitution of Nepal, 2015, p. 7.
69 Dipendra Jha, no. 65, pp. 98-101.
70 "Tarai stir: Madhesi parties turn up heat for cadres' release", *The Kathmandu Post*, 13 August 2016, https://kathmandupost.com/national/2016/08/13/tarai-stir-madhesi-parties-turn-up-heat-for-cadres-release (accessed on 23 October 2024).
71 "Statement on the situation in Nepal," 20 September 2015, Ministry of External Affairs, Government of India.
72 "China congratulates Nepal on the promulgation of the constitution", *The Kathmandu Post*, 21 September 2024, https://kathmandupost.com/national/2015/09/21/china-congratulates-nepal-on-the-promulgation-of-the-constitution (accessed on 23 October 2024).
73 Dipendra Jha, no. 65, pp.132-133.
74 "India sees red over UN officials' meet with Nepal Maoists", *The Times of India*, 09 November 2007, https://timesofindia.indiatimes.com/india/india-sees-red-over-un-officials-meet-with-nepal-maoists/articleshow/2529830.cms (accessed on 23 October 2024).
75 Ian Martin, Special Representative for the Secretary-General in Nepal, Interview by Sumit Sharma on Nepal 1 Television, 5 February 2008, at http://www.unmin.org.np/downloads/interview/2008-02-05-UNMIN.SRSG.Interview.Nepal1.ENG.pdf. (accessed on 25 September 2021).
76 Krishna Hari Pushkar, "Seeds of ethno-civil war in Terai", *Nepal Monitor*, 20 December 2007, at http://www.nepalmonitor.com/2007/12/seeds_of_ethno-civil_war_in_nepal_terai.html. (accessed on 25 September 2021).
77 This perspective was conveyed to the author by Pramod Jaiswal, a Madhes based researcher who is linked to the Maoists, who asserted that he had talked about these matters with the Indian ambassador at the time.
78 Prashant Jha's interview with Upendra Yadav, "Koirala must resign", *Nepali Times*, Issue #401 (23–30 May 2008).
79 Author's interactions with a Madhesi leader, who wished to remain anonymous, in Kathmandu in July 2018.
80 Keshav Prasad Mainali, "India's stand on Madhesh issue is self-contradicting", *Telegraph Nepal*, 1 July 2008, at http://www.telegraphnepal.com/news_det.php?news_id=3654. (accessed on 25 September 2021)
81 Author's interaction with a senior leader of the NSP in Patna on 29 February 2009.
82 Krishna Hari Pushkar, "India's Neighbourhood Intervention in Madhesh", *Nepal Monitor*, 14 February 2008, at http://www.nepalmonitor.com/2008/02/inviting_indias_neighbourhood_intervention_in_madhesh.html (accessed on 25 September 2021).
83 "Nepal events hitting India Inc: FICCI", *Hindustan Times*, 6 May 2009, at http://www.hindustantimes.com/StoryPage/StoryPage.aspx?sectionName=HomePage&id=f72535b7-ed67-45c6-bf91-cd8493bba7a3&ParentID=c9fcc197-033e-4766-8a19-9b9128b5bdfe&Headline=Nepal+events+hitting+India+Inc%3a+Ficci.(accessed on 25 September 2021)
84 "Nepal crisis may hit Pancheshwar dam", *Business Standard*, 7 May 2009, at http://www.business-standard.com/india/news/nepal-crisis-may-hit-pancheshwar-dam/357257/. (accessed on 25 September 2021).
85 "Nearly 20 terrorists entered India via Nepal: Indian envoy," ndtv.com, 29 April 2010, at http://www.ndtv.com/news/india/nearly-20-terrorists-entered-india-via-nepal-indian-envoy-21997.php.(accessed on 25 September 2021).

86 "IM has shifted to Nepal after Bangladesh crackdown", *The Times of India*, 10 March 2010.

87 "ISI-backed bombing plot by Khalistan group foiled", *The Times of India*, 05 May 2010, at http://timesofindia.indiatimes.com/india/ISI-backed-bombing-plot-by-Khalistan-group-foiled/articleshow/5891417.cms (accessed on 25 September 2021). On 15 March 2010, a 55-year-old Pakistani woman was arrested at the Tribhuvan International Airport in Kathmandu with fake Indian currency worth Rs 3 million.

# *Chapter Four*

# *The Maoists and Marginalised Groups*

The 1990s represented a significant turning point in Nepal's political history. At the onset of the decade, Nepal transitioned to a multiparty democracy as enshrined in the newly adopted constitution. This development provided a platform for marginalised groups and civil society to articulate their perspectives with greater autonomy and creativity. The revised political framework led to increased competition among various political parties, particularly with the rise of leftist movements. Furthermore, this period witnessed the resurgence of multiple ethno-cultural movements in Nepal, which had previously been suppressed, discriminated against, and marginalised by the State under the Panchayat system.

In the post-1990 era, Nepal experienced four significant movements led by marginalised groups that effectively mobilised their constituencies to draw the attention of the State. As noted by Mukta S. Tamang, these movements were spearheaded by women, Dalits ('low caste'), Madhesis, and Adivasi Janajatis (indigenous peoples). These groups actively participated in the first people's movement of 1990, which reinstated democracy and expanded the opportunities for organised collective action.[1]

The emergence of these social movements and others opposing discrimination received significant impetus and additional backing with the proclamation of the Maoists' 'People's War' against the State in the mid-1990s. This was a reaction to the state's alienation of communist parties as they sought to establish a government.[2]

At that time, public sentiment indicated that the fundamental cause of

Nepal's poverty and uneven development stemmed from an undemocratic political system characterised by potent identity-based power dynamics. Although many Nepalese initially perceived democratisation as a comprehensive solution, its faltering execution yielded limited outcomes. The inaugural decade of democratisation in Nepal was characterised by political instability, marked by the occurrence of three parliamentary elections and the succession of nine distinct governments.[3]

In this context, the Maoist movement in Nepal has been distinctive in its ability to transform the armed struggle into a transformative socio-political movement despite the theoretical complexities involved. Within a relatively brief period, the Maoist movement emerged as a significant socio-political uprising by capitalising on societal fault lines. A substantial number of Dalit and Janajati youths actively participated in the Maoist movement, which enabled the swift propagation of protests against the state in remote regions.[4]

## Political Discrimination

The Communist Party of Nepal (Unity Centre), later rechristened as CPN-Maoist, also known as UCPN-Maoist, took part in the 1991 general elections and secured nine seats in the lower house under the 1990 Constitution[5] of Nepal. In 1994, the Unity Centre broke up, with the Election Commission not recognising the faction led by Baburam Bhattarai and the Maoists. This forced the Maoists to boycott the 1994 mid-term elections. In February 1996, the Maoists submitted a list of 40 demands (Appendix VII) to the then Prime Minister Sher Bahadur Deuba.

However, Maoist demands did not emerge for the first time in 1996, and their roots could be traced back to the democratic movement of 1990.[6] After the government failed to address their demands, the Maoists declared an armed struggle against the state. The 'harassment of the local cadres of United People's Front [of] Nepal in various districts, including Rukum, Rolpa and Gorkha,'[7] after the 1991 parliamentary elections reportedly forced the Maoist leaders to launch a people's war. The armed struggle was launched from two districts of Nepal's mid-western region, namely Rukum and Rolpa, on February 13, 1996.

Political unrest and violence grew in the western regions of Nepal owing to poverty, lack of economic development, social discrimination, exploitation, absence of civic administration in remote areas and increasing marginalisation.

In early 1990, Nepal was considered one of the poorest countries, ranking 113.[8] According to CPN-Maoist literature, from 1996 to 1997, the total stagnation of society and the absolute low level of productive forces were reflected in a mere US$180 per capita GDP (second lowest in the world).

A mere 1.25 percent of the labour force was engaged in industrial activities, while 71 percent of the population lived below the poverty line, and 60 percent was illiterate. The pronounced degree of class polarisation and inequality was evidenced by the fact that only 10 percent of landlords and affluent peasants controlled 65 percent of cultivable land, in stark contrast to 65 percent of impoverished peasants who possessed only 10 percent of arable land. Furthermore, the wealthiest 10 percent of society accumulated 46.5 percent of the national income.[9]

Apart from these domestic factors, the Maoists were inspired by people who were against the state worldwide. The Revolutionary Internationalist Movement (RIM)[10] played a critical role in linking and inspiring Nepali Maoists' with Peru's left-wing guerrilla movement, the Sendero Luminoso (Shining Path),[11] India's Naxalite movements and guided by the ideological teachings of Marxism, Leninism and Maoism (MLM).[12] The strategy of the Shining Path was a significant source of inspiration for the CPN-Maoist because Peruvian geography, topography, political, economic and social conditions were similar to that of Nepal in the 1990s.

The Peruvian Maoists achieved a strategic equilibrium in a relatively short timeframe. However, as both organisations were members of the Revolutionary Internationalist Movement (RIM), they were able to effectively exchange strategies and information. It is posited that several senior Maoist leaders from Nepal visited Peru during the 1990s to gain insights into Peruvian methodologies. While the Marxist-Leninist-Maoist (MLM) ideology directed the Nepalese Maoists, they were primarily influenced by Mao Zedong rather than by Marx and Lenin, as the theoretical foundations proposed by the latter were more applicable to European contexts. At the same time, Mao's revolution was based on the peasantry,[13] which was also the dominant class in Nepal.

The Maoists primarily aimed at replacing the country's semi-constitutional monarchy with a republican system. According to them, 'capitalism is more progressive than feudalism. The existence of bureaucratic capitalism, a hybrid of feudalism and imperialism, makes the matter more complicated, and things cannot be taken at their face value.'[14] During its Third Central Plenum in March 1995, the party chalked out a detailed politico-military policy and the strategy to launch the people's war.[15]

Later in September that year, the party's Central Committee meeting adopted the 'Plan for the Historical Initiation of the People's War,' which defined the war's theoretical basis and goal and formulated a detailed plan and programme for the final preparation and initiation of the decisive people's war against the state.[16] As a part of this preparation, a series of countrywide mass meetings under the banner of the Maoists' political wing, United People's Front–Nepal (UPF), were organised.

## Strategy and Tactics

The Armed 'People's War' (PW) in Nepal commenced in 1996 under the leadership of the Communist Party of Nepal-Maoist, with the articulated objective of establishing a 'New Democratic socio-economic system and state through the overthrow of the existing socio-economic structure and political apparatus'.[17]

According to the military theory of Mao Zedong, a 'protracted armed struggle' passes through six phases (three intense political-social-military phases, generally called military phases and three political-military phases) before setting up a communist state. Those phases are identified as strategic defensive, strategic equilibrium, strategic offensive, 'New Democracy', socialism, and Communism. As per the Maoist revolutionary strategy, there is always a pressing need to convert a protracted armed struggle from 'quantitative development' to a 'qualitative transformation.'[18] Therefore, the people remain a central element in the revolution. The party uses existing social fault lines and economic situations to seek public support for political and military purposes. The state response intensifies, and the party adopts different tactics to uphold public support.

The guerilla war's overall strategic and tactical aim is to preserve one's force and destroy the enemy's force.[19] According to Thomas A. Marks, 'The Maoist movement advances along five lines of operations. Those are mass lines, the united front, violence of various sorts, and political warfare,[20] and then the movement strives for international attention to strengthen the domestic struggle. They all go simultaneously.'[21]

During the strategic defensive phase, when the state was formidable, and the insurgents occupied a defensive stance, the Maoists capitalised on local grievances to swiftly augment their networks and support base, thereby severing the connections between the populace and the state. The masses, under the leadership of the revolutionary party, engaged in resistance against the powerful 'reactionary state' with minimal resources.

In the context of conducting a people's war, the 'grievance guerrillas', who were ideologically and politically equipped with Marxism-Leninism-Maoism, prepared themselves militarily by appropriating arms from the security forces. Subsequently, they guided the guerrilla combatants in establishing a People's Liberation Army (PLA) and achieving both political and military dominance over the state. The party's ideological, political, and military capabilities enabled it to orchestrate the conflict and develop a foundational base area that would serve as the epicentre of the revolution and the locus of popular political authority.[22]

Thomas A. Marks posits that the strategic phases of the Maoist movement adhere to a coherent progression. Initially, the revolutionary endeavour is likely to adopt a defensive posture, subsequently reach a stalemate, and ultimately shift to an offensive phase. Each phase is distinguished by specific forms of warfare with the combination of political and military campaigning that influence the overarching dynamics, albeit not always in a quantitative manner. During the strategic defensive phase, tactics characterised by terror and guerrilla warfare are predominant.[23]

In Nepal, as per the decisions of the Third Central Plenum,[24] the CPN-Maoist adopted the three-pronged Maoist path of armed struggle. The strategic defensive phase has several tactical stages: final preparation of initiation, development of guerrilla zones, and development of the base areas.[25] This began in 1996 and continued up to 2001. The People's War started in seven target areas[26] from three different regions of the country with a small group of people led by the CPN-Maoist and equipped with locally available weapons like knives, sticks, sickles, homemade explosives and old-fashioned guns.

The selection of these seven targets across various districts and regions was executed with careful consideration of Nepal's geophysical and sociopolitical contexts, ensuring that the opposing forces would be unable to concentrate their repressive military capabilities in any specific area. This strategy was subsequently complemented by propaganda efforts, including the dissemination of leaflets, posters, street programmes by the cultural wings of the party, and nationwide strikes.[27]

Over a three-week period, approximately 5,000 actions took place across roughly 65 districts nationwide. Of these actions, about 85 percent were classified as propaganda efforts, 12 percent as sabotage activities, and 3 percent as guerrilla operations. The more advanced forms of action were primarily observed in the districts of Rolpa, Rukum, Jajarkot, and Sallyan in the western hills, as well as in Sindhuli, Kavre, and Sindhupalchowk. Terai regions are in the eastern hills, and Gorkha is in the central hills.[28]

Gradually, the organisation expanded its guerrilla zones, mobilised forces, and established militias to create a parallel governance structure in its strongholds (mid-west districts) by selecting locations distant from state-controlled territories. This initiative by the Maoists aptly reflects Mao's tactics that "we must take care to lay a solid foundation in the central districts so that we shall have something secure to rely on when the White terror (Japanese) strikes."[29]

According to the loss-of-gradient (LSG) theory by Halvard Buhagh, a rebel group will be more effective if it sets up its base area far from the (state) capital and 'push further towards the capital—or manage to gain increasing levels of self-determination—as they grow stronger.'[30] The rebel groups also decide where the conflict should occur, considering easy recruitment, financing opportunities, types of terrain and an assessment of relative military effectiveness.[31]

The Maoists ordered the implementation of a new curriculum as an indoctrination programme in the schools in the areas under their control to train students along Maoist lines and impart education on military science. 'After six months, it formed its first squad of fighters and began on their path of guerrilla warfare. The initial raids were carried out against local feudal forces, police, rival political workers, government spies (informers), moneylenders, rapists, wife-beaters, smugglers and corrupt officials.'[32] 'In the areas under their influence, they created governing bodies, judicial entities, underground economies and collective farming systems.'[33]

**Table 5: Violent Incidents in Nepal from 1996-2006**

| *Year* | *Violent Incidents* | *Police Station/ Army Camps Attacked* | *Banks Looted* |
|---|---|---|---|
| 1996-2000 | 26 | 8 | 4 |
| 2001 | 11 | 8 | 0 |
| 2002 | 109 | 9 | 7 |
| 2003 | 163 | 7 | 3 |
| 2004 | 193 | 4 | 0 |
| 2005 | 178 | 10 | 1 |
| 2006* | 86 | 7 | 1 |

* Till 30 April 2006
*Source:* Compiled from English Media Reports and The Worker.

Table 5 reflects that although the armed struggle was declared in 1996, the number of violent incidents, attacks on police stations and looting of banks increased after the setting up of base areas in 2001. In the initial five years of the armed struggle, the Maoists focused on garnering public support, establishing base areas, and monitoring the activities of the Royal Nepal Army (RNA) by collecting comprehensive information on its political, military, and financial status. As the movement evolved, the frequency of incidents escalated from 11 in 2001 to 109 in 2002, accompanied by assaults on police stations and financial institutions as the organisation sought to acquire additional weapons and resources to sustain the movement. Maoist manuals indicate that once the guerrilla phase commences, it should not be interrupted.

As part of its political strategy during this period, the CPN-Maoist tried to create a rift between the political parties and the King. They even lured the youth, women, ethnic and indigenous people, and Dalits and created a 'united front' of various political forces to smash the existing political system. By the year 2000, it had 25 front organisations.[34] The National Convention of the CPN-Maoist in February 2001 formulated several tactics for urban insurrection by carrying out activities through its frontal organisations. The purpose was to weaken the state's central power, instigate revolt within the security forces and seek the support of mainstream political parties.[35]

## Social-Economic Survey

As elaborated in the preceding chapter, the ethno-cultural movements in Nepal made numerous unsuccessful attempts to compel the state to address their grievances until the onset of the Maoist insurgency. Although certain indigenous nationalities, such as the Limbus and Rais, resisted the unification of Nepal in 1769 and sought the establishment of a separate autonomous region in the eastern part of the country, these movements did not garner support from other marginalised groups at that time. It is noteworthy that pre-Maoist insurgency ethno-cultural movements in Nepal were largely fragmented and confined to specific regions, resulting in limited access to exert influence in Kathmandu. Additionally, inadequate physical connectivity hindered inter-ethnic coordination efforts aimed at articulating a collective voice against the state. Most significantly, as these movements were predominantly localised, the state was able to effectively suppress them through coercive measures or by co-opting their leaders.

The same phenomenon occurred with the initial Madhesi movement. Moreover, the ruling elite capitalised on India's security apprehensions concerning the Himalayan region, particularly regarding border disputes with China. India seemingly prioritised the 'twin-pillar' theory over Madhesi matters. India's stance on the Madhesi changed when it recognised that the UCPN-Maoists' presence in the Terai, along with their connections to Indian Maoists (Naxalites), could potentially threaten India's internal security.

The UCPN-Maoist documents on strategy and tactics in the armed struggle indicated that the Maoist leaders were aware of the level of angst of the ethnic groups against the state and their demands. As a general practice, the rebel groups, in general, and the Maoist outfit, in particular, survey the socio-economic situation of a society, the level of political awareness of the masses, the military strength of the enemy (state), and possible international responses before declaring an armed struggle against the state. Referring to a 1995 strategic document of the UCPN-Maoist,[36] Krishna Hachhethu observed that the UCPN-Maoists had been confident about a successful outcome to the insurgency on the following accounts:

- The geographical situation (of Nepal) is favourable for waging guerrilla war.
- A good mass base for guerrilla war can be created from the members of ethnic groups who have been oppressed.
- There is no possibility of a direct military clash with the enemies who hold political power. The people's armed forces could take advantage

of this to seize a definite area.

- Guerrilla warfare can be initiated and used in different parts of the country, with the peasant revolution as the backbone of the insurgency. By centralising activities in rural areas and relying on and uniting with poor peasants, guerrilla warfare can be used in different parts of the country.
- The people's support for the insurgency will increase if the revisionists are thoroughly exposed and the tactics of armed struggle are painstakingly pursued.
- The pace of development of the armed struggle to establish the people's alternative revolutionary power would be faster, inspiring us to undertake bold tactics to achieve the same.
- Nepalese people working in foreign countries—mainly those working in India—would be mobilised if we were to conduct political work among them and use Indian territory to provide logistical support for the armed struggle in Nepal.[37]

The Maoists' strategic framework suggested that the organisation had engaged in preliminary discussions or negotiations for support with certain ethnic groups strategically positioned to facilitate the establishment of guerrilla zones for the UCPN-Maoists. Following two years of declaring an armed struggle, the UCPN-Maoists established their first ethnic front—the Tamang National Liberation Front (TNLF)—for both political and military objectives.

## Blending of Two Separate Aspirations

The UCPN-Maoist required substantial popular support to alter the political and military equilibrium in opposition to the state. The mobilisation of millions of socially and politically disenfranchised individuals may have prompted the Maoist leaders to devise strategies against the governmental authority. The Maoists facilitated the empowerment of marginalised segments of society and reignited the fighting spirit of populations that had been suppressed for centuries. Consequently, these marginalised groups articulated their demands for rights that they had previously deemed unimaginable.

The Maoists implemented a series of strategies to harness public discontent. Unlike earlier ethno-political movements, the Maoist movement integrated issues of class division and social discrimination into its framework.

Ideologically, they delineated class adversaries, which facilitated a clearer target for the masses to confront.

### *Tapping the Grievances*

In the context of political campaigning, the Maoists capitalised on the grievances held by Janajati communities towards the state. The organisation utilised these grievances as a basis for both political and military mobilisation against the state apparatus. They engaged in negotiations with Janajati representatives to address longstanding demands that the state had been overlooked. The Maoists assured these indigenous groups that their concerns would be prioritised following the dismantling of the existing feudal state structure. The emergence of the Maoist movement served as a unifying force among various ethnic groups, a role that NEFIN was unable to fulfill. Consequently, there emerged a convergence of interests between the Janajatis and the Maoists in their collective struggle against a shared adversary, the monarchy, which was emblematic of the state.

Initially, in addition to establishing ethnic coalitions, the organisation made concerted efforts to incorporate Janajati representatives across its various branches. To tap into the frustrations and grievances of the Janajatis toward the state, as well as to leverage their combat proficiency in mountainous terrain, Janajatis were designated as zonal commanders of the People's Liberation Army and heads of the central military commission. Prominent Janajati and Madhesi figures, such as Ram Bahadur Thapa, Barshaman Pun, Nanda Kishore Pun, Gopal Kirati, and Matrika Yadav, were integral members of the PLA's core strategy team. Aside from a few high-ranking Brahmin and Chhetri individuals, approximately 40 percent of the PLA personnel and other divisions of the UCPN-Maoists comprised individuals from various ethnic groups, encompassing both women and men. An additional 30 percent were drawn from Dalit and other marginalised communities, including the Madhesis. Furthermore, members from upper caste groups, such as Chhetris and Brahmins, were included, either motivated by ideological convictions or a sense of economic disenfranchisement. This structure enabled the organisation to cultivate an inclusive and pluralistic framework in opposition to the state's unitary system. By implementing this organisational model, the group secured sustained support and loyalty from its members in exchange for their eventual integration into various state institutions, particularly within the Nepalese Army.

### *Cultural Campaigning*

Furthermore, the outfit created a cultural wing or drama club (Jananatya Mandali) in the organisation. One former Maoist cadre shared that "her task was to go from village to village with her group, playing songs and staging 'song-plays' that depicted the valour and sacrifices of the Maoists, as well as their dreams for a better future.... The leaders told me it was easy to produce a leader, but it took special talents to become an artist."[38] By having this arrangement, the ethnic groups got a guarantee of protection, preservation and timely celebration of their festivals.

The party directed the members of the drama club to incorporate local folklore, traditional ethnic music, and dances during their visits to rural communities. The drama club successfully revitalised numerous cultural programs that had been suppressed by the state. Additionally, Maoist leaders actively participated in and greeted community members during the festive periods of various ethnic groups. These clubs also served as a means to attract new recruits to the party.

### *Maoist Local Government*

As the movement advanced and the insurgency transitioned from a strategic defensive to an equilibrium phase, guided by the principles of Prachandapath, the organisation established local governance structures. Several of these local governments were designated in accordance with the predominant ethnic groups of the respective regions, addressing the demands for autonomous governance. This parallel governance framework instituted by the Maoists bolstered the confidence of the ethnic communities in the insurgents while simultaneously addressing the administrative void in terms of both security and developmental initiatives. According to Krishna Hachhethu, "By contextualising the ideology of class war with poverty, injustice and exploitation, and by ethnicising the insurgency, the CPN (Maoist) has been able to appropriate a large number of people belonging to the poor and excluded groups."[39] The Maoist Party responded to the grievances of various ethnic groups. Additionally, it capitalised on the aspirations and ambitions of the younger generations within marginalised communities by enlisting them as armed cadres. These affiliates were provided with a monthly stipend, assured socio-economic security for their families in the event of the ciders' death, uniforms, identification cards, and armaments.

### *Two Front Tactics*

The presence of Maoists emerged in a dual-front confrontation against the state by marginalised groups. In rural areas, these groups employed guerrilla tactics, while in urban settings, they leveraged front organisations such as the NEFIN and support from NGOs and INGOs. This dynamic illustrates that it was not solely the Maoists who required the backing of ethnic groups; rather, the marginalised communities were afforded the opportunity to engage in a collective struggle against the state, bolstered by both military and political support from the Maoists.

By blending the deprivations of the marginalised groups with ideology, the movement spread rapidly. The Maoists had control over a two-thirds portion of Nepal's territory and were able to upgrade the movement to a strategic equilibrium phase in 2002. Socially and economically, "the Maoist war changed the landlord-labour relations. Tharus began to assert as Maoists raised their issues. Many of the Zamindars who exploited them fled the areas, selling their land."[40] The rulers allotted these lands to their sympathisers by abolishing the traditional landholding system of the ethnic groups.

However, for the Maoists, everything was not hunky-dory. It was not easy to navigate through the social and political contradictions in the society. In certain places, they had to use force to garner public support. One former Maoist cadre shared: "First, Maoists tried to win people's hearts. If they failed, they used force, such as kidnapping or killing."[41] Moreover, although the Maoists supported the marginalised groups against the state, there were differences between Madhesi and Janajatis in the organisation. Matrika Yadav shared that "the top Maoist leaders were initially reluctant to raise the Madhesi discrimination issue and demands in the organisational meetings. My (his) viewpoints in the meetings were often ignored."[42] It appears that around 2001 and 2002, Madhesh became important to the CPN-Maoists, when the outfit realised the strategic necessity of the region for two purposes.

Initially, the conventional Maoist strategy of encircling the capital without involving Madhesh in the encirclement of Kathmandu proved to be unfeasible. Economically, the Terai region holds significant importance for Kathmandu, particularly in terms of food production, agriculture, and industrial activities. Over fifty percent of Nepal's population resides in this area. From a communication perspective, it serves as a crucial link between eastern, western, and central Nepal via the Mahendra Highway. The infrastructure in the Terai region facilitates the efficient movement of goods, including fossil fuels, to Kathmandu and other urban centers in Nepal from India. Furthermore, as the insurgency expanded into new territories and the state's response intensified, the Maoists recognised the necessity of gaining support from Madhesh and the Madhesi population to secure access to Indian cities for refuge, as well as to obtain arms and ammunition from illicit manufacturing operations in Bihar. Additionally, Nepali labourers in India constituted a major source of revenue for their efforts. In this context, the Akhil Bharatiya Ekta Samaj (ABES) was established in India.

## The 40-point Demands

In 1995, the CPN-Maoists presented a comprehensive set of 40 demands to the government. Among these, three specific demands were exclusively focused on addressing the concerns of marginalised groups. Those were:

- All racial exploitation and suppression should be stopped. Where ethnic communities are in the majority, they should be allowed to form their autonomous governments.
- Discrimination against downtrodden and backward people should be stopped. The system of untouchability should be eliminated.
- All languages and dialects should be given equal opportunities to prosper. The right to education in the mother tongue up to higher levels should be guaranteed.

These issues exerted a profound influence on Nepal's socio-political landscape. For the first time, a political organisation openly endorsed the demands of the Janajati community. This significant development instilled a sense of empowerment among the marginalised groups, thereby legitimising their aspirations to confront the state.

### *Jan Adalat*

The outfit established Jan Adalat, or Kangaroo courts, within their stronghold areas, providing immediate redress to individuals who had been marginalised or excluded from the formal justice system in the early 1990s in Nepal. This mechanism facilitated expeditious and accessible justice. The organisation garnered substantial popular support, with local communities exhibiting greater trust in the Maoists than in the state.

The operational framework of the Jan Adalat, however, exacerbated societal divisions. Any individual within the village could petition this court in pursuit of justice, and it addressed a wide array of issues, including corruption, familial disputes, matrimonial conflicts, property disputes, dowry issues, public intoxication, rape, and the molestation of women. The Jan Adalat emerged as one of the party's most effective political instruments against the exploitation and discrimination perpetrated by landlords in rural areas. Reports indicated a significant reduction in harassment cases against marginalised groups under the auspices of the Jan Adalat. Nevertheless, several media and human rights organisations reported concerns that Jan Adalat was also utilised to instill fear among the populace.

## Major Maoist Ethnic Front Organisations

The Maoists established various fraternal organisations to boost their popularity by carrying out over-ground political activities and mobilising on their behalf. By 2000, there were more than 20 such organisations.[43] The operations and activities of these frontal organisations were coordinated through the ethnic and regional front coordination committee of the CPN (Maoist).

### *Magar National Liberation Front*

The Magar National Liberation Front (MNLF), an affiliate of the CPN-Maoist, was established in 1999. Its political objectives were aligned with those of the CPN-Maoist, advocating for ethnic-based federalism and the establishment of a Magar province. The front sought to preserve and protect Magar culture, designate Magar as the official language in the proposed Magarat province, implement a directly elected presidential system of governance in Kathmandu, and ensure proportional representation of the Magar community in governmental positions and the Constituent Assembly.

In 2010, the MNLF declared a campaign against anti-federalists, contending that their activities were incompatible with democratic principles and fostered autocratic regimes. The organisation attributed the dissemination of rumours and efforts to undermine the achievements of the people's movements to the Chhetri Samaj and Brahmin Samaj. The MNLF vowed to engage in a non-violent struggle and to address these challenges by forming alliances with like-minded parties and organisations.[44]

### *Leaders*

Santosh Budhamagar was the president, and Sharun Bathamagar was the general secretary on the front. Other senior leaders of the front were Onsari Ghartimagar, Basanta Ghartimagar, Lal Bahadur Susling Magar, Dipak Chartimagar, Narayan Burjamagar and Shuva Gurmachhan Magar as vice-chairmen.

Other than this, the Magars had been part of the Maoist movement and contributed to the task/responsibility allocated by the Maoist party. For example, Suresh Ale Magar headed the All-Nepal Janajati Federation, Ram Bahadur Thapa alias Badal had played a key role in building a political base for people's war in the Rapti hills, Mani Thapa (Anukul, Anup) was in charge of Sagarmatha-Janakpur Regional Bureau, Varshaman Pun (Ananta) was the Eastern Division commander, Nanda Kishor Pun (Pasang) was Western Division commander, Man Bahadur Thapa Magar was the leader of the then United People's Front, Ganesh Man Gurung (Rashmi) was the deputy head of the Magarat Autonomous Regional People's Government and Parivartan Memorial Ninth Brigade commissar, etc.[45]

## *Tamang National Liberation Front (TNLF)*

The Tamang National Liberation Front (TNLF) was established in 1998 with the backing of the CPN-Maoist. Prior to the formation of the TNLF, the Tamang community had created a Tamang Committee in 1956, primarily aimed at the preservation of their cultural heritage and language. The members of this Committee operated clandestinely in opposition to the State. In the post-1990 era, a coalition known as Nepal Tamang Ghedung, comprising 25 Tamang organisations, was established.[46] Upon the creation of the TNLF, numerous disillusioned and radicalised youths affiliated with the Ghedung aligned themselves with the Maoist movement, anticipating the establishment of an autonomous Tamang province.

The Maoists had consented to all the demands of the Tamangs and assured the establishment of ethnic-based federalism following the conclusion of the people's war.

Similar to other front organisations, the TNLF orchestrated regular rallies in its predominant territories. A significant number of Tamang youth affiliated with the PLA, many of whom were members of the local government established by the UCPN-Maoist. It is posited that the TNLF transformed into the Tamsaling Nepal Rastriya Dal in the lead-up to the 2008 Constituent Assembly elections, aiming to ensure a robust representation of Tamang constituents and advocate for their interests on a sustained basis.

*Leaders*

Ganga Bahadur Tamang (Dorje) was the general secretary of the TNLF. Many other Tamang leaders had played a prominent role in the social and political transformation movement under the UCPN-Maoists. For example, Hit Bahadur Tamang (Shamsher) was head of the Tamang Autonomous Regional People's Government. Similarly, Dawa Tamang (Kshitij) was an alternate central committee member and head of the Sindhupalchowk People's Government. Kumari Moktan (Samjhana) was an alternate central committee member, acting head of the Tamang Autonomous Regional People's Government and head of the Makwanpur People's Government.[47]

### *Tamu (Gurung) National Liberation Front (TNLF)*

The TNLF, a sister organisation of the UCPN-Maoist, was established in 1999. The political aspirations and objectives of the front were aligned with those of the UCPN-Maoist. The front advocated for ethnicity-based federalism and the creation of a Gurung province in the mid-western region of Nepal. It emphasised the preservation and protection of Gurung culture, the designation of 'Tamukwi' as the official language of the Gurung province, the implementation of a directly elected presidential system of governance, and the proportional representation of the Gurung community in governmental positions and the Constituent Assembly.

Similar to other front organisations, the TNLF orchestrated regular demonstrations in the regions under their influence. A significant number of Gurung youths also enlisted in the PLA, many of whom were constituents of the local government established by the Maoists.

In the post-conflict period, the TNLF organised the inaugural Kathmandu district conference in November 2007, establishing a 29-member executive committee under the leadership of Jit Bahadur Ghale. The committee comprised Vice President Raju Tamu, Secretary Mahendra Tamu, Joint Secretary Bijaya, Treasurer Rajman, and Joint Treasurer Manraj. Its members included Kamala, Man Kumari, Dil, Tek, Som, Dilu, Yumaya, Durgesh, Nim Bahadur, Prithvi, Rohit, Prem, Ash Bahadur, Ashuta, and Prem Bahadur.[48]

## *The Limbuwan National Liberation Front (LNLF)*

The LNLF, a sister organisation of the UCPN-Maoist, was established in 1999. The political aims and objectives of the front were aligned with those of the UCPN-Maoist. The front advocated for an ethnicity-based federalism and the creation of the Limbuwan province in the mid-western region of Nepal, as well as the preservation and protection of Limbu culture. Additionally, it sought the recognition of 'Limbu' as an official language within the Limbu province, the implementation of a directly elected presidential system of governance in Kathmandu, and proportional representation of the Limbu community in government positions and the Constituent Assembly.

In January 2010, the United Limbuwan Front, an alliance comprising nine Limbuwan organizations, including the Limbuwan National Liberation Front, issued a warning of potential reprisals against the UCPN-Maoist unless the latter promptly rescinded its declaration of Kochila and Kirat autonomous states. The Front accused the Maoists of attempting to fragment the Limbuwan region by advocating for the establishment of the Kirat and Kochila states.

K.P. Palungwa, in charge of the Federal Limbuwan State Council, said that the Maoists disfigured the history of the Limbuwan land in the garb of Kirat and Kochila states. Kumar Lingden, the council's central chairman, accused the Maoists of trying to divide the Limbuwan region. The leaders, including Bir Nembang, chairman of the Limbuwan Liberation Front, also claimed they would foil any move on federalism in their area.[49]

### *Kirat National Front (Maoists)*

The Kirat National Front (KNF) was established in July 2003 through the amalgamation of a faction of the Khumbuwan National Front and the Kirat Workers' Party. The merger was facilitated by then Chief of the Communist Party of Nepal (Maoist), Prachanda, along with prominent leader Baburam Bhattarai. Subsequently, the KNF integrated into the CPN (Maoist).

This political party was established with the great and sacred purpose of establishing a Khambuwan Autonomous state of the Khambuwan Nation.

Bhaktaraj Kandangwa, a member of the Maoist Revolutionary People's Council and the head of the people's government of Tehrathum, has been elected as the new chairman of the KNF. The necessity for reunification has been highlighted as a strategy to fight against discrimination. At the same time, the Maoists aimed to expand their influence in the eastern region by merging two factions that were advocating for separate sovereign states of Khumbuwan and Limbuwan, into their organisational framework.[50]

Furthermore, a splinter faction, the Kirat Janabadi Workers' Party, dissociated from the Maoists following the 2006 Comprehensive Peace Accord (CPA). This group underwent additional fragmentation and engaged in violent activities primarily focused on extortion, ultimately relinquishing its limited arsenal only in 2015.[51]

### *Madhesi Rastriya Mukti Morcha (MRMM)*

The MRMM, also known as the Madhesi National Liberation Front (MNLT), was formed in 2000 (along with similar 'liberation fronts' for some of Nepal's larger marginalised groups). In 2004, differences with the Maoist leadership led the head of the MRMM to part ways and form the Janatantrik Tarai Mukti Morcha (JTMM–Democratic Tarai Liberation Front) to create an independent state in the Terai.[52]

The CPN-Maoist had formed other smaller minority groups' fronts, which were mutually beneficial, like the Nepal Dalit Liberation Front, Tharuwan National Liberation Front, Karnali Regional Liberation Front, Thami Liberation Front, Majhi National Liberation Front, and Newa Khala. The CPN (Maoists) also declared several autonomous regions designated based on geography and ethnicity for more comprehensive public support. These are

(1) Seti-Mahakali Autonomous Region, (2) Bheri-Karnali Autonomous Region, (3) Tharuwan Autonomous Region, (4) Magarat Autonomous Region, (5) Tamuwan Autonomous Region, (6) Tamang Saling Autonomous Region, (7) Newar Autonomous Region, (8) Kirant Autonomous Region, and (9) Madhesh Autonomous Region.

## Strategic Equilibrium Phase

After completing the initial phases of the Maoist strategic offensive in August 2001, the Maoists declared that they were now in the phase of strategic balance. This power balance is defined as the state of 'strategic equilibrium', a state in which the people's strength and the enemy's strength are, in a certain sense, equal.[53] However, the equilibrium between the Maoists and the state does not mean absolute numerical equality in purely military terms; instead, it reflects the qualitative situation between the Maoists and the masses on the one side and the reactionary state on the other.[54] This phase was significant because it led to two states, two armies and two political systems in Nepal.

This phase witnessed a significant transformation in the equilibrium of political and military power on both sides. Politically, the CPN-Maoist consolidated its position by uniting with other revolutionary entities, such as the Kirat Workers' Party, which had been engaged in a national liberation struggle. In this context, the organisation reinforced its stance by declaring national and regional autonomy and advocating for the right to self-determination to address the contradictions engendered by the state. Militarily, the PLA escalated its strength to the brigade level in strategically important areas. Additionally, the PLA succeeded in dismantling military bases and confiscating weaponry.[55]

As the people's war progressed through various phases, it gained strength owing to widespread mass support. During the strategic offensive phase, the Maoists employed mobile or manoeuvre warfare,[56] urban insurrections,[57] and extensive mass mobilisation[58] efforts. Ultimately, they dismantled and supplanted the repressive former government with a new revolutionary regime.

In this context, it is imperative to evaluate whether the Maoists in Nepal attained a pivotal strategic offensive phase subsequent to the king's capitulation in April 2006. The Maoists' alteration in tactics, favouring the strategy of a 'united front' rather than relying solely on military campaigns, suggests that the strategic offensive phase did not align with their ideological framework.

Despite possessing substantial mass support, including backing from the Janajatis and Madhesis, various internal and external factors influenced the Maoists' shift in Nepal from a traditional Maoist armed struggle approach toward the acceptance of constitutional democracy.

During the armed conflict, the Maoists frequently employed a strategy of ceasefires and negotiations as deemed necessary. It is posited that the Maoists formed alliances with political parties to augment their support base in urban areas. This was primarily due to their limited presence in cities, which stemmed from their inclination towards extreme violence, persistent solicitation of 'donations' from government officials and shopkeepers, and a significant military presence.[59]

Maoist spokesperson Krishna Prasad Mahara said: 'We have a controlling presence in the rural areas across Nepal, except for the district headquarters, market towns and the strip running along the highways.'[60] Urban warfare constituted a fundamental aspect of the standard operating procedure (SoP), with popular support being crucial for the sustainability of the movement. Had the Maoists initiated SoP in urban areas without widespread backing, it would likely have resulted in significant setbacks. This necessity was, in part, dictated by their inability to seize control of the capital city.

Furthermore, the Maoists had already demonstrated their capacity as significant political actors and legitimate power centres in Nepal with their proclamation in August 2004 that they had achieved the strategic equilibrium phase, which commenced in August 2001. Geographically, the Maoists were active in all 75 districts of Nepal, with the exception of Kathmandu city and the district headquarters.

Politically, the Maoists established a quasi-governmental structure in their areas of influence through the establishment of 'village committees.' They implemented taxation, maintained public order, engaged in developmental initiatives, and administered justice through Jan Adalats. The Maoists demonstrated the ability to mobilise substantial numbers of individuals against the monarchy, bolstered by the support of various front organisations and marginalised minority groups that had been neglected by the autocratic regime.

This substantial mass support, which was intermittently assessed through street demonstrations and road blockades, coupled with the increasing unpopularity of the autocratic monarchy, prompted the Maoist leaders to transition their revolutionary agenda towards a democratic framework.

In stark contrast to such a system, since the peace process began, the Maoists have been trying to become a part of mainstream politics in the democratic process, something they had been opposing since 1996. They have agreed to work with other political parties that they had earlier dubbed corrupt and 'revisionists'.[61] Based on the exact charges, the Maoists left the political space provided to them in the Nepalese political system before their desertion.

It is important to note that the 12-point agreement (Appendix VIII) between the Maoists and the Seven Party Alliance (SPA) was established on November 22, 2005, in New Delhi. This agreement advocated for collaborative action to terminate the autocratic monarchy and to ensure free and fair elections to the Constituent Assembly. The agreement significantly altered the political landscape in Nepal and facilitated the Maoists' emergence as a legitimate center of power.

In fact, the Maoists were amenable to engaging in political negotiations until 2001, despite declaring an armed insurrection in 1996. Three peace dialogues between the government and the Maoists were conducted at the onset of 2001. However, the royal massacre on June 1, 2001, coupled with the ascendance of King Gyanendra, compelled the Maoists to escalate their armed resistance against the monarchy, feudalism, and bureaucracy. Concerned that the king would undertake actions detrimental to the democratic movement, the Maoists "argued that the time had come to institutionalise a republic in Nepal as the end of Monarchy was complete with the massacre of King Birendra."[62]

However, the king's takeover on February 1, 2005, changed the political scenario in Nepal. The king emerged as a common enemy against the Maoists and the political parties. According to Prachanda, the king's takeover was a turning point in the decisive battle between autocracy and republic, and the party repeated its call for a 'united front' against the feudal aristocracy.[63] The takeover also changed the opinion of the political parties in favour of setting up a new constituent assembly.

Simultaneously, this development empowered the CPN-Maoist, which had been endeavouring to initiate an offensive against the monarchy in light of military disparities, to extend the movement to Kathmandu. Both the Maoists and the political parties recognised the necessity of forming a united front to oppose the king. Consequently, the 12-point agreement, signed in November 2005, marked the commencement of a new epoch in Nepal's fragmented political landscape.

Subsequently, the 19-day pro-democracy movement in April 2006 compelled the monarchy to reinstate the House of Representatives. Following the restoration of democratic governance, the Maoists declared a ceasefire and expressed their willingness to engage in negotiations with the SPA to achieve a peaceful resolution to the conflict.

## Minority Response to Ceasefire

The Nepal Tamang Student Ghedung (NTSG) and the Nepal Magar Students' Association (NMSA) expressed their dissatisfaction with the agreement reached on November 8, 2006. They advocated for equitable representation of indigenous populations. A press release of the NTSG said, 'We appeal to the Tamang community and students to be ready to fight for their rights.'[64] Alleging that the agreement between the Maoists and the SPA had overlooked the Madhesis' problems, the Madhesi Jana Adhikar Forum-affiliated Nepal Madhesi Students' Front on November 08, 2006 staged a protest rally at Rajbiraj in Saptari district. District chairman of the Front, Arun Yadav, said, "There is no alternative but to launch a strong movement because conspiracies have been hatched against the Madhesi people for the past 238 years in Nepal."[65]

**Table 6: Top Five Political Party Positions in the 2008 Constituent Assembly**

| *Sl. No.* | *Party Name* | *FPTP* | *PR* | *Total* |
|---|---|---|---|---|
| 1. | Communist Party of Nepal (Maoist) | 120 | 100 | 220 |
| 2. | Nepali Congress | 37 | 73 | 110 |
| 3. | Communist Party of Nepal (UML) | 33 | 70 | 103 |
| 4. | Madhesi People's Rights Forum, Nepal | 30 | 22 | 52 |
| 5. | Tarai Madhes Loktantirk Party | 9 | 11 | 20 |

*Source:* Election Commission of Nepal.

**Table 7: Quota Provisions**

| *Quota Provisions (%)* | *UCPN-M* | *NC* | *CPN-UML* |
|---|---|---|---|
| Madhesis (31.2) | 29 | 28.77 | 30 |
| Dalits (13) | 14 | 12.33 | 12.85 |
| Janajatis (37.8) | 30 | 36.99 | 34.28 |
| Backward region (4) | 4 | 2.74 | 2.86 |
| Women (50) | 50 | 49 | 50 |
| Others (30.2) | 30 | 32.88 | 30 |

*Source:* Election Commission of Nepal.

## Withering Support Base

The marginalised groups and the UCPN-Maoist derived significant advantages from the armed struggle. This movement heightened public awareness regarding the failures of the state and the systemic discrimination faced by minority communities. It also established the Maoists as a pivotal political entity in Nepal during the monarchy. The UCPN-Maoist emerged as the dominant political party, securing 220 seats in the Constituent Assembly (CA) elections held in April 2008. Mainstream political parties, such as the Nepali Congress and the CPN-UML, attained second and third positions with 110 and 103 seats, respectively (Table 6). Notably, for the first time, a newly established regional political party, the Madhesi Janatantrik Forum, claimed the fourth position in the CA elections.

There could be numerous factors accountable for the success of the Maoists. However, the Maoists' advocacy for marginalised groups was pivotal. The primary issue was the failure of the two principal parties—the Nepali Congress and the CPN-UML—to fulfill the aspirations of the populace in general and the marginalised groups in particular over the two decades prior. Consequently, the UCPN-Maoist emerged as a viable alternative. Additionally, there was a widespread acknowledgement that the Maoist decision to engage with the democratic mainstream was a favourable development, while the alternative appeared quite daunting. From personal interactions with ordinary citizens in and around Kathmandu in April 2008, one discerned that voters found the Maoist slogan of a 'New Nepal' to be credible.

The UCPN-Maoists' effective populist campaign addressing critical issues such as republicanism, federalism, land reforms, integration of the PLA into the Nepali Army, and job security resonated with indigenous nationalities,

Dalits, and Madhesis, who collectively account for over 70 percent of the total population.

However, the circumstances underwent a significant transformation during the second Constituent Assembly elections in 2013, wherein the UCPN-Maoist attained a third-place ranking. This pattern was replicated in the first parliamentary elections in 2017, indicating a substantial erosion of the party's political standing, performance, and popularity. This decline can be attributed to the repudiation of the UCPN-Maoist by the electorate, including marginalised groups, primarily due to the party's compromises on its core political agenda, which had initially been pledged to the common people in its 2008 election manifesto. By the time of the 2013 elections, the Maoist party had altered its stance regarding the republican system, ethnic-based federalism, and the integration of Maoist combatants into the Nepali Army. Further, prior to the elections, the party experienced a schism over these contentious issues.

Most significantly, the party compromised the interests of its cadres in favour of the political ambitions of individual leaders. Additionally, allegations of extensive corruption and the mismanagement of PLA cantonment funds among certain senior Maoist leaders diminished their credibility. Consequently, the Maoist cadres experienced a profound disenchantment with the leadership.

## NOTES

1 Mukta S. Tamang, "Social movements and inclusive peace in Nepal", *Accord*, issue 26, pp. 97-98.

2 Narayan Khadka, "Communist Opposition in Nepal's Multi-Party Democracy", Rivista di Studi Politici Internazionali, Vol. 61, No. 2 (242) (Aprile-Giugno 1994), pp. 210-232.

3 Paul K Davis, et. al, "Public Support for the Maoists in Nepal" in *Understanding and Influencing Public Support for Insurgency and Terrorism,* RAND, 2012, p.120.

4 Mukta S. Tamang, no.1, p.101.

5 Despite King Birendra's resistance to the democratic movement by the Nepalese political parties in 1990, he agreed to the formation of the interim government. The interim government was formed with K.P. Bhattarai as Prime Minister from the Nepali Congress on 19 April 1990. This marked the change from Nepalese old party less *Panchayat* system to a multi-party Democracy. The government was assigned to prepare the Constitution and conduct free and fair elections. Although the Constitution was promulgated, the demand for a Republic came both from within and outside of the interim government. Finally, undermining the demands, the interim government had conducted general elections in 1991.

6 Padmaja Murthy, "Understanding Nepal Maoists' Demands: Revisiting Events of 1990,"*Strategic Analysis,* Vol. 27, No.1, January-March 2003.

7 Chaitanya Subba, "The ethnic dimension of the Maoist conflict, Dreams and designs of liberation of oppressed nationalities", in Lok Raj Baral (ed.) *Nepal Facets of Insurgency*, Adroit Publishers, New Delhi, 2006, p. 31.

8 Paul K. Davis, et al, no. 03.

9 "One Year of People's War in Nepal: A Review," *The Worker*, Issue 3, February 1997, www.cpnm.org (accessed on 25 September 2021).

10 RIM came into being on March 1984, when delegates and observers of various Marxist-Leninist-Maoist organizations held the second international conference and adopted a document, 'Declaration', and formed the RIM. RIM help revolutionaries advance their ideological and political level through the political magazine *A World To Win* and get acquainted with revolutionary developments taking place the world over.

11 Shining Path, established in the late 1960s by a former university professor Abimael Guzman, was a militant Maoist group that tried to install a peasant revolutionary authority in Peru. The group took up arms in 1980, and its ranks once numbered in the thousands. Not only did the rebels win control of large areas of the countryside, but they also struck repeatedly at targets in the capital, Lima, giving rise to fears that the group would eventually succeed in taking over the country. Peru's intelligence services, however, work better in the capital than in the rugged mountain and remote jungle regions where the Sendero Luminoso (Shining Path) had grown strong. Guzman and most of the members of the Central Committee of his organisation were captured, which triggered the near total political and military collapse of the insurgent organisation. But despite the Peruvian government's successful anti-terrorist campaign, the rebels retain a small number of sympathisers among the rural poor. For more details about the Shining Path, see Simon Strong, *Shining Path: The World's Deadliest Revolutionary Force*, London Harper Collins Publishers, 1992.

12 Prachanda Path is the fusion of the armed insurrection and the protracted war adopted by the Communist Party of Nepal-Maoist in 2001. Prachanda Path was declared on the line of Peruvian Maoists' Shining Path.

13 Abi Narayan Chamlagi, "Maoist Insurgency an Ideological Diagnosis," in Lok Raj Baral (ed.) *Nepal Facets of Insurgency*, Adroit Publishers, New Delhi, 2006, p. 14.

14 "Internal Debate within the Communist Party of Nepal (Maoist)," in *Monthly Review*, July 2005, www.monthlyreview.org (accessed on 03 November 2024). Baburam Bhattarai's interview was conducted by *Tehelka* and published in their issue of 9 July 2005.

15 "Strategy and Tactics of Armed Struggle in Nepal," Third Plenum of the Central Committee of CPN -Maoist in March 1995, at www.cpnm.org/worker/issue3/document.htm(accessed on 29 June 2014)

16 "One Year of People's War in Nepal: A Review," *The Worker*, Issue 3, February 1997.

17 Baburam Bhattarai, "Politico-Economic Rationale of People's War in Nepal," in *Human Rights Server*, at http://www.humanrights.de (accessed on 20 July 2008). Also see Baburam Bhattarai "Politico-Economic Rationale of People's War in Nepal," Utprerak publication, Kathmandu, 1998.

18 "The People's War in Nepal: Taking the Strategic Offensive," *A World To Win*, at www.awtw.org (accessed on 09 October 2006).

19 "The Nature, Target and Motivating Force of Armed Struggle in Nepal," *The Worker*, Issue 3, February 1997, at http://www.cpnm.org/worker/issue3/document.htm (accessed on 18 July 2009).

20 Major Monte R. Bullard, United States Army, in the article "Political Warfare in Vietnam," says the political warfare system is an organizational attempt to solve deep-rooted, non-combatant military problems involving loyalty and civil military relations, at https://

calldbp.leavenworth.army.mil/eng_mr/txts/VOL49/00000010/art7.pdf#search=%22China%2C%20political%20warfare%22 (accessed on 10 October 2016).

21 Interview with Thomas A. Marks in September 2006. Marks is Professor of Insurgency, Terrorism, and Counterterrorism at the School for National Security Executive Education (SNSEE) of National Defense University (NDU) in Washington, DC and the author of Maoist Insurgency Since Vietnam (London, 1996), considered the current standard on the subject of 'people's war'.

22 "The People's War in Nepal: Taking the Strategic Offensive," *A World To Win,* at www.awtw.org (accessed on 18 July 2010). Also see www.cpnm.org (accessed on 18 July 2010). To know more on Strategic Offensive consult *Selected Military Writings of Mao Tse-Tung*, Foreign Language Press, Peking, 1967.

23 Thomas Marks, "Insurgency in Nepal", *Faultlines*, Volume 15, 2004.

24 The Third Central Plenum of the CPN-Maoist held in March 1995 decided the detailed politico-military policy and programmes of the three strategic phases of starting an armed struggle. The Plenum document titled "Strategy and Tactics of Armed Struggle in Nepal" is available on www.cpnm.org(accessed on 18 July 2010)

25 Base areas formation technically mean when revolutionaries win the battle with the state and take control of the governance of a particular area. It is the strategic base of any people's war and which later would be converted to new communist republic. However, before the formation of a base area, the rebel groups set up guerrilla zones, which is a transitional phase for base areas. Mao argued that the survival and growth of an armed struggle required the following conditions: (1) a sound mass base, (2) a sound party organisation, (3) a fairly strong Red Army, (4) terrain favourable to military operations, and (5) economic resources sufficient for sustenance.

26 As planned on February 13 (1996), one police outpost each in Rolpa and Rukum in Western Hills, an Agricultural Development Bank and a distillery factory in Gorkha (district) in Central Hills, a police outpost in Sindhuli and the house of (a) feudal-usurer in Kavre in Eastern Hills and the factory of a multi-national company (Pepsi Cola) in the Kathmandu Valley, were systematically attacked by armed squads (accompanied by mass supporters at several places) with great precision to herald the historic initiation.

27 *The Worker*, Issue 3, February 1997.

28 *The Worker*, Issue 2, June 1996, at http://www.cpnm.org/worker/issue2/w2_1p.htm (accessed on 18 July 2010).

29 "Selected Military Writings of Mao Tse-Tung," Foreign Language Press, Peking, 1967, p. 21.

30 Halvard Buhaug, "The Geography of Armed Civil Conflict," NTNU, 2005 (Doctoral Thesis), pp. 19-20.

31 Scott Gates, "Recruitment and Allegiance: the Microfoundations of Rebellion," *Journal of Conflict Resolution*, 46 (1), 2002.

32 Dev Raj Dahal, "Nepal: Changing Strategies of the People's War," in *Nepal Democracy,*www.nepaldemocracy.org (accessed on 25 September 2021).

33 David G. Wiencek, "China Views The War on Terrorism in Nepal," *The Jamestown Foundation,* Vol. 2, Issue 11, 23 May 2002, in China Brief section at www.jamestown.org (accessed on 25 September 2021).

34 Dev Raj Dahal, no. 32. Following are some important front organisations of the CPN-M—All Nepal Women's Association (Revolutionary)-women's wing, All Nepal National Independent Students' Union (Revolutionary) - student wing, Akhil Bharatiya Nepal Ekta Samaj (ABNES), Magarat National Liberation Front, Tamuwan National Liberation Front, Taruwan National Liberation Front, Tamang National Liberation Front, Thami National Liberation Front, Majhi National Liberation Front, Madhesi National Liberation Front, Newa Khala, Nepal Dalit

Liberation Front, Karnali Regional Liberation Front, Young Communist League, All Nepal Trade Union Federation (ANTUF).

35 Ibid.

36 Text of Strategy and Tactics of Armed Struggle in Nepal, Adopted by the Third Expanded meeting of the Central Committee of the CPN (Maoist) in March 1995.

37 Krishna Hachhethu, "The Communist Party of Nepal (Maoist): Transformation from an Insurgency Group to a Competitive Political Party," further details are not available. A link of the article is given here. https://himalaya.socanth.cam.ac.uk/collections/journals/ebhr/pdf/EBHR_33&34_03.pdf . The PDF version of the article was accessed on 15 April 2022, p-61.

38 Saif Khalid and Gyanu Adhikari "Nepal: The Maoist dream" *Aljazeera*, 2016, https://interactive.aljazeera.com/aje/2016/nepal-maoist-dream/index.html (accessed on 25 April 2022).

39 Krishna Hachhethu, no. 37.

40 Saif Khalid and Gyanu Adhikari, no. 38.

41 Ibid.

42 Authors telephonic discussion with Matrika Yadav on 16 April 2022.

43 "Nepal's Maoists: Their Aims, Structure and Strategy," *International Crisis Group*, Asia Report N°104 – 27 October 2005, at https://www.refworld.org/pdfid/43bd262c4.pdf (accessed on25 September 2021).

44 "Magar front launches struggle against federalism opponents", *The Himalayan*, 06 March 2010, at https://thehimalayantimes.com/kathmandu/magar-front-launches-struggle-against-federalism-opponents (accessed on 25 September 2021)

45 "Nepal's Maoists: Their Aims, Structure and Strategy," no. 43.

46 Anne Kukuczka, "Negotiating Ethnic Identity in the Himalaya-The Tamang in Nepal", FORUM. Further details are not available. The article is accessible online at https://edoc.hu-berlin.de/bitstream/handle/18452/18605/393.pdf?sequence=1 (accessed on 25 September 2021).

47 "Nepal's Maoists: Their Aims, Structure and Strategy," no. 43.

48 Rishi Singh "Tamu meet concludes", in Brief, *The Himalayan*, 04 November 2007, at https://thehimalayantimes.com/kathmandu/in-brief-358 (accessed on 25 September 2021).

49 "Limbuwan warns against Maoists", *The Himalayan*, 11 January 2010, at https://thehimalayantimes.com/nepal/limbuwan-warns-against-maoists (accessed on 25 September 2021)

50 Allied: Dambar Krishna Shrestha in Himal Khabarpatrika, 1-17 August, *Nepali Times*, Kathmandu, From Issue #157 (08 AUG 2003 - 14 AUG 2003), at http://archive.nepalitimes.com/news.php?id=3566#.X6Q1PvMzbIU (accessed on 25 September 2021).

51 Deepak Thapa, "Post-war armed groups in Nepal", *Accord*, Issue 26, pp. 107-108, at https://rc-services-assets.s3.eu-west-1.amazonaws.com/s3fs-public/PostWarArmedGroupsInNepal.pdf (accessed on 25 September 2021).

52 Ibid.

53 "The People's War in Nepal: Taking the Strategic Offensive," *A World To Win*, at www.awtw.org (accessed October 2006).

54 Ibid.

55 Ibid.

56 Mobile warfare is a mixture of manoeuvre and attrition warfare. It attempts to defeat the enemy by incapacitating its decision-making through shock and disruption. In mobile warfare the Maoist armed cadres, who were engaged in guerrilla warfare in strategic defensive and strategic equilibrium phase, fight against the enemy openly.

57 Urban uprising or insurrections is a Maoist strategy by mobilising masses to put pressure on

the opponents on a specific issue. It could be both violent and non-violent in nature. Maoist urban uprising are basically supported by its front organisations and sympathisers.

58 Maoists characteristically attempt to win popular support and consolidate their power by mobilising the population in mass meetings, street demonstrations, parades, and other gatherings.

59 Bertil Lintner, "Nepal's Maoists Prepare for Final Offensive", Asia Pacific Media Services Limited, at http://www.asiapacificms.com/articles/nepal maoists/ (accessed on 12 September 2006).

60 Rita Manchanda, "Nepal's challenges," *Frontline*, Vol. 20, Issue 12, 7-20 June 2003, at http://www.hinduonnet.com/fline/fl2012/stories/20030620008206100.htm (accessed on 31 October 2024).

61 Biplab Dasgupta, "The Naxalite Movement", Allied Publishers, Bombay, 1974, p. 7. The concept Revisionists or Reformists was used by the ultra-leftists in 1967 against those who were taking part in the state government under a bourgeoisie constitution and failed to adhere to the Maoist ideology. Also see exclusive interview with CPI-Maoist spokesperson Azad (pseudonym) on Nepal Developments on *People's March,* a publication which reports on the activities of the Indian Maoists in July 2006. Part of the interview was published in "Indian Maoists Criticise Prachanda", *The Hindu*, 24 July 2006.

62 Abi Narayan Chamlagi, "Maoist Insurgency an Ideological Diagnosis," in Lok Raj Baral (ed.) *Nepal Facets of Insurgency*, Adroit Publishers, New Delhi, 2006, p. 20.

63 "The People's War in Nepal: Taking the Strategic Offensive," *A World To Win,* at www.awtw.org (accessed on 10 October 2006).

64 "Historic Agreement Fails to Woo Janajatis," *The Himalayan Times*, 09 November 2006.

65 Ibid.

# Chapter 5

# The Constitution Drafting: Issues and Debates

Following over five decades of political turbulence, the 2006 Jana Andolan II instilled hope for genuine democracy in Nepal through the unification of democratic forces opposing the monarchy. This culminated in an accord among seven prominent political parties, leading to the integration of the Maoists into the political mainstream and, subsequently, to elections for the Constituent Assembly (CA)[1] and the dissolution of the monarchy. Prior to this, democratic factions waged separate campaigns for democratic governance against the authoritarian regime. The primary objective of the 2008 Constituent Assembly, henceforth referred to as 'CA-I,' was to draft a new constitution and finalise the peace process. Although the peace process objectives were largely fulfilled through extensive negotiations among key political parties, the constitution ultimately drafted after two rounds of CA elections has been fraught with controversy, achieving only a partial fulfillment of its intended aim of inclusivity as asserted by marginalised groups in Nepal.

Following the failure of the CA-I to draft a constitution, despite four extensions, the Supreme Court mandated its dissolution and the organisation of new elections for a successive CA-cum-Parliament. These elections served as a significant indicator of public aspirations for democracy and reform. In the aftermath of the polls, a preliminary analysis of the Nepalese media and scholarly writings regarding the state of Nepalese politics revealed a prevailing sentiment of discontent among the populace concerning the conduct of political parties, resulting in widespread disillusionment with the democratic process in Nepal.

The explanations provided by observers in Nepal for the shortcomings of democracy encompass a range of factors, including cultural incompatibility, irreconcilable group interests, persistently weak socio-economic conditions, and enduring external interventions. In light of this context, it is imperative to analyse the evolving democratic process in Nepal, examining the people's experiences with the representative system, the influence of political parties, the dynamics of leadership, as well as the aspirations of various ethnic and regional groups, and the strategies of external actors. This comprehensive analysis is essential to achieve a nuanced understanding of then the state of democracy and its potential trajectory in Nepal.

## Nepalese Perspective on Democracy

Before analysing the democratic process in Nepal, it is essential to comprehend Nepalese perspectives on democracy. Democracy encompasses various interpretations and manifestations. However, several common characteristics are universally adhered to in order to ensure the success of the democratic process. The Western perspective is predominantly shaped by Robert Dahl, who articulated five criteria necessary for a robust democratic framework: effective participation, voting equality, enlightened understanding, control of the agenda, and the inclusion of all individuals to whom the established rules will apply.[2]

Citing an opinion poll by K. Hachhethu in 2004, Gellner found that many in Nepal think democracy is the best political system. It is an 'opportunity to change the government through elections, freedom to criticise those in power, equal rights, and fulfillment of basic needs for food, clothing, and shelter.' They also feel that the most essential characteristic of democracy is to fulfil citizens' basic needs.[3] David N. Gellner also observed that there are four main democratic ideologies in Nepal. They are king-led, liberal, leftist and multicultural.[4]

According to Citizen Survey 2013, 'democratic principles included periodic elections, the multiparty system, rule of law, separation of powers, an independent judiciary, fundamental rights, human rights, rule of the majority, respect for the minority, popular sovereignty, rule by the people through their elected representatives, and so forth.'[5] When individuals were queried regarding their anticipations of the electoral process and their representatives, approximately 80 percent of respondents indicated that good governance, to them, encompassed well-constructed infrastructure, reliable access to safe drinking water, guaranteed employment opportunities, consistent electricity supply, effective maintenance of public order, transparency in government operations, inclusive developmental practices, and food security.

The people also anticipated that the Constitution would be completed within a year. Interestingly, contentious issues such as ethnic-based federalism, proportional representation methods, and the structure of the political system under the new constitution did not prominently feature in their list of expectations.[6]

Therefore, in the context of Nepal, adherence to democratic principles is of greater significance than the tangible outcomes produced by political leaders. The people often place greater trust in democratic ideals, values, and institutions than in their political leaders and parties. This phenomenon might be transient, as constituents have expressed dissatisfaction with the performance of the Constituent Assembly-I and the major political parties.

While Western democracy prioritises participation, Nepalese democracy, from the perspective of its leaders, aims to perpetuate its hold on power by employing various strategies. For instance, the CA-I was tasked with drafting the constitution within a two-year timeframe while simultaneously functioning as the Parliament. Regrettably, the political parties in Nepal approached the Constituent Assembly elections as if they were parliamentary elections, presenting party manifestos that primarily emphasised good governance. This approach fostered an environment of intense competition among the political parties.

## Evolution of Democracy

The trajectory of democracy in Nepal has undergone several tumultuous phases. In the initial period (1950-1959), alongside the influence of the political transition in India following its independence, the protracted authoritarian Rana regime fostered a strong demand for democratic governance in Nepal. Democratic factions, bolstered by support from King Tribhuvan, who was in exile in India, led the anti-Rana movement. This movement culminated in success through a tacit agreement between King Tribhuvan and the democratic forces in 1951, contingent upon the establishment of a constitutional monarchy.

As per the agreement, Nepal appointed its first interim prime minister and established an interim constitution, subsequently leading to elections. The king purposefully delayed the electoral process for nine years, obstructing the drafting of a new constitution by the elected representatives. Notably, India, which played a pivotal role in promoting democracy in Nepal, refrained from strongly opposing the king's anti-democratic measures during this period. Conversely, the democratic factions placed their trust in India's intentions and did not contest the king's actions.

Rather than seeking to establish internally a framework for conducting elections in the early 1950s, the democratic forces anticipated India's intervention to exert pressure on the monarchy. This approach diminished the prospects for a robust multiparty democracy in Nepal. In 1959, the Nepali Congress (NC) achieved a two-thirds majority in the parliamentary elections. Notably, the newly formed parliament lacked inclusivity, being predominantly comprised of upper-caste representatives, and there were no provisions for affirmative action.

In a notable setback to the emerging democratic framework, King Mahendra dissolved the parliament in December 1961. Following this event, Nepal was governed under a party-less Panchayat system for a duration of 30 years. The Civil Code of 1854 was superseded by a new Civil Code in 1963. The monarchy implemented various strategies for security and protection in response to demands for a pluralistic society, which included the introduction of a uniform language and dress code. This approach exacerbated the marginalisation of ethno-cultural groups within the country.[7]

In 1990, Nepal established a newly elected government and constitution. However, the revised constitution failed to adequately address the grievances of marginalised groups. Political parties were predominantly influenced by the hill upper-class—Chhetris and Bahuns. Between 1990 and 2008, Nepal experienced a tumultuous political landscape with 11 prime ministers, three elections, and six constitutions. During this period, proponents of democracy, political analysts, and civil society organisations contended that the monarchy inhibited the proliferation of democratic governance. The reigning monarch(s) frequently misused their constitutional prerogatives, instigating conflicts among leading political party figures for the crown's gain. Nevertheless, the political parties themselves were deeply fragmented, with their vested interests taking precedence in their actions. One Nepalese scholar articulated that "the break-up of multiparty democracy was not entirely the monarchy's fault, but a series of factors, chief among those being the politicians who pretended to represent citizens but served only their narrow interests."[8]

Interestingly, those who were critical of the monarchy and advocated for a new constitution under a multiparty, inclusive constituent assembly, alongside the abolition of the monarchy, were afforded the opportunity to govern Nepal following the monarchy's dissolution. Since 2008, Nepal has witnessed six administrations led by both leftist and liberal socialist parties, as well as bureaucrats, prior to the conduct of the inaugural parliamentary elections in 2017.[9] Moreover, the Constituent Assembly was characterised by its inclusivity, ensuring representation from diverse sectors of society.

The Marginalised groups have not yet been integrated into mainstream politics or afforded adequate representation in the nation-building process. They have voiced dissent regarding the new constitution, which may stem from intra- and inter-party rivalries, leadership crises, the politicisation of democratic institutions, corruption and inefficiency within these institutions, and, most significantly, the entrenched biases of upper-caste populations.

Throughout the political transformations of the 1950s and the subsequent phases of democratic movements in the 1990s and 2006, India played a pivotal role in shaping these transitions in Nepal. Democratic forces heavily relied on India's influence. During this tumultuous period, India's support oscillated between endorsing democracy and backing the monarchy, influenced by geostrategic considerations within the region. India implemented a twin-pillar policy in 1950 and refrained from directly endorsing the anti-democratic actions of the then-royal regime. However, India demonstrated a lack of commitment to bolstering the capacity of democratic forces in their struggle against the authoritarian regime.

This decelerated the process of democratic consolidation in Nepal. In the post-monarchy era, when India advocated for a domestically-driven resolution to the political impasse and constrained its involvement to the promotion of democratic consolidation, certain political leaders and parties solicited support from extra-regional powers—such as China, the European Union, and the

United States—as a means to rationalise their undemocratic actions and maintain their authority in opposition to India's recommendations.

## Issues that Led to the First CA Dissolution

### *Consensus Phase*

The consensus among political factions—specifically the Seven Party Alliance (SPA)—and the Maoists was instrumental in addressing contentious issues prior to the establishment of a CA-I. This consensus was initiated through the diplomatic engagement of India, which sustained the momentum of the process, culminating in the signing of a 12-Point Agreement in November 2005 in New Delhi. It was advantageous that the various political entities advocating for a transformative agenda in Nepal were unified in their opposition to the absolute monarchical rule instituted by King Gyanendra in February 2005.

The first point of the agreement reads:

> It is our clear view that without establishing absolute democracy by ending autocratic monarchy, there is no possibility of peace, progress and prosperity in the country. Therefore, an understanding has been reached to establish absolute democracy by ending autocratic monarchy, with all forces against the autocratic monarchy centralising their assault against autocratic monarchy from their respective positions, thereby creating a nationwide storm of democratic protests. (Appendix VIII)

The signatories to the agreement committed to the establishment of multiparty democracy through the restoration of parliamentary governance via organised agitation, the formation of an all-party government endowed with comprehensive authority, and the conduct of elections for a Constituent Assembly. They also reached a consensus to collaboratively initiate *Jana Andolan II* in opposition to the autocratic tendencies of the monarchy. Following the successful culmination of *Jana Andolan II* in April 2006, the role of the monarchy was effectively suspended, and parliamentary governance was reinstated in Nepal. The Interim Government, led by G.P. Koirala, officially declared an indefinite ceasefire with the Maoist insurgents on May 03, 2006, and announced that the government would no longer classify them as terrorists. An interim government was subsequently established in April 2007, presided over by G.P. Koirala, with the support of eight political parties, including the Maoists.

During this phase, divergences among the leaders of the SPA concerning the distribution of cabinet portfolios emerged. There were also notable discrepancies between the Maoists and the SPA regarding the appointment of an international observer to oversee the peace process. Additional points of contention included the methodologies for arms surrender, the management of surrendered arms in conjunction with the Nepali Army, the formal declaration of a republic, the integration of Maoist combatants into the Nepali Army, the establishment of a new constitution, and other related issues. On a positive note, there were observable advancements in building consensus. Some of the significant events in this process are highlighted below.

- 21 November 2006: Comprehensive Peace Agreement (CPA)
- 8 December 2006: Agreement on the Monitoring of Management of Arms and Armies
- 1 April 2007: Interim Constitution of Nepal promulgated
- 7 August 2007: Agreement between the Government and Janajatis
- 1 April 2008: 10-point commitment for a peaceful, impartial, free and credible election from top leaders.
- 30 August 2007: Agreement between the Government of Nepal and the MJF

### *Majoritarian Phase*

Following the CA election, significant fissures emerged within the political framework of Nepal. What was anticipated to be a consensus government transformed into a majoritarian phase. In a consensus government, the absence of opposition is paramount. Consensus is typified by inclusivity, negotiation, and compromise. However, substantial opposition arose against the prevailing majoritarian system in Nepal.

Several explanations are offered regarding the development of fault lines in the consensus government. First, criticism has been that the 12-Point Agreement was an 'alliance of compulsion.'[10] The agreement and the CPA were 'based more on a temporary convergence of interests than on a deeply shared vision for reshaping Nepal.'[11]

Second, there was distrust between the SPA and the Maoists before the CA elections. Atul Kumar Mishra observed that 'there was no consensus before the elections. There were only individual interests.'[12] The king's role as a shared adversary and the Constituent Assembly election as a collective objective fostered unity among the factions. This circumstance provided the Maoists with a strategic opportunity to advance their people's war agenda. The interim government's suspension of the monarchy on December 28, 2007, catalysed a competitive race for power among political parties in Kathmandu, a dynamic that was evident in their electoral manifestos.

Third, the Maoist victory was initially indigestible for status quo supporters and later unacceptable. The Maoists' emergence as the largest winning party, contrary to the confident assertions of the NC and CPN-UML that the Maoists would be trounced in the electoral battle, embittered the major political parties. Padmaratna Tuladhar observed: "To bring the Maoists under control, the major political parties demanded amendments in the interim constitution from a two-thirds majority to simple majority to form a government by any political party." In Tuladhar's view, this brought the consensus politics to an end.[13] Matters have worsened since the election.

According to Nischal Nath Pandey, 'Until the CA, the signatories to the 12-Point Agreement had one agenda: to conduct the CA election. After the CA elections, these forces suddenly found several other issues and agendas.'[14] Therefore, a controversy was provoked when the 'Maoist leadership proposed en-bloc integration of all verified Maoist cadres into the Nepali Army (NA). This was neither in line with the letter nor the spirit of the previous agreements. The NC's preconditions, like dismantling the Maoists' parallel youth organisation, the Young Communist League (YCL), and return of private property captured by the Maoist cadres, were also against the Maoists' hidden agenda.'[15] According to Ram S. Mahat,

> Since entering the peace process, the Maoists have committed themselves to a competitive multiparty political system, periodic elections, fundamental rights, press freedom, and the rule of law in all formal documents. They have now [2008] set the goal of a people's republic, a euphemism for totalitarian communist rule, as their next agenda.[16]

Maoist leaders countered the allegations by saying that 'NC and UML could not stand by the Maoist victory as the largest party in the CA and tried to create a roadblock in the political process by setting conditions. The mandate of the CA election was a consensus government led by the Maoists. Without a Maoist-led government, the peace process would not be completed.'[17] Criticising seven conditions made by the NC to join the Maoist-led government, a UCPN-Maoist central committee member, Khim Lal Devkota, said that the NC violated the consensus by demanding changes in the interim constitution. India should not have supported the UML and NC government, which has been against people's verdicts. Without Maoists, what would be the meaning of the peace process?"[18]

There was limited discourse on crucial issues, such as the integration of Maoist combatants into the security forces. Nonetheless, this issue was addressed in the 12-Point Agreement and the Comprehensive Peace Agreement (CPA) prior to the first Constituent Assembly elections. Initially, the non-Maoist parties proposed postponing the implementation of this matter until after the CA-I elections, operating under the erroneous assumption that a significant defeat of the Maoists would weaken their position regarding integration. However, the Maoists' impressive electoral victory only served to enhance their assertiveness. Transitioning from a private acceptance of the necessity to accommodate a few thousand ex-People's Liberation Army (PLA) combatants in the Nepali Army at lower ranks before the elections, they subsequently demanded group-level entry and a presence within the Army's command structure following the election results.[19]

Also, the Maoists' provocative statements following their election victory engendered significant skepticism among the principal non-Maoist parties and the international community regarding the former insurgents' adherence to multiparty democracy. In the April 2008 Constituent Assembly elections, the leftist parties secured approximately 60 percent of the votes, marking an unprecedented achievement for Nepal. This success emboldened the Maoists to pursue a coalition government with other left factions. Conversely, the non-Maoist parties, apprehensive about the Maoists' professed intent to transform the Nepali Army into a 'democratic force,' regarded the Army as the sole bulwark against a complete Maoist takeover.[20] Therefore, they were against group entry of former rebels into the Nepali Army.

The Maoists exhibited discomfort with the Nepali Congress leaders' alliance with India and endeavoured to marginalise the party within Nepal's political framework. The Maoists had yet to fully acclimate to democratic politics, and mainstream political avenues did not facilitate their integration into the political landscape. The Maoist leaders articulated a call for renewed revolutionary struggle and the "capture of state power." Numerous aspects of the peace agreement remained unresolved or unimplemented. With few exceptions, the Maoists failed to honour their repeated commitments to return property confiscated during the conflict, nor did they effectively disband parallel governance structures.[21]

## Faultlines in the Constitution-Making Process

### *Political Trust Deficit*

The Nepali Congress and the CPN-UML harboured suspicions that the Maoists were pursuing a long-term agenda of state capture by infiltrating their operatives into the military, bureaucracy, and other institutions. Conversely, the Maoists suspected that the NC, in collaboration with the Nepali Army and India, sought to suppress their movement. Table 1 illustrates the significant divergences among the major political parties regarding contentious issues. While the Maoists proposed the establishment of 14 federal units, the NC and CPN-UML expressed uncertainty about the appropriate number.

Conversely, the Madhesi parties advocated for the establishment of only three provinces based on geographical zones. Likewise, only a limited number of prominent political parties opted for a presidential system of governance. Although the parties successfully addressed the issue of integration, their divergent perspectives regarding the structure of government, electoral system, federalism, and economic policy significantly delayed the constitution-making process.

### *Distrust Between the Army and the Maoists*

The Army and the Maoists fought against each other for ten years. The Army believed that "it was not a defeated Army. It was betrayed by the political leaders,"[22] who treated the Maoists at par with them. The Army had strong

**Table 8: Political Parties and Contentious Issues in First CA**

| *Major Parties* | *Seats in Parliament* | *Maoist combatant's rehabilitation** | *Form of Government* | *Electoral system*** | *Federalism* | *Basis for forming federal unit* | *Economic policy* |
|---|---|---|---|---|---|---|---|
| **UCPN-M** | 232 | Hardliner-group integration. Moderate-5 to 6 thousand | President to be elected directly by people | PR based on caste and ethnicity | 14 federal units and three sub-provinces in Terai | Ethnic Basis | New Transitional Economic Policy |
| **NC** | 116 | No integration or Integration as suggested in CPA | In the parliamentary system, the President is elected indirectly | Majoritarian system | Seven federal units | Geographical, Cultural, Social and economic aspects | Open market system |
| **CPN-UML** | 109 | As suggested in the CPA | PM directly by people | Mixed system | 15 federal units | Geographical, economic and natural resources | Mixed Economy |
| **MJF** | 55 | No integration | President to be elected directly by people | PR system | One Madhes, One Pradesh | Ethnic and geographical | Not clear |
| **TMLP** | 21 | As suggested in CPA | PM to be elected by Lower House | PR System | One Madhes One Pradesh | Ethnic and geographical | Not clear |

*Note: * and **:* Issues resolved under CA-I.

*Source:* Compiled by the Author from English media.

reservations about the Maoists' obsession with democratising the NA and group integration of their combatants into the Army.

Emboldened by the divisions in Nepal's body politics, the Army came out with a statement on national security that implied that the Maoist government was not legitimate. The Army Chief General Rookmangud Katuwal said that the 'military would only abide by the "legitimate" orders of the legitimate government.'[23] The Army handed over a 106-page National Policy and National Defence Policy to the National Interest Preservation Committee, clearly overreaching its authority in the constitutional scheme. The report said:

> (Nepal) should look beyond the conventional security concept and develop a comprehensive security concept that considers the changed global, regional, and national security atmosphere and the country's geopolitical situation to promote and preserve national interests towards achieving national goals and objectives.[24]

### *The Maoists' Ambivalence*

Although the Maoists were elected as the largest party in the April 2008 CA elections and subsequently headed a coalition government, they kept saying that the 'people's revolution continues'. Then the Prime Minister, Prachanda, himself threatened several times to carry out protests against the state and warned of 'another people's revolt if reactionary forces obstructed the peace process'.[25]

In his speech before the PLA commanders in the Shaktikhor cantonment in Chitwan district in January 2008, Prachanda said:

> The revolution is continuing but in a different form. But the gist is the same ... political parties and the Army feel terror because of the PLA. Your number has not decreased. Instead, it has been increased from earlier 8,000 to 35,000. We have not shrunk, but grown ... the PLA in cantonments will be used by the party to prepare for revolt and ultimately capture the state ... even a tiny number of their [PLA cadres] entry into NA is enough to establish complete Maoist control over the army. This was why Army Chief Rookmangud Katuwal was against our soldiers' entry into the military.[26]

The Maoists' resolutions in the Kharipati conclave in December 2008 clearly showed their future agenda. Some of these resolutions said:

- Of the three stages of the Maoist People's War, Nepal's Maoist revolution has reached the stage of strategic offence with its indigenous characteristics.
- Prepare the PLA politically and ideologically for the offensive to complete the revolution.
- The PLA will undergo ideological and political training on *Prachandapath* and MLM (Marxism, Leninism, and Maoism) at introductory, intermediate, and advanced levels.
- The integration of the PLA will be used to further the cause of proletarianism and revolution. The issue of army integration should be used in this context.

### *External Forces' Interests*

In the post-Constituent Assembly election phase, the Maoist party emerged as China's preferred political ally, significantly fostering unity among the various communist factions. China also advocated for a stable unitary political system to mitigate anti-China sentiments in Nepal. Prior to Jhala Nath Khanal assuming leadership of the CPN-UML, a four-member Chinese delegation visited Kathmandu on May 10, 2008, engaging with Khanal as well as other Maoist leaders. Additionally, a senior delegation from the Communist Party of China, led by Vice Minister Liu Hongcai, attended the inaugural ceremony of the eighth national convention of the CPN-UML in February 2009.

When India protested against the Maoists' initiative to form a communist alliance and suggested creating a national government by including the NC, the Maoists interpreted India's suggestion as patronising the NC and interfering in the internal affairs of Nepal. 'Beginning with the signing of the 12-Point Agreement to the declaration of Republic, India played quite a positive role in Nepal … now, India is expansionist, and its attitude is purely hegemonic,' a Maoist leader declaimed.[27] The Maoists' anti-India campaigns intensified after Prachanda's resignation as Prime Minister in May 2009, who declared, 'Signing of 12 point agreement in New Delhi is a liability on the peace process.'

Media reports indicated that China had facilitated the modernisation of the Nepali Army and the integration of Maoist combatants into its ranks. During his official visit to China in September 2008, Nepal's former Defence

Minister, Ram Bahadur Thapa, formally requested assistance in this regard. China expressed a desire to support the incorporation of Maoist combatants into the Army and paramilitary forces for its strategic advantage. The inclusion of Maoist elements within Nepal's security forces could potentially afford China a degree of operational influence over these entities and enhance its capacity for effective management of anti-Tibetan refugee initiatives in Nepal.

The United States' views on PLA integration were not too well articulated. The CPN-Maoist, the United Revolutionary People's Council and the PLA were included in the US State Department's Terrorist Exclusion List (TEL) till September 2012.[28] State Department spokesman Sean McCormack, talking to media on May 8, 2008, said, 'I don't think that the US has changed its policy in looking at the Maoists...having said that, I must reiterate that there is no change as such in looking at the Maoists…it remains as usual.'[29]

The EU member states were worried that the CA-I would fail to complete its tasks. They were pushing for an inclusive constitution. Given the EU's active engagement in the peace process and on the federalism issue, civil society groups approached to pressure the major political parties to settle on ethnic-based federalism and proportional representation arrangement in the constitution. The member countries started engaging with the stakeholders such as civil society groups, ethnic organisations and women groups to find an amicable solution to the stalemate over issues like federalism, transitional justice, proportional representation arrangement in the electoral system and other human rights issues.

## Tussle Over Power Sharing

The contentious power-sharing dynamics between the Nepali Congress and the Maoist party culminated in the failure of consensus-building efforts during the post-2008 period. Prior to the 2008 CA-I elections, the NC exhibited a lack of seriousness regarding the integration of Maoist combatants, as former Prime Minister and NC President G.P. Koirala intended to utilise these combatants as a contingency against potential incursions from the monarchy. This strategy was predicated on the need to mobilise the Royal Nepal Army (RNA), now known as the Nepali Army, in opposition to democratic forces, given that the NA remained inscribed within the coercive apparatus of the monarchy at that time.

Prachanda and G.P. Koirala established a tacit understanding regarding Koirala's candidacy for the position of the first President of Nepal following the elections. As the Maoists ascended to prominence as the largest political party and Nepal transitioned into a Republic, the Nepali Congress and the CPN-UML began to endorse the Nepali Army's stance on the integration issue. Concurrently, radical factions within the Maoist party argued that Koirala should not be permitted to assume the presidency without instituting amendments pertaining to the powers and functions of the Prime Minister within the interim constitution. This situation precipitated a misunderstanding between the NC and the Maoists, resulting in a three-month delay in the NC's transfer of power to the Maoists after the 2008 elections.

Amidst the trust deficit between the major political parties, the Army and civil society, the CA-I failed to generate consensus on critical issues such as the form of government, federalism, electoral system and economic policy (see Table 8). Since the Maoist Party and the marginalised groups had a strong presence in the Constituent Assembly, the NC and the CPN-UML found it challenging to reconcile the Maoist Party's demand for ethnic and based federalism and the adoption of a directly elected Presidential form of government. The failure of the first CA in May 2012 was a significant blow to the democratic process in the post-monarchy period. Overall, the CA was the most representative body in Nepal's history.

There are several immediate reasons offered for that failure. First, the CA and the political parties did not stick to democratic norms. For example, the CA failed to implement the Interim Constitution (IC) clause on the inclusion of marginalised groups despite the stated right in Article 21 of the IC, 2007, to participate in state structures based on proportional inclusion and various laws and policies.[30] Dalits and Janajatis were underrepresented, while Madhesis and those from the 'Other' category were overrepresented relative to their national population.[31] Unfortunately, the CA was dissolved after the failure to generate consensus on the nature of federalism that should be adopted in the new constitution.

Second, a significant number of leaders who were unsuccessful in the elections subsequently joined the government. For instance, Bamdev Gautam, the then-home minister under the Prachanda-led administration, did not secure a seat in the first Constituent Assembly elections. Similarly, Madhav Kumar

Nepal, who succeeded Prachanda as prime minister, was also not elected as a member of the CA-I. Approximately 40 percent of the ministers in the government were not elected during the CA elections. This trend continued with the third government led by Jhalanath Khanal, who appointed Bharat Mohan Adhikari as Deputy Prime Minister despite his rejection at the polls in the 2008 elections. Nearly 30 percent of the ministers in the Khanal administration were not granted electoral endorsement by the electorate.[32]

Third, many portfolios and constitutional committees were dominated by upper-caste hill Bahuns and Chhetris. Despite the strong presence of marginalised groups in the CA, they were not consulted on contentious issues, especially federalism.

Finally, prolonged political instability hindered democratic decentralisation. Without a constitution, local body elections were not held for 16 years. These elections required a constitutional regulatory framework, which the state organs found challenging to keep.

## Problems with the CA-II

The CA-II elections were conducted in accordance with the Supreme Court's directive following the inability of the CA-I to fulfill its obligations within the designated timeframe. The mandate of the CA-II was to finalise the outstanding tasks of the CA-I and promulgate the constitution in a timely manner.

While marginalised groups were relatively well represented in the CA-I, their representation significantly declined in the CA-II. Notably, the representation of the Madhesi community, alongside Janajatis, decreased in CA-II. There was a prevailing sentiment in Nepal that the CA-II was less inclusive than its predecessor. According to the Election Commission, only ten women, 63 Janajatis, and two Dalits were elected through direct polls. In contrast, the total number of women candidates in the 2008 Constituent Assembly was 30.

The number of Janajati elected CA members was 63, down from 74 under the FPTP system. Of them, 25 were elected from UML, 23 from NC, 11 from UCPN (M), three from Madhesi Janaadhikar Forum-Loktantrik (MJF-L) and one from Nepal Majdoor Kisan Party. There were 219 representatives (74 elected and 145 from proportional representation) from the indigenous communities in the last CA. The National Population Census 2011 shows that Janajatis comprise 37 percent of the country's population.[33] Therefore, the second CA was less inclusive than the first one. Interestingly, those who were, to some extent, responsible for the historical exclusion of many people had returned to power (see Figure 2).

Other challenges encompassed insufficient public consultations and the local population's limited engagement in the constitution-making process. Most importantly, the contentious issues that led to the dissolution of the CA-I remained unresolved, with the positions of the affected parties on these matters largely unchanged. This continuity of stance significantly influenced the discourse in the CA-II regarding these contentious issues (Table 9).

**Table 9: Comparison of Major Challenges during AC-I and CA-II**

| *CA-I* | *CA-II* |
|---|---|
| Public expectations: Constitution drafting, peace and governance | Public Expectations: Governance, political stability and constitution |
| The most considerable presence of Maoists and alliances | NC, UML and rightist groups dominant |
| Substantial presence of minority groups | Number reduced drastically |
| First elected members | 60 percent of new members |
| Only integration and electoral systems are resolved. | Major contentious issues - federalism, structure of the future political system, judiciary, reservations of jobs for marginalised groups |
| Only UCPN (Maoist) | Two Maoist parties |
| 50+ political parties | 128+ political parties |
| 3 Madhesh based parties | 13+ Madhesh-based parties |

## CA-II Changes and Their Impact on Debates

### *Composition and Restructuring of CA-II*

The November 2013 CA-II elections yielded results that astonished many observers. The Maoist party, which had previously attained the largest party position in the first Constituent Assembly (CA-I), experienced a decline and finished in third place. The Nepali Congress (NC) emerged as the predominant party, followed by the Communist Party of Nepal-Unified Marxist Leninist (CPN-UML).

Figure 2: Nepal: Constituent Assembly Election 2013 under FPTP: Breakdown of Elected Candidates by Caste/Ethnicity

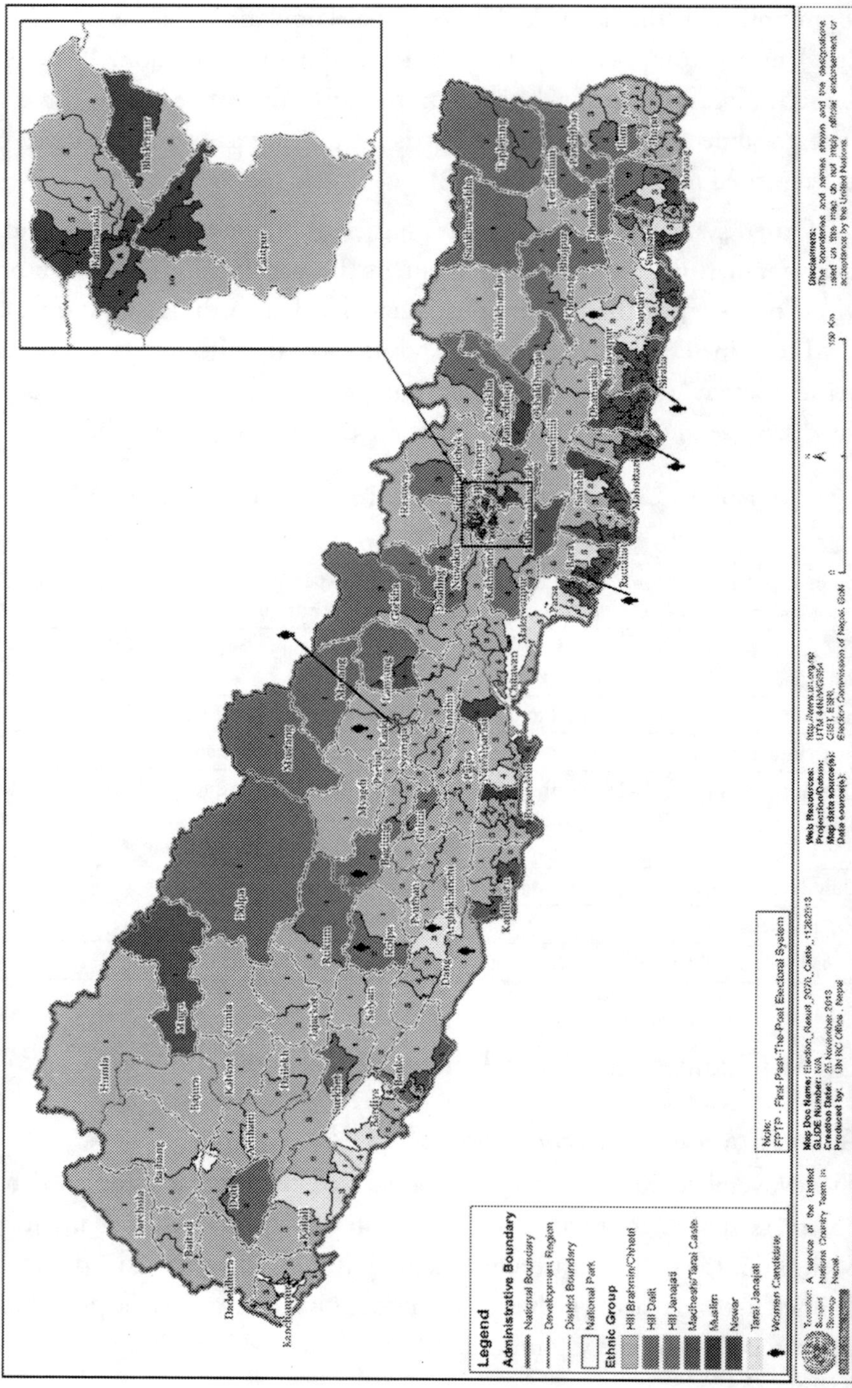


*Source:* United Nations, Resident Coordinator Office, Nepal, 26 November 2013.

As previously highlighted, the composition of CA-II was less inclusive than that of CA-I, primarily due to diminished representation of minority groups, including women. Despite the implementation of a proportional representation system and the allocation of reserved seats for minorities in the interim Constitution, both the NC and UML did not fully comply with these provisions. Notably, despite their subpar performance, the Maoist party retained a majority of the minority representatives in CA-II.

The supremacy of the two major political parties, predominantly led by the Hill-upper-caste groups, undermined the Constitution's fundamental objectives. Many contentious issues resolved in CA-I were subsequently proposed for re-evaluation in the constitution drafting committees. Furthermore, with the alteration in the composition of CA-II, numerous committees were restructured to incorporate newly elected members, who were largely affiliated with the two major parties. These committees were strategically manipulated to prevent any acknowledgement of the Maoists' contributions to the adoption of the new constitution.

This realisation began to crystallise both domestically and internationally around April 2008, when the Maoist party ascended to the position of largest party in CA-I. Some EU member states were optimistic about the Maoists' success, but other important international players, including China, were ambivalent over their rise to prominence. At that juncture, the Maoists sought ideological, political, security, and economic support from China. This perception among global actors resonated with the perspectives of the NC, UML, and the Nepali Army, all of which have played pivotal roles in the peace process since 2006.

### *Leadership*

The most consequential event that influenced the debates and discussions throughout the Constituent Assembly (CA) drafting process favouring the Hill-upper caste ruling classes was the election of former Prime Minister of Nepal and CPN-UML chairman K P Sharma Oli to CA-II. Oli had previously lost in the CA-I elections. He was elected as the parliamentary party leader of the CPN-UML following the CA-II elections. Ideologically, Oli was a fervent adversary of the Maoists. In a meeting with the Indian Ambassador in Kathmandu in 2012, Oli asserted that "given an opportunity, he would cut the Maoist party into four pieces." He is believed to have played a pivotal role in the fragmentation of the Maoist party in June 2012.

Culturally, as a Brahmin hailing from the eastern Terai of Nepal and a nationalist, he vocally opposed the demands for ethnic-based federalism from Janajati and Madhesi-based parties, as well as the call for "One Madhesh, One Pradesh." Politically, Oli maintained connections with several communist leaders in India, attributed to his involvement in the Jhapa uprising of 1969 and his membership in the CPN-UML. Before 2014, the Indian establishment regarded him as one of Nepal's favoured leaders. Oli was crucial in formalising the Mahakali Hydro Project Treaty between India and Nepal. Given his extensive association with India and personal contacts there, former Indian Ambassador to Nepal, Rakesh Sood, remarked, "Mr. Oli is no stranger to India."[34]

Subsequently, Oli's influence in the CA debates regarding various contentious issues became increasingly pronounced following his ascendancy to the chairmanship of the CPN-UML on July 17, 2014. He emerged as a key figure in negotiating the 16-point agreement between the Nepali Congress (NC), the CPN-UML, and the Maoists to expedite the remaining phases of the Constitution drafting process immediately after the April 2015 earthquake. Dipendra Jha noted that the "16-point agreement departed from what the parties had agreed upon under CA-I."[35] Oli served as the principal interlocutor, uniting the Maoists and the NC under a common platform and formulating a power-sharing arrangement between the NC and UML.

It is important to recognise that the 16-point agreement constituted a transformative development in the completion of the Constitution drafting process. Regrettably, India remained unaware of this due to its disconnection with the CPN-UML generally, and Oli in particular. Indian agencies and diplomats stationed in Kathmandu relied on input from certain Madhesi intellectuals, who consistently provided misleading information.

This emergent rapport between select Indian officials and Madhesi intellectuals provoked Oli and segments of civil society in Kathmandu. As India leveraged its influence in Kathmandu to accommodate Madhesi's demands in the Constitution, Oli began to distance himself from India, adopting a non-cooperative stance towards Indian engagement during the constitutional processes. The communication chasm between Oli and India further widened when India failed to assist Nepali officials in maintaining the no-man's-land along the India-Nepal border free from Madhesi protestors in 2015, contrary to the stipulations of the 1950 Treaty agreement and previously established border regulations.

In conjunction with Oli, Maoist Party chief Prachanda, NC party president, and then Prime Minister of Nepal, Sushil Koirala, experienced a communication gap stemming from a trust deficit with India for distinct reasons. In line with his party's opposition to India's policies, Prachanda expressed discontent regarding what he perceived as India's influence over the Nepal President's office in reinstating General Rookmangud Katwal. This situation ultimately led to his resignation as Prime Minister in May 2009.

Similarly, during this period, Sushil Koirala discreetly disregarded many critical recommendations from India, as he was not convinced of India's support for Sher Bahadur Deuba as Party President in the 2016 Party's General Convention. Concurrently, Koirala considered the nomination of Shashank Koirala. Prime Minister Koirala was perplexed by New Delhi's inadequate coordination among various agencies and ambivalence regarding Nepalese affairs; while one Indian agency supported him, others backed Deuba.

Moreover, India's Madhesi-centric policy preceding the adoption of the Constitution compelled these leaders to unify, culminating in the 16-point agreement. Given the historical tensions between the Madhesi and the ruling classes of Nepal, these leaders opted to align with the sentiments of the hill communities to safeguard their political constituencies. Although the constitution has been adopted and amended, the remnants of the anti-constitution protests continue to adversely affect India-Nepal relations.

### *Geopolitics*

Given Nepal's strategic geopolitical positioning and its diplomatic relations with major powers since the Rana regime, the domestic developments in Nepal at any given time cannot be disentangled from the dynamics of global and regional power equations. Furthermore, India has played a pivotal role in significant political transformations in Nepal since 1950, especially in comparison to other contemporary global actors. There exists a prevalent perception in Nepal that the composition of the Indian government and the degree of political clarity in New Delhi regarding Nepalese matters could, to some extent, influence the political landscape in Kathmandu. Consequently, Nepalese citizens often find themselves in a position of both complimenting and critiquing India.

India was again instrumental in resolving the Maoist conflict and reinstating multi-party democracy through the formulation of the 12-point agreement in Delhi in December 2005, which was brokered between the Maoists and seven political parties of Nepal. The governmental composition in New Delhi at that time proved to be crucial. The UPA-I was a coalition government led by the Indian National Congress (INC) and supported by various Communist parties of India and other regional entities. The UPA-I was able to leverage the communist Party's influence and persuade the Maoists to engage in the peace process and transition to parliamentary democracy, facilitated by personal connections between the Communist leadership and Maoist figures. Notably, former Communist leader Sitaram Yechuri played a significant role in this engagement. As a result, India adopted a constructive and conciliatory policy towards the Maoists, with dual objectives: maintaining the northern front free from conflict and political instability while simultaneously disrupting the strategic and ideological affiliations between the Nepali and Indian Maoists, also known as Naxalites.

In contrast, the UPA-II, which was again led by the Indian National Congress under Dr. Manmohan Singh, emerged as a coalition government devoid of the Communist Party's support. It assumed power in May 2008, at a juncture when the Nepal peace process was ongoing. Merely a month prior to the establishment of the UPA-II, the Maoists had ascended to the status of the largest party in the April 2008 Constituent Assembly elections. Surprisingly, in the absence of the Communist Party, the UPA-II's policy orientation towards the Nepalese Maoists underwent a remarkable reversal. New Delhi gradually discerned that endorsing the Maoists for their role in drafting a new constitution in Nepal could potentially embolden the Naxalites within India and, concurrently, draw the Nepalese Maoists ideologically closer to China.

Another compelling rationale for the UPA-II to contemplate the adoption of a revised policy concerning the peace process in Nepal was its longstanding affiliation with the Nepali Congress. Both entities staunchly advocate for multiparty democracy and the supremacy of the constitution. In 2008, considerable discrepancies emerged between the Nepali Congress and the

Prachanda-led government in Kathmandu. Following his ascension to power, Prachanda reneged on his prior agreement to support G P Koirala's candidacy for the presidency, a commitment established before the elections. Consequently, the Nepali Congress leader's evaluation of the Maoists' strategies and tactics in the context of the post-peace agreement was given significant consideration in New Delhi.

India was also perturbed by Prachanda's alignment with China, his party's anti-India resolutions, and, most critically, his initiative to undermine the integrity of the Nepali Army by dismissing the then-Nepali Army chief, General Rookmangud Katwal. This action was particularly contentious, as India had assumed the role of guarantor in safeguarding the Nepali Army from Maoist influence following the 12-point agreement and the subsequent peace process. In response to India's interference concerning General Katwal's situation, Prachanda, in May 2009, articulated that India "denied support" to his government in its efforts to uphold "civilian supremacy," contending that its "lack of support" for institutionalising democratic norms engendered suspicion, and he attributed blame to New Delhi for "breaking politics of consensus."[36]

The political communication between New Delhi and Kathmandu took a new turn following Prime Minister Modi's assumption of power in May 2014. While Prime Minister Modi's inaugural overseas visit to Nepal was a significant step towards resolving various misunderstandings, there appears to be an opportunity for New Delhi to further build on this initial success and maintain the positive momentum established during the visit. Prime Minister Modi's proposal for a Nepali Constitution that would encompass the aspirations of all segments of Nepali society—a notion he expressed as "Har Nepali ko lage ki yeh ek aisa guldasta hai jismein mere ek phool ki bhi mahak hai"[37]—was positively received by Nepali leaders. However, the relationship significantly declined due to visiting of then-Indian foreign secretary Dr S Jaishankar, as the special envoy of PM Modi, just two days before the promulgation of the constitution and protests by the Madhesi at the open border. Dr Jaishankar suggested that "the window until the promulgation of the new constitution be used effectively to push for its wider acceptance. India remains concerned by the lack of broad ownership of the current draft and by ongoing protests in the Tarai region that borders India. India remains worried about spillover effect of protests in Tarai".[38] It seemed that the Nepalese leaders were not pleased with India's last-minute suggestion to delay the drafting process. As the constitution was adopted in Nepal as scheduled, India responded somewhat lukewarmly to the constitution.

At the governmental level, despite achieving a diplomatic masterstroke by arranging PM Modi's two visits to Nepal in 2014, the Bharatiya Janata Party (BJP) faced ideological dilemmas concerning engagement with Nepali political parties. As a right-wing entity, the BJP was inherently uncomfortable with communist factions domestically. This ideological schism posed a barrier to engagement with the CPN-UML and the Maoist party, both of which played significant roles in the constitution drafting process. Regarding the Nepali Congress, the BJP perceived it as a party with a longstanding association with the Indian National Congress, adopting an initial policy of caution towards it. While the BJP was ambivalent about engaging with major political parties during this period, some Madhesi leaders and intellectuals endeavoured to bridge the gap by positing the Madhesis as India's cultural and political ally. Confidence in engaging with Nepalese political parties only materialised after the BJP was elected to power in 2019.

### *USA*

India's strategic pivot towards the Maoists in 2008 was rapidly endorsed by the USA, which had staunchly opposed the 12-point agreement due to the Maoist party being designated on the USA's terrorist list. The USA corroborated New Delhi's approach of engaging and mainstreaming the Maoists, given the concurrent finalisation of the civil nuclear deal between the two nations. The USA also aligned with the Nepali Army's assessment of the Maoists and India's intervention in preserving the integrity of the organisation against Maoist encroachment. Ideologically, the USA was reluctant to ascribe any credit to the Maoists regarding the constitution's formation.

### *China*

In addition to India and the USA, China appeared disinclined to support the Maoists' ascension in Kathmandu. Although Chinese officials extended congratulations to Prachanda upon his premiership, the Chinese Communist Party exhibited a preference for the CPN-UML over the Maoists during Nepal's post-monarchical phase. Chinese authorities expressed ongoing scepticism regarding the Maoist leaders' allegiance, given their historical context of spending considerable time in India during the Nepalese people's war. From a Chinese perspective, the Maoist movements in South Asia did not constitute authentic revolutionary endeavours aimed at socio-political transformation in the region. Mao Zedong's grandson, Mao Xinyu, a general in the Chinese army, remarked that "the ideas of China's Great Helmsman were being misused by groups such as the Maoists in India."[39] Furthermore, China harboured concerns regarding political and structural changes instigated by a revolutionary party in Nepal, particularly due to its geographical proximity to Tibet, which raised apprehensions about potential political ramifications in Tibet.

### *Poor performance of the Maoist Party*

The Maoist Party's subpar performance in the Constituent Assembly II (CA-II) constituted a considerable setback for the discourse surrounding constitutional matters. Several factors contributed to the Maoists' lackluster showing in 2013. Primarily, the party leadership's failure to meet the elevated expectations of its cadres significantly undermined support. Many party members assumed that the Maoist Party's majority in the CA would effectively address their developmental aspirations, including employment, rural infrastructure, educational facilities, health services, and the rehabilitation of ex-combatants into the Nepal Army. However, the mandate of the CA was predominantly focused on drafting a new constitution. It is noteworthy that Nepal's political parties had disseminated their electoral manifestos prior to both the CA-I and CA-II elections. Consequently, the Maoist Party's impressive performance in the initial CA-I elections stood in stark contrast to its electoral outcomes in CA-II.

Secondly, a party that emerged to power by championing the grievances of marginalised groups found itself increasingly excluded in the constitutional debates that commenced in 2013 due to a lack of representation in the CA-II. Furthermore, the party's top leadership struggled to maintain its ideological commitments, succumbing to pressures from rival parties and compromising on core issues, particularly those concerning the aspirations of marginalised communities. This compromise was exacerbated following the Supreme Court's January 2014 ruling that prohibited the granting of amnesty for serious human rights violations committed during the decade-long Maoist insurgency.[40]

Thirdly, during the initial phase of the People's War, the Maoists had committed to establishing ethnic-based federalism and regional official languages in various provinces to garner popular support. However, many of its supporters, particularly from the Janajati community, became disillusioned with the party. This discontent was amplified by strong resistance from major political parties, resulting in the first CA-I's failure to achieve consensus on these issues. By 2007, the Maoists had also lost support among the Madhesi population due to their altered stance on the demand for a separate Madhesh Pradesh advocated by Madhesi parties. In March 2007, a violent clash in Gaur resulted in the deaths of approximately 25 individuals, including two women, and left around 40 others injured. The confrontation occurred between Maoist cadres and activists of the Madhesi Janaadhikar Forum (MJF). Consequently, the Maoists suffered a significant erosion of their electoral base related to federalism issues in the 2013 CA-II elections.

Fourthly, the Maoist party experienced a decline in its support and cadre strength over the integration of Maoist ex-combatants into the Nepali Army. After the Maoist government was established in Kathmandu, the party did not implement the promised reforms in the security sector or achieve the mass integration of Maoist combatants, which had been a pledge during the People's War. However, dissatisfaction grew among party members when, by 2011, the integration process had facilitated the inclusion of only a little over a thousand ex-combatants into the Nepali Army, with many opting for financial settlements instead.

Fifthly, beyond political promises, the Maoist Party historically benefited from the presence of the Young Communist League (YCL), the radical youth wing of the former UCPN (Maoist), particularly in rural areas. During the first CA election, YCL cadres employed intimidation tactics, effectively suppressing the activities of Nepali Congress and CPN-UML leaders. They also employed coercive measures against non-Maoist voters. However, the YCL underwent regulation and restructuring into a more moderate youth wing in 2012. The diminishing relevance of ex-combatants who had been part of the YCL following the integration into the Nepali Army led to a decline in the organisation's radical fervour, thereby significantly impacting its role in the CA-II elections. In January 2016, Prachanda remarked, "The party's journey of defeat had begun with the decision to dissolve the Young Communist League."[41]

Lastly, the split within the Maoist Party in June 2012 further compounded its challenges, resulting in a division of its support base. This fragmentation has imposed considerable strain on its affiliated organisations, including those representing minority communities.

### *Fragmented Madhesi*

The second phase of the Madhesi movement, which commenced in the first quarter of 2007, represented a pivotal moment in the constitution-writing process of Nepal. This movement compelled the major political parties based in Kathmandu to amend the Interim Constitution to incorporate the principle of federalism. Following this amendment, the Madhesi movement, initially perceived by the hill elites as a cultural endeavour, evolved into a significant political movement. Four registered Madhesi-centric political parties participated in the first Constituent Assembly (CA-I) elections, securing 83 seats out of a total of 575 in the assembly. This marked the first occasion in which Madhesi representation was notably pronounced within the CA-cum-Parliament of Nepal. The Madhesi demands, encompassing federalism, proportional representation, citizenship, and linguistic rights, garnered considerable attention during the Constituent Assembly debates.

However, this momentum dissipated during the second Constituent Assembly (CA-II), as the Madhesi-based parties fragmented into multiple factions. Ultimately, nine parties represented the Madhes region in CA-II, with only 36 members. The divided Madhesi factions appeared more focused on consolidating power and attaining constitutional positions rather than advancing the Madhesi agenda. Consequently, they were unable to effectively oppose the Kathmandu-based political parties on various contentious issues during the constitution drafting process. In response, they enacted an economic blockade against Kathmandu by staging protests at the India-Nepal border.

## What Lies Ahead

Overall, there has been no substantial change in the democratic framework compared to the monarchical era. The primary distinction lies in the replacement of a singular monarch with multiple leaders who exhibit a profound desire for power. The newly elected representatives demonstrate an unwillingness to distribute power equitably among marginalised groups.

Similar to the monarchy, the political culture of seeking external support (rather than external influence) to attain power persists.

Political analysts believe the conflict might relapse if the post-conflict political set-up does not address grievances. In this regard, quoting Huntington, one Nepalese scholar observed that "an unstable social, economic, and political environment coming out of a civil war, a shift to democracy that is too rapid may prove counterproductive if the newly created political institutions cannot accommodate pressures for political participation."[42] This trend has been observed in Nepal during the post-constitution era. Marginalised groups have united to advocate for the revision of the constitution. Certain Maoist splinter factions, such as those led by Netra Bikram Chand and Mohan Vaidya, have categorically rejected the new constitution. Additionally, royalist factions are demanding the reinstatement of the 1990 constitution, the restoration of which would inherently re-establish Nepal as a Hindu state. In this context, the potential resurgence of social and political tensions cannot be discounted if the provisions of the new constitution are not effectively implemented and minority groups continue to experience marginalisation. It is imperative for the nation to promptly address the grievances of these excluded groups to preempt another cycle of conflict or mobilisation by marginalised communities.

## NOTES

1 The first Constituent Assembly (CA-I) concluded its mandate in 2013 without fulfilling its designated tasks. Subsequent elections for the second Constituent Assembly (CA-II) were held in 2013, culminating in the promulgation of the Constitution in September 2015. To prevent ambiguity, the first Constituent Assembly will henceforth be referred to as CA-I, and the second as CA-II.

2 Mahendra Lawoti (ed.), "Contentious Politics and Democratization in Nepal", Sage, Los Angels, 2007, p. 52.

3 David N. Gellner, "Democracy in Nepal: four models", *Seminar*, 576, August 2007, p. 55.

4 Ibid.

5 "Citizen Survey 2013: Nepal in Transition", Nepal Democracy Survey Round III, June 2013. Joint survey by State of *Democracy in South Asia/Nepal chapter / and International IDEA*.

6 Author's interaction with the Nepalese in November 2013.

7 Krishna Hachhethu, et al., "Nepal in Transition: A study on the State of Democracy", International Institute for Democracy and Electoral Assistance, Stockholm, January 2008, p. 73.

8 Ganga Bahadur Thapa, "Is there a Transition to Democracy in Nepal?" *Indian Journal of Nepalese Studies*, Vol. 13, 2007, p. 7.

9 The evidence contradicts the prevailing narrative that attributes political instability in Nepal to the monarchy. It appears that the monarchy capitalised on the rivalries among political

leaders to consolidate its power.

10 Author's interaction with Uddhab Pyakurel in Kathmandu. Pyakurel is a political analyst and faculty with Kathmandu University.

11 "Nepal Faltering Peace Process," International Crisis Group, *Asia Report* No. 163, 19 February 2009, p. 2.

12 Author's interaction with Atul Kumar Mishra, a Kathmandu based journalist reports on developments in Terai region and senior editor, *The Kathmandu Post*, in Kathmandu.

13 Author's interaction with Padmaratna Tuladhar in Kathmandu.

14 Author's interview with Nischal Nath Pandey in Kathmandu. Pandey is director, Center for South Asian Studies in Kathmandu.

15 Author's interaction with Ram S. Mahat in Kathmandu. Mahat is a former Minister and Central Committee member of the Nepali Congress.

16 Ram S. Mahat, "Betrayal of the peace process?" *Kantipuronline*, 14 December 2008, at http://www.kantipuronline.com/kolnews.php?&nid=170406 (accessed 01 August 2009).

17 Author's interaction with Baburam Bhattarai, former senior Maoist leader and Prime Minister of Nepal, in Kathmandu.

18 Author's interaction with Khim Lal Devkota, a Supreme Court lawyer and former Maoist leader, in Kathmandu.

19 Author's interaction with a member of the Technical Committee on the Maoists integration into the Nepali Army of CPN-UML, in Kathmandu.

20 Prashant Jha, "Deepening Distrust," *South Asia Intelligence Review*, 7 (35), 09 March 2009, at http://www.satp.org/satporgtp/sair/Archives/7_35.htm#assessment2 (accessed on 28 September 2021).

21 "Nepal Faltering Peace Process," International Crisis Group, *Asia Report* No. 163, 19 February 2009, p. 2.

22 Author's interview with Brigadier General Ramindra Chhetri (Retd.), Director of Public Relations, The Nepali Army, in Kathmandu.

23 "Recruitment of political activists in NA a strict no-no: Army chief", *Nepalnews*, 04 January 2008, at http://www.nepalnews.com/archive/2009/jan/jan04/news10.php (accessed on 03 October 2024).

24 "The Army's ideas," *Nepali Times*, 19 February 2009, at http://www.nepalitimes.com.np/2009/02/19/163 (accessed on 16 April 2022).

25 "Dahal issues revolt threat," *MyRepublica*, 23 April 2009, at http://www.myrepublica.com/portal/index.php?action=news_details&news_id=4202 (accessed on 27 September 2021).

26 The videotape of the speech was published in *Nepalnews*, 05 May 2009, at http://www.nepalnews.com/archive/2009/may/may05/news12.php#1 (accessed on 27 September 2021).

27 "Nepal's Maoist influential leader spits venom against India", *The Telegraph Nepal*, 10 May 2009, http://www.telegraphnepal.com/news_det.php?news_id=5386 (accessed on 27 September 2021).

28 "Country Reports on Terrorism 2008," US Department of State, USA, 30 April 2009.

29 "US stance on Nepal Maoists, a volte-face," *The Telegraph Nepal*, 16 May 2008, at http://telegraphnepal.com/news_det.php?news_id=3424 (accessed on 27 September 2021).

30 "Deadlines, Democracy and a Popular, Democratic Constitution", Policy Paper, No. 05, June 2011, Martin Chautari, Kathmandu, p.7.

31 Ibid, p.8.

32 Ibid, p.10.

33 "CA stokes inclusion fears," *The Kathmandu Post*, 28 November 2013, at http://

www.ekantipur.com/the-kathmandu-post/2013/11/27/news/ca-stokes-inclusion-fears/256251.html (accessed on 11 May 2014).

34 Rakesh Sood, "Restoring goodwill in India-Nepal ties", Comment, *The Hindu*, 18 February 2016.

35 Dipendra Jha, "Federal Nepal: Trials and Tribulations", AAKAR Books, Delhi, 2018, p. 34.

36 "Will not tolerate any kind of interference, says Prachanda" *mint*, 07 May 2009, https://www.livemint.com/Politics/yM38sLXgSjctpEnKUEa4EM/Will-not-tolerate-any-kind-of-interference-says-Prachanda.html (accessed on 03 November 2014).

37 "Summary of Prime Minister's address to Constituent Assembly of Nepal (August 3, 2014)", 05 August 2014, https://www.mea.gov.in/press-releases.htm?dtl/23817/Summary+of+Prime+Ministers+address+to+Constituent+Assembly+of+NepalAugust+3+2014 (accessed on 03 November 2014).

38 "Utilise time before statute promulgation", *The Kathmandu Post*, 19 September 2015, https://kathmandupost.com/miscellaneous/2015/09/19/utilise-time-before-statute-promulgation (accessed on 03 November 2014).

39 "India's Maoists are misusing Mao's name", *The Hindu*, 20 April 2012, https://www.thehindu.com/news/international/indias-maoists-are-misusing-maos-name/article2982482.ece (accessed on 03 November 2014).

40 "Nepal Supreme Court Prohibits Amnesty for Serious Human Rights Violations Committed during Armed Conflict", International Justice Resource Center, San Francisco, USA, 08 January 2014, https://ijrcenter.org/2014/01/08/nepal-supreme-court-prohibits-amnesty-for-serious-human-rights-violations-committed-during-armed-conflict/ (accessed on 03 November 2014).

41 "Dissolution of YCL led to UCPN-M's downfall says Dahal", *The Himalayan*, Kathmandu, 25 January 2016, https://thehimalayantimes.com/kathmandu/ycls-dissolution-led-to-ucpn-maoists-downfall-says-dahal (accessed on 03 November 2014).

42 Ganga Bahadur Thapa, "Is there a Transition to Democracy in Nepal?" *Indian Journal of Nepalese Studies*, Vol. 13, 2007, p. 8.

# *Chapter 6*

# *Democracy, Peace and International Community: Contributions and Controversies*

The marginalised groups' demand for making the Nepali state inclusive and recognition of their cultural identity by the state was mostly an internal issue until the 1970s. Despite its cultural diversity, Nepal did not have any significant ethnic violence except the Limbu ethnic groups' demand for the restoration of the *Kipat* system in the eastern parts of Nepal. In post-1970, many marginalised groups had organised resistance movements against depriving their territorial, cultural, and political rights. Apart from other factors, it is widely believed that those movements could not be sustained since Nepal was not a party to the international conventions against discrimination.[1]

The marginalised groups' interaction with the international community began around the late 1960s when certain Western diplomatic missions in Kathmandu took an interest in Nepal's cultural and social issues. Meanwhile, since the state response to the demands of the ethno-cultural groups was slow, certain sections of the ethnic groups approached the international community present in Kathmandu. The international community had put pressure on the Nepali State to join the international conventions against discrimination. The role of the international community in the cultural and social issues of Nepal further increased after Nepal ratified International Conventions on the Elimination of All Forms of Racial Discrimination on January 30, 1971, which allowed international non-governmental organisations (INGOs) to work at the community level.

With the introduction of multiparty democracy in 1990, Nepal began to ratify many international instruments of human rights.[2] For example, Nepal ratified the Convention on the Rights of Children on September 14, 1990, and the Convention on the Elimination of All Forms of Discrimination against Women on April 22, 1991. The International Covenant on Civil and Political Rights and its Optional Protocol and the International Covenant on Economic Social and Cultural Rights were acceded/ratified on May 14, 1991. After these ratifications, any group or individual in Nepal could form their own organisations and express their views freely against deprivation and discrimination.

In all these developments, UN agencies, INGOs, and local non-governmental organisations (NGOs) funded by Western countries, including Scandinavian countries, played an important role. UNDP shared its expertise on community development and encouraged the state and civil society to strengthen networks, encourage dialogue, and build capacity in Nepal. For example, the United Nations country team involved minority civil society organisations representing various ethnic and women's groups in developing the United Nations Development Assistance Framework (UNDAF) and in-country programming processes.[3]

Within this focus area, UNICEF promotes the effective participation of minorities in mapping, planning, implementation, monitoring and evaluation. This, coupled with relevant advocacy initiatives within and for minority communities, facilitates the development of tailored initiatives to meet their needs. In Nepal, the Decentralized Action for Children and Women programme employs an evidence-based framework informed by data disaggregated by ethnicity and engages participatory approaches with marginalised groups such as Dalits.[4]

Nepal has ratified a multitude of significant international human rights conventions, including the International Labour Organization (ILO) Convention No. 169. According to the Nepal Treaties Act of 2047 (1990), in instances of discrepancy between the stipulations of Nepalese law and those of an international treaty to which the nation is a signatory, the provisions of the treaty shall take precedence.

International human rights instruments, in particular ILO Convention No. 169 and the United Nations Declaration on the Rights of Indigenous Peoples (UNDRIP), establish a solid normative framework for legislative and policy reforms aimed at enhancing the promotion and protection of indigenous peoples' rights. Nepal voted in favour of its adoption in the UN General Assembly in September 2007, an international public commitment of its support and recognition of indigenous peoples' rights both nationally and globally.[5]

In addition to the support provided by multilateral institutions in empowering marginalised groups, numerous countries have engaged in bilateral assistance to the Nepalese government, promoting democracy, human rights, the eradication of social discrimination, and community development initiatives. Given that Nepal maintains diplomatic relations with 179 nations, many of these countries have shared their experiences and contributed technical support concerning democratic governance, the empowerment of marginalised populations, and capacity-building programs within society. Furthermore, considering Nepal's strategic geographic position, several countries have fostered special relationships and emerged as significant stakeholders in the socio-economic and political transformations occurring in Nepal.

In this context, this chapter primarily examines the role and nature of the linkages between China, India, the USA, the UK, and the EU in the empowerment of marginalised groups within Nepal.

## China

Despite geographical proximity and socio-cultural linkages with Nepal, China has remained relatively reticent regarding issues pertaining to marginalised groups in the country, except for the discourse on ethnic-based federalism during the constitution-making process from 2008 to 2015. Its engagement with Nepal has largely been confined to strategic and economic considerations. China's apparent distancing from these social issues may be attributed to two primary factors. First, as a non-democratic state, it has limited frameworks to offer Nepal in terms of democracy and human rights. Second, China has historically pursued the assimilation of cultural minority groups into the Han culture in regions such as Tibet and Xinjiang. A Chinese scholar observed that the "Cultural Revolution affected ethnic minorities in China greatly. Under the mission of destroying old objects that remind people of traditions and capitalism, Mao's government severely persecuted ethnic minorities across the nation, destroying their cultural objects and forcefully assimilating them."[6]

Since the establishment of diplomatic relations with Nepal in 1955, China has consistently extended robust support to the monarchy. Its annual aid, along with economic and diplomatic initiatives, has been strategically channeled through state mechanisms. Furthermore, China's engagement with Nepal has predominantly been driven by security considerations, including the monitoring of anti-Chinese activities among Tibetan refugees in Nepal, countering the influence of other nations in the Himalayan region, particularly India, and safeguarding the authoritarian regime against democratic movements.

China, in fact, endorsed the Nepali ruling classes' understanding that the security of monarchy was equal to the security of the country. Even China's special development programmes in the 15 bordering districts[7] of Nepal were targeted at monitoring and preventing anti-Chinese activities by the Tibetan refugees and other countries' activities near the border areas. These border districts are dominated by indigenous groups. Initially, the Tibetan autonomous government used to supply food and other essential goods to these districts.

In the post-monarchy period, China upgraded its development programmes in these districts keeping in mind the growing influence of India and the role of Western countries in the constitution-making process. In this regard, China proposed to the Nepal government that it be allowed to undertake special development projects. In 2014, a deal was signed between the two countries. China had agreed to provide 10 million Yuan ($1.63 million) annually from 2014 to 2018 to help Nepal develop its northern districts bordering China's Tibet Autonomous Region. The Chinese aid was spent on health, education and road sectors to improve the livelihood of the residents of those districts.[8]

China reviewed the strategy in 2019 by providing direct developmental support to the local bodies in 15 districts. This proposal came from China's side during Prime Minister K.P. Sharma Oli's visit to Beijing in 2016. Under the agreement, the China International Development Cooperation Agency (CIDCA) would provide developmental and logistic support to the northern districts for another five years. As agreed, the Nepal government permitted the CIDCA to provide development assistance and create capital in 15 northern districts of Nepal to meet their developmental needs. The Chinese side also agreed to provide material support like dozers, solar lights, blasting equipment, construction materials for schools and libraries, among others.[9]

It is pertinent to note that although the entirety of Nepal requires developmental funding, China has concentrated its efforts on merely 15 bordering districts. This indicates that China's assistance to these particular districts is motivated more by security considerations than by a genuine commitment to enhancing the socio-economic conditions of marginalised groups in Nepal. Most notably, China has consistently opposed ethnic-based federalism since its emergence by the Maoists in the mid-1990s.

In June 2012, a month after Nepal's Constituent Assembly failed due to differences in federalism, Ai Ping, a senior Chinese party official, visited Nepal. He met senior leaders during the visit, including Pushpa Kamal Dahal alias Prachanda. During the meetings, Ai Ping strongly expressed China's reservations about ethnic-based federalism. A very senior Maoist leader told *The Hindu*: 'Their message was China prefers a unitary Nepal, but if federalism has to happen, it should not be based on ethnicity.'[10]

Ai Ping expressed significant concern regarding the number of provinces in the northern regions of Nepal. He advised Nepali leaders to maintain a minimal number of provinces in this area for security considerations.[11] Consequently, China's stance on social discrimination in Nepal appears minimal. Despite China's opposition to one of the fundamental demands of the Janajati community, its engagement with Nepal is perceived as benign and amicable. There is a notable scarcity of critical discourse in Nepal concerning China's position on federalism, particularly from marginalised groups.

In the post-constitution period, the Social Welfare Council Nepal (SWCN) and the China NGO Network for International Exchanges (CNIE), a consortium of Chinese NGOs, formalised an agreement through a memorandum of understanding to facilitate the operation of Chinese NGOs within Nepal. This MoU was established concurrently with the government's formulation of the National Integrity Policy (NIP), aimed at regulating the activities of NGOs and INGOs, as certain organisations were identified as trying to break communal harmony and proselytising in Nepal. According to the MoUs, "a majority of Chinese NGOs are interested in working in the fields of agro-based livelihood, health care, education, disaster management, and skill training, among others."[12] This suggests that the Chinese NGOs are positioned to function as development-oriented entities rather than rights-based organisations.

## India

Unlike China, Nepal exhibits mixed sentiments regarding India's contribution to democratising Nepali society. India assumes multiple roles in this context. Despite India's significant contributions, both direct and indirect, towards empowering indigenous nationalities and other minorities and reinforcing multiparty democracy, its efforts have not been adequately recognised.

Since 1950, India has played a crucial role in political transformations within Nepal. India advised King Tribhuvan to collaborate with democratic parties and draft a new constitution. Unfortunately, this recommendation was later perceived as interfering in internal matters, even though the broader Nepalese population benefited from it.

Several factors may contribute to the rise of anti-Indian sentiment. Firstly, the ruling elite interpreted India's actions as indirectly encouraging democratic forces to challenge the monarchical system. This perception appears linked to the Madhesi demand for Hindi as an official language in Terai and their support for the democratic movement in Nepal.

Secondly, the Maoists' critical perspective on India during the People's War period significantly influenced the Janajati understanding of India-Nepal relations. The Maoists depicted India as an expansionist nation, embedding this notion deeply in the collective consciousness of the populace. Of the 40 issues articulated in the Maoists' 40-point demands in 1996, the first five specifically targeted India. The Maoists' anti-India narratives, to some extent, intensified Janajati groups' perception of India as a domineering neighbour. Furthermore, it was widely believed that some Western-funded INGOs utilised the Maoists to create rifts in the cultural ties between India and Nepal at the community level.

Thirdly, and perhaps most critically, there exists a prevalent perception in

Nepal that while India supports the minority groups, such support is predominantly directed towards the Madhesis. This perception has arisen due to several factors. One, Madhesh shares a border with India, and its population comprises a diverse caste group with deep cultural ties to India. However, India-Nepal cultural relations extend beyond the Madhesi region; they represent a pan-Nepal phenomenon. Unfortunately, local north-Indian media have portrayed these cultural linkages narrowly, often referring to them as "roti-beti reeshta," which misrepresents the broader context and confines India's cultural and political connections to a specific region in the post-monarchical era.

This sentiment intensified after the Maoist conflict as Madhesi-based groups advocated for a separate Madhesh Pradesh, the recognition of Hindi as an official language, and equitable representation in the interim constitution. The Janajatis presented similar demands, with the notable distinction that the Madhesi movement persisted longer and became more violent, ultimately achieving its objectives. This outcome differed for the Janajatis. Regrettably, the Kathmandu elites and Janajatis perceived India as having supported and instigated the Madhesi demand for a separate state, believing the movement would not have sustained itself without India's backing.

Two, it is important to recognise that the nature and dynamics of the Madhesi movement differed markedly from those of the Janajatis due to topographical and demographic factors. The Madhesis are not a homogeneous group; nonetheless, they united in their struggles against the perceived discrimination by the Kathmandu elites based on cultural and demographic identity. The geographical characteristics of Terai, being a flat region, facilitated communication and coordination among various caste groups. In contrast, the Janajatis, scattered across the nation and hindered by the Himalayan topography, faced challenges in maintaining cohesive communication.

### *Community Empowerment Programmes*

As previously noted, in the context of India-Nepal relations, India has not only addressed security concerns but has also actively advocated for multiparty democracy in Nepal. However, in contrast to Western nations, India has not distinctly articulated its stance on the promotion and safeguarding of minority rights.

It was only when the 2015 constitution failed to address the minority groups' demands that India anticipated that there could be a spillover effect in its northern front in case they indulge in violent activities against the state. In this regard, India brought the attention of the UN body for human rights violations and ethnic discrimination and reiterated its message that Nepal should consolidate its constitution by accommodating all sections of society.[13]

Unlike the Western countries, who have been using INGOs and NGOs to promote the rights of minority groups, India primarily provided technical support for the promotion of democracy by sharing experiences on parliamentary democracy, electoral process and other technical details for holding the elections by sending officials to Nepal, supplying of transport vehicles to ferry electoral officials and security personnel, electronic voting machines, and stationary for peace and smooth running of the elections.

Another factor could be India's direct engagement in community development initiatives and its provision of funding to local governmental bodies in Nepal, rather than relying on NGOs and INGOs. Notably, despite a deep and multifaceted relationship with Nepal, no Indian NGOs are operating within the country. In contrast, Western nations concentrate more on empowerment issues by granting direct funding to local NGOs and INGOs, a practice curtailed by a new legislative measure introduced in 2019. This may elucidate the heightened involvement of Western countries in addressing human rights concerns and promoting democratic governance in Nepal.

### *Development Aid*

India has been Nepal's foremost development partner. It has been engaged in wide-ranging social and economic development programmes since the 1950s. The Indian Aid Mission in Nepal was set up in 1954. India provides substantial financial and technical assistance (IC 12,000 crore for the year 2020-2021) to Nepal for the implementation of small development projects/high-impact community development projects (HICDPs).

HICDPs are short-gestation projects. These grassroots projects have been implemented to create adequate capacity building and construction of new infrastructures such as hospitals, schools, colleges, drinking water facilities, sanitation and drainage systems, rural electrification and hydropower plants, embankment and river training works, etc. They have contributed to enhancing the quality of life and all round development of the people of Nepal. Since 2003, over 523 HICDPs have been taken up by the Government of India, of which 467 have been completed and the remaining 56 projects are ongoing. The total cost of these projects is around INR 706 Cr (NRs 1130 Cr).[14]

The open border arrangement has been extremely helpful for the poor people on both sides in terms of getting jobs, accessing medical facilities and educational institutions and other meaningful economic activities. Over three million Nepali diaspora live and work in India. India provides around 3000 scholarships annually to Nepali nationals to study in India and in Nepal at all levels of education in a wide range of disciplines. Under the Indian Technical and Economic Cooperation (ITEC) programme, professional training is offered annually to about 250 officials from Nepal at various technical institutes in India. Since 2007-08, more than 1700 ITEC alumni of Nepal have received training under the ITEC programme of India.[15] Manmohan Memorial Polytechnic was the first polytechnic of its kind in Nepal providing technical education in three engineering streams as well as several vocational courses.

India's community empowerment programmes do not focus on any particular community, caste, religion, or region, in contrast to initiatives in other countries. Instead, these programs are designed for the overall development of Nepal. They are primarily guided by the principles of a special relationship with Nepal and humanitarian considerations, under the "Neighborhood First" policy.

## Nepal and Western Countries

Nepal maintains diplomatic relations with several prominent Western nations. Numerous countries have established embassies in Kathmandu, while others continue to operate from their missions in New Delhi. Among these Western nations, the UK's Department for International Development (DFID), the United States Agency for International Development (USAID), and the European Union have significantly contributed to advancing democracy and civil rights within Nepal.

Simultaneously, there are concerns regarding the promotion of proselytisation under the guise of supporting local NGOs and INGOs. These organisations have faced scrutiny, and their operations have occasionally raised suspicions within the Nepali government. This issue has been addressed in various forums, including government officials and Nepali media discussions.[16]

Similar to the dynamics with India and China, the UK and EU member states do not possess substantial strategic interests in Nepal. Nevertheless, some EU member countries and the UK provided support to the US-led initiatives during the global campaign against terrorism in Nepal amidst the Maoist insurgency from 1996 to 2006. Since 2005, the EU and certain member states, such as Sweden, Denmark, Switzerland, and Germany, have primarily focused on humanitarian endeavours and conflict resolution efforts within the country. These nations are particularly noteworthy due to their significant financial contributions, support for peace-building initiatives, and sustained engagement with Nepal.

## Nepal and USA

Nepal and India established diplomatic relations in 1948. Since then, the United States has significantly contributed to Nepal's political, social, and economic development. Initially, strategic concerns during the Cold War drove US involvement in Nepal. However, this engagement expanded over the decades to include a broader range of issues such as democracy promotion, empowerment of marginalised groups, peacebuilding, disaster management, and economic development.

### *Economic and Development Assistants*

Economically, over the years, the US investments in Nepal have focused on rural economy enhancement, mainly through strengthening the farming and agriculture sector, infrastructure development, and investment in various services sectors. The United States accounted for $52.4 million worth of foreign direct investment (FDI) in Nepal, representing 3.1 percent of the total FDI, making the US one of Nepal's top 10 foreign investors. In 2023, the US pledged to invest more than $1 billion in Nepal over the next five years, focusing on green energy, electrification, small and medium enterprises, and women-led businesses.[17] Total bilateral trade has been $300 million annually, making the US among Nepal's top half-dozen trade partners.[18]

The USA is also one of Nepal's top five development partners. The USAID has been the largest bilateral donor to Nepal. Since 1951, the US has provided over $1.6 billion in assistance to Nepal. USAID's programs in Nepal focus on fostering a democratic, prosperous, and resilient society. In 2023, the US Department of State and USAID committed $643 million in assistance to Nepal in the next five years.[19]

USAID's work is focused on five key development objectives:

1. Promoting inclusive and effective governance.
2. Supporting sustainable economic growth to reduce extreme poverty.
3. Increasing human capital, including education, health, and disaster resilience.
4. Strengthening Political Parties, Electoral and Legislative Processes
5. Supports marginalised groups to engage in political processes

These mutually reinforcing objectives contribute to Nepal's long-term stability and prosperity. USAID has also supported innovative investment policies, sustainable natural resource management, and disaster preparedness efforts, particularly given Nepal's vulnerability to natural disasters such as earthquakes and floods.[20]

### *Democracy and Peace Building*

The United States played a crucial role in fostering political transition in Nepal in 1990. This assistance was pivotal for conducting free and fair elections, the cornerstone of any democratic system. Moreover, the support also reinforced democratic institutions.

During Nepal's civil war, the US recognised the threat posed by the Maoist insurgency, which gained ground due to the legitimate grievances of marginalised communities. The US government emphasised the importance of unity among Nepal's political forces and supported efforts to address the underlying issues that fuelled the civil war. At the same time, the US also extended support to Nepal's security forces to reinforce the need for improved human rights practices while providing the tools necessary to combat the insurgency. This support included non-lethal equipment, training, and modern rifles.[21]

### *Post-Conflict Period*

USAID provided technical and financial support to the Nepal Transition to Peace Forum (NTTP), facilitating structured negotiations on sensitive issues outlined in the Peace Accord. USAID's assistance in this area helped to build Nepal's capacity for conflict analysis and dialogue facilitation, supporting sustainable peace-building efforts.[22]

In addition to supporting the peace process, the US strengthened Nepal's security sector reforms. That included supporting training and making the army inclusive by recruiting ethnic minority groups. Also, an emphasis was placed on improving the human rights records of the Army, which has been a concern due to past allegations of abuses.[23]

Since Nepal transitioned to federalism, the United States supported the implementation of federal policies at the local level. The US worked closely with Nepal's newly elected local governments to help them implement disaster management plans, improve the delivery of quality public services, and address the needs of underserved communities. These efforts were designed to help Nepalese authorities meet the commitments made to their constituencies and ensure effective governance at the local level.[24]

In 2023, USAID provided $58.5 million to strengthen democratic processes and institutions, enhance public financial management, and support the development of independent civil society and media in Nepal. These initiatives aimed to enhance fundamental freedoms, promote accountability, and ensure that all citizens have a voice in the democratic process.[25]

Nevertheless, the United States has taken a strong interest in promoting human rights and religious freedom in Nepal. Following the promulgation of Nepal's new constitution in 2015, US officials expressed concerns over restrictions on freedom of religion, including the rights to convert and proselytise. US officials have consistently raised these issues with Nepali counterparts and have worked to promote religious diversity and tolerance through public engagements and financial support for preserving and restoring religious sites.[26]

## Nepal and EU

Nepal's diplomatic relations with the European Union (EU) and its member countries are across many levels—regional, bilateral, and multilateral. European countries have contributed to Nepal's socio-economic development as part of the EU and at the bilateral level in various ways.

The EU began interacting with Nepal as a development partner in 1973. Regarding regional engagement, the European Commission (EC) represents the EU in Nepal.

In the late 1940s, the US replaced the UK as a major power at the international level with growing interest in South Asia. It was natural, therefore, that among other Western countries, a relationship with the US would acquire greater significance for Nepal in the subsequent days. In the early 1970s, when the US shifted its aid diplomacy to East Asia after its rapprochement with China, the EU, as a regional organisation, made its presence felt in Nepal and focused on democracy, governance and development-related issues.

In the 1990s, the European Union and its member states exhibited varying perspectives regarding the political system and governance in Nepal. It has been observed that Scandinavian countries showed support for the CPN-UML by viewing it as aligned with social democratic principles. During this period, the CPN-UML garnered sympathy from certain Scandinavian nations. However, with the emergence of the Maoist movement in 1996, some Scandinavian countries shifted their support from the CPN-UML to the Maoists. Other European countries supported constitutional monarchy. The UK especially played the role of a 'proxy superpower' in the Himalayan sub-region because of its long association with Gurkha soldiers and as a trusted ally of the US. The UK, along with the US, supported the monarchy as a factor of stability. Their support remained intact until the Maoists joined mainstream politics in 2008.

Unlike the US, at the individual level, most of the member states of the EU, except perhaps for the UK, have been actively engaged in the processes of conflict resolution and restoration of democracy in Nepal, and they have acquired a 'distinct image as development partners of Nepal.'[27] As a non-EU member country, Norway had liberally contributed funds to the United Nations Nepal Peace Fund (UNPFN) and worked with EU member countries in other development and peace-building programmes in Nepal.

At the collective level, the EU gave Nepal a total of €240 million from 1977 up to 2006 for irrigation, watershed management, livestock, reproductive health, primary education, refugees and institutional capacity building. Between 2007 and 2013, the EU assisted with €120 million in Nepal, focusing on three areas: education, stability and peacebuilding, and trade facilitation and economic capacity building.[28] The EU allocated €360 million of assistance to Nepal for the period 2014-2020.[29] The EU is also engaged in human rights assistance (energy, food, and elections) and has supported civil liberty and democratic movements since 2001, with an approximate yearly budget of more than €30 million. It also attempted to resolve the problems of Bhutanese refugees living in the two eastern districts of Nepal.

According to the EU Country Strategy Paper, the EU funding to Nepal fluctuated after the commencement of intense internal conflict between the Maoists and the state in 2001. The EC allocated €70 million in aid for the period 2002–2006. The aid did not achieve its developmental objectives due to some technical problems. As a protest against the royal takeover in February 2005 ensued, many important programmes initiated by the EU were put on hold. In the post-conflict period, however, at the request of the government, the EC prioritised education, peace building, capacity development, governance issues, trade facilitation and economic capacity building as areas of intervention.[30]

There are perceptions in Nepal that there were economic and security interests behind Western aid to Nepal. One Nepalese scholar observed that Western international donors, including EU members 'since the late 1970s, started making their aid programme conditional behind the veil of good governance and structural adjustment policies. Their objectives were to carry out market-oriented neo-liberal policies that would promote their economy and shape their long-term political interests.'[31] In the case of Nepal, the government brought out policy changes as instructed by the donors.

There are occasions when Western international donors[32] have supported projects directly without channelising the funds through the government mechanism.[33] Interestingly, Thomas Gass, former Switzerland's ambassador to Nepal and co-chair of the 13 Basic Operating Guidelines (BOG) signatories, and Robert Piper, former UN Resident and Humanitarian Coordinator, another Co-Chair of the 13 BOG group, during a media interaction on November 23, 2012, had agreed that some 60-70 percent aid is spent through the government channels.[34]

## EU Countries and the Peace Process

During the conflict phase, European NGOs co-funded projects on family health, literacy and poverty eradication, along with campaigns to prevent human trafficking. The EC also contributed to conflict mitigation through support to core legal institutions, improving peace research capacities and assistance programmes to victims of the Maoist insurgency.[35] The EC also supported the Office of the High Commissioner for Human Rights (OHCHR) mission with a contribution of €5 million (around 30 percent of the budget). The first EU Troika, led by the Dutch presidency, the European Commission, and the high representative, visited Nepal from December 13-15, 2004.

It was part of the EU mandate to support all efforts to promote multi-party democracy within the framework of a constitutional monarchy and human rights.[36] In September 2007, the European Parliament (EP) launched the 'Friends of Nepal Group', a political campaign to improve parliamentary dialogue between the EP and the Nepalese parliament. The EP also sent several missions to Nepal over the next two years to support the new democratic reconstruction efforts.[37]

In the post-conflict period, especially when the first CA failed to deliver the constitution on time and neglected minority groups' demands, the international community led by the EU and Nordic countries played a proactive role in ensuring addressing social exclusion and supporting the transition towards a more inclusive state and society. The International Work Group for Indigenous Affairs (IWGIA) report highlighted that a joint commitment was formulated in the BOG for development work in Nepal signed by a number of development organisations, including the EU, DANIDA, Swiss Agency for Development and Cooperation (SDC), DFID and the Embassy of Finland, which were updated and reaffirmed by the signatories in 2007, saying that international aid would 'ensure that our assistance tackles discrimination and social exclusion, most notably based on gender, ethnicity, caste and religion'.[38]

This commitment to social inclusion and the eradication of discriminatory practices was reflected in a number of donor-funded initiatives in post-war Nepal, including the Norwegian-funded Social Inclusion Research Fund, the World Bank, DFID-funded research in gender—and ethnicity-based exclusion, the large DFID cooperation with Nepal Federation of Indigenous Nationalities

(NEFIN), the Danish and Norwegian support to ILO's promotion of Convention No. 169, and the Asian Development Bank.[39]

The IWGIA report indicated that all those international donors who had promised to extend all kinds of support for an inclusive state and society reportedly withdrew funds support for indigenous people by 2011. The report did not mention the reasons for that. It said, 'Some observers talked specifically about DFID's withdrawal of funding for NEFIN's large Janajati Empowerment project in May 2011, in response to NEFIN's continued involvement in organising street protests and national close-downs (*bandhas*).'[40]

At the same time, the NEFIN accepted that the decreased donor interest in supporting their activities had severely limited their access to dialogues with the international community and negotiations on federalism.[41] It would be interesting to note that around the same time, the NEFIN witnessed a vertical split by the formation of Adivasi Janajati Rastriya Andolan (AJRA) under the leadership of Padmaratna Tuladhar. Many NEFIN leaders, including the then NEFIN Chairman Nagendra Kumal, opposed his leadership.[42]

While the international community reduced its support for NEFIN by citing its continued involvement in organising street protests, AJRA leader Tuladhar and others criticised NEFIN for not being able to carry out protests regarding the rights of indigenous nationalities.[43]

The differences between the AJRA and NEFIN were predominantly political in nature. The AJRA ardently advocated for a singular ethnicity-based federalism and expressed a degree of sympathy towards Pushpa Kamal Dahal. In contrast, NEFIN's Chairman, Nagendra Kumal, was an elected representative of the Constituent Assembly of the Nepali Congress. At the same time, NEFIN's General Secretary, Pemba Bhote, was affiliated with the CPN-UML and maintained close ties with CPN-UML leader K.P. Sharma Oli. Both the CPN-UML and the Nepali Congress opposed the implementation of ethnic-based federalism.

## The EU and Post-Conflict Nepal

In the post-Maoist conflict period, the EU and some of its member countries supported the peace process, the 2008 CA elections and the constitution-making process by providing technical and financial assistance. EU member countries were the most prominent donors for integrating and rehabilitating the former Maoist combatants. As a part of the conflict resolution programme, they had put pressure on the then interim government(s) to formation a Truth and Reconciliation Commission (TRC) and Commission on Investigation of Disappeared Persons by adhering to the international norms to deliver justice to the civil war (February 13, 1996, to November 21, 2006) victims.

Apart from that, the EU supported the creation of women and *Janajati* caucuses in the 2008 Constituent Assembly. They also funded research and activism on identity issues. Although some of the EU member countries have been supporting these issues for a long time, their support to these causes was criticised by the upper caste elites when the 2008 CA was dissolved without a new constitution being written and as the demand for ethnic-based federalism remained unresolved.

This controversy led to division among the EU members. While Switzerland, Sweden and Denmark supported identity-based federalism for justice and equality in Nepal, the UK stopped funding the cause due to serious ethnic polarisation, especially after ethnic conflicts in far-western districts in 2012.

Moreover, there were rumours made in Kathmandu regarding the establishment of the High-Level Political Committee (HLPC), which was created to assist the Chief Justice-led government in mediating disputes among political parties and was influenced by certain European Union countries seeking to maintain support for advocating for ethnically based federalism. However, no substantial evidence was presented to substantiate that claim. Although the EU countries had welcomed the second CA election held on November 19, 2013, and declared additional financial support to the Nepal Peace Trust Fund (NPTF)[44] with a view to supporting the elections, there was a perception in Nepal that the EU supported to identity-based federalism might scuttle the election process. None other than UCPN-Maoist vice-chairman Baburam Bhattarai, observed that 'European countries are lobbying hard against CA elections.'[45] Although Bhattarai had failed to mention specifically, their anti-election activities, many Nepalese believed that the newly formed Federal Socialist Party, Nepal of Ashok Rai, enjoyed the sympathy of some European countries.

The European Initiative for Democracy and Human Rights (EIDHR) funded community-based awareness campaigns and engaged in conflict mediation, which has been mired in controversy since the Janajatis and Madhesis launched their demand for identity-based federalism in Nepal. Since then, the Ministry of Foreign Affairs (MoFA) in Nepal has asked the donor countries to focus on infrastructure and development. Many scholars have observed that this state regulation of the INGOs without a credible and stable political system may create social tensions in the future.

The EU members were concerned about the delay in writing the new constitution and political instability in Nepal. They made several attempts to forge a consensus between the major political parties to form a national unity government. Still, these efforts have been termed by both the government and some political parties as interference in Nepal's internal affairs. Some non-Maoist parties raised concerns about the possibility that EU members may be sympathetic toward the Maoists.

### *EU Aid and Federalism*

EU support for the development programmes in Nepal was not free from controversy. There has been a growing perception in Nepal that aid from European countries has contributed to the movement for ethnic federalism, with possible violent ethnic conflict. During the visit of ministers from Norway and the UK after the dissolution of the CA on 27 May 2012, the Nepali media raised questions about the social tensions in Nepal arising from the funds being pumped into the country by various INGOs.

During a media interaction programme in Birgunj on 22 May 2010, Kamal Thapa, the then chairman of the Rastriya Prajatantra Party-Nepal, said, 'They [the European countries] have been pouring in huge sums of money in the conversion drive that they are carrying out in Nepal.'[46] He also alleged that religious conversions have increased in the post-conflict period. According to K.B. Rokaya, around 800 Christians in Nepal in 1978. In comparison, he said:

> It was estimated that by the year 2000, the number of Christians in Nepal crossed 800,000. The growth rate of Christians in Nepal has been rising sharply after Nepal became a republic and a secular state.[47]

Interestingly, conflicting reports have been published about the increase in the Christian population in Nepal. Since the Christian population was not included in the 2001 census, the exact growth of the population in the last ten years has been ambiguous. While the ultra-rightist groups argue that the number of Christians was between 1.5 and 2 million, the 2011 census said the Christian population in Nepal was 3,75,699, which was 1.4 percent of the total population of 26,444,504,[48] while the Christian population was 0.4 percent in 2007 of the then total population.[49]

In fact, challenging the Christian population number released in the 2011 Census, the Federation of National Christians-Nepal (FNCN) claimed that 'there were more than 8,500 churches and over 2.5 million Christians across the country [Nepal].'[50] According to Yuvaraj Ghimire, a journalist and political analyst, 'certain donor countries such as Denmark, Norway, Switzerland and Britain have provided assistance to ethnic organisations that espouse extreme views in the name of empowerment. Such assistance has increased the danger of social and ethnic tensions and social violence.'[51]

These issues became official in 2010 when the government of Nepal objected to a planned meeting between visiting European parliamentarians and the armed Limbuwan and Khumbuwan groups in May that year. In a statement, the Ministry of Foreign Affairs (MoFA) said that 'the EU parliamentarians should abstain from meeting the armed groups as they were illegal and they did not represent any social or political groups.'[52]

Although there has not been any strong evidence to back these allegations, to avoid controversy due to criticism over promoting ethnic federalism by EU donors, UN Resident and Humanitarian Coordinator and 13 signatories of Basic Operating Guidelines (BOG) on November 23, 2012, came out with a media statement about their commitment to impartiality and preventing the misuse of aid by any civil society organisations and promised not to support activities that would lead to violence during the election period.[53]

The alacrity of the EC and other European countries in establishing the TRC in the post-CA dissolution period has again been criticised by the government of Nepal. The MoFA criticised such activities as 'foreign interference into Nepal's internal affairs. This was against the nicety of diplomatic decorum and has been perceived as an attempt to drag the constitutional Head of State into political issues.'[54] This reaction came after representatives of the EC and the ambassadors of some European countries met President Ram Baran Yadav on September 07, 2012, despite MoFA disallowing such a meeting. Some media reports indicated that the CA was dissolved due to the external support given to the Janajatis by the EU and Madhesis by India on the federalism issue.

During the period of armed conflict and constitution-making in Nepal, the EU and certain member countries were able to justify their support to the social empowerment. However, the role of the EU in fostering social harmony and peace in Nepal was called into question by the first democratically elected government in 2018. While responding to the election report prepared by the Nepal Election Observation Committee (NEOC), Prime Minister K.P. Sharma Oli warned the European Union not to 'undermine the constitution, social cohesiveness and the achievements made by Nepali people.' The NEOC was formed under the EU Election Observation Mission (EUEOM), which, in its report, had asked the Nepal government to remove the reservation quota allocated to Khas Arya. The Election Commission of Nepal had also stated that the report violated the memorandum of understanding between the poll authority and the observer.[55]

Most importantly, the role and functioning of the EU came under strict scrutiny under the new constitution with introducing a new policy by the Oli government on barring International Non-Governmental Organisations from financing religious and political institutions. The Social Welfare Council, Government of Nepal, in June 2019, introduced a new policy. The new Development Cooperation Policy of the government, which was made public, stated that foreign NGOs while mobilising their resources directly or through domestic NGOs, should fund development works other than religious and political institutions and the country's sensitive areas.[56]

The policy was introduced amid complaints that some foreign NGOs were involved in religious conversions. Political leaders and lawmakers have also found to have made foreign trips under the sponsorship of foreign NGOs. The annual report, 2018-2019, of the Office of the Auditor General blamed the SWC for poor monitoring despite reports finding that some of the NGOs—both domestic and foreign—were involved in some religious activities.

The audit report mentioned that Himalayan Bible Study Academy, an NGO, was found to have run computer and sewing training and business and employment generation training only for the Christian community. Likewise, the Witness Society, another NGO, was found to have spent Nepalese NRs 264 million (approximately US$ 1.98 million) for purchasing land and running religious and social activities for Christians in 15 towns and 19 wards in 11 districts. Nepal Christian Bal Sikshya Sangati was found to have spent NRs 5.6 million (approximately US$ 0.042 million) for providing Bible education to children and teachers.[57] Although there was no direct evidence of EU support for these NGOs' involvement in religious activities, its aid and assistance were affected due to the new policy.

## The UK and Minority Rights

Among the EU countries, the UK has the oldest association with Nepal in terms of employing Gorkha soldiers, whose remittances contributed to socio-economic development in Nepal. Besides that, the UK has been the second-largest bilateral donor to Nepal after Japan. As per the Development Cooperation Report 2014-2015 by the Ministry of Finance, Nepal, the UK remained the top Official Development Assistant (ODA) provider (based on disbursement) with a total assistance of $168.07 million in the Fiscal Year 2014/2015.[58] However, the disbursement amount was 38 million pounds in 2023.[59] The DFID programmes aimed to reduce poverty and social exclusion and establish the basis for lasting peace.[60] The UK has also invested significant political and financial resources in conflict prevention and resolution.[61]

The DFID was key in empowering minority groups, developing community programmes, and setting up socio-economic infrastructure in remote areas. Given its historical association with Nepal and deep diplomatic relations, the UK provided military assistance to the Nepal government to fight the Maoists during the conflict. While the other EU members more or less analysed the civil conflict as a political movement caused by the grievances in society, the UK treated the Maoists as terrorists.

Interestingly, the UK's development programmes in Nepal contradicted its state-to-state relationship. While most of the DFID programmes were targeted at the marginalised groups of the society, which was a major support base of the Maoists, the UK's arms supply against the Maoists and branding them as terrorists was baffling and contradictory. Most importantly, like the US, the UK was a strong supporter of the monarchy, which was the progenitor of social discrimination in Nepal. The military assistance of the UK to Nepal increased after the terrorist attack on the US mainland on September 11, 2001, and the deployment of the Nepali Army against the Maoists in November 2001.

In the post-conflict period, when Nepal was struggling to complete the integration of the Maoist combatants into the Nepali Army, the UK offered a proposal for the modernisation of the Nepali Army. The issue was discussed during British Army Chief General Sir David Julian Richards's visit to Kathmandu in February 2010. General Richards also emphasised the strengthening of relations between the two countries' armies. Surprisingly, while the international community was busy consolidating the peace process, the UK's offer to strengthen the army created further distrust between the then-ruling party, CPN-UML, and the Maoists.

The UK's policy towards Nepal has taken a distinct approach compared to that of the EU, which prioritises a negotiated settlement. It is worth noting that UK policy has sparked some debate. Various media reports have indicated that the UK embassy and DFID supported certain local NGOs, which has raised questions about promoting cultural activities. Media reports said that in 2011, the Nepal government observed that the DFID has been funding various programmes run by the NEFIN. DFID had decided to discontinue funding to NEFIN after it supported the *banda* (general strike) organised to demand more rights for the indigenous nationalities in the new constitution during the first Constituent Assembly.[62]

Again, the UK embassy's involvement and sympathy towards minority groups in Nepal were exposed. On December 15, 2014, Andrew Spark, the deputy chief of mission in Kathmandu, wrote an open letter to the Constituent Assembly members of Nepal to ensure that the people's rights to change their religion are protected in the 2015 Constitution.[63]

In a press release in February 2006, the DFID and SDC justified their support of Nepali initiatives promoting human and civil rights, democracy and inclusion. These organisations launched the rights, democracy and inclusion fund (RDIF). The fund was utilised to increase awareness of human rights at the grassroots level and strengthen state and society collaboration to make the government more responsive to addressing local rights violations.[64]

Amidst concerns regarding the involvement of certain foreign NGOs in religious conversions, the Nepalese government enacted the Development Cooperation Policy in June 2019. However, despite efforts to regulate the financing of political activities, this policy lacks clarity regarding the definition of political institutions and the criteria for their characterisation. Furthermore, the frequent changes in government in Nepal have hindered the effective implementation of the regulation.[65]

## Conclusion

Although the international community worked against the discrimination faced by the minority groups in Nepal at different times and in different phases of political transition, it encouraged the minority groups to play a significant role in the constitution-making process. While India broadly worked towards strengthening democracy by extending support to the major political parties and front organisations, international organisations, with the support of some Western countries, empowered minority groups at the grassroots level and put pressure on the state to ratify international conventions.

Despite having an 'inclusive' constitution, minority groups are still critical of some of the provisions in the constitution. They feel that a large number of their historical grievances have not been addressed by the new constitution. The marginalised groups also feel that despite constitutional provisions to bring to an end all the discrimination, the state and ruling elites have failed to implement that. For example, the state institutions are still dominated by the upper castes.

Therefore, the Constitution might say that discrimination has ended, but it still exists socially and psychologically. Social tensions are far from over. In this regard, the role of the international community would be to continue putting pressure on the state to ensure the enforcement of the constitutional provisions and the protection of minority rights.

NOTES

1 Mahendra Lawoti, "Ethnic Politics and the Building of an Inclusive State", in Sebastian, et al. (eds), *Nepal in Transition: From People's War to Fragile Peace*, Cambridge University Press, Cambridge, 2012, p. 133.

2 Krishna Bhattachan, "Indigenous Peoples and the right to Participate in decision-Making in in Nepal", paper presented on 20-22 January 2010.

3 "Promoting and Protecting Minority Rights: A Guide for Advocates", UNHR, Geneva and New York, 2012, at https://www.ohchr.org/Documents/Publications/HR-PUB-12-07_en.pdf

(accessed on 27 September 2021).

4 Ibid.

5 Raja Devasish Roy and John B. Henriksen, "Inclusion of Indigenous Peoples' Rights in the New Constitution of Nepal," 11 February 2010 (Rev), other publication details are not available. The report can be accessed on https://www.ilo.org/wcmsp5/groups/public/--ed_norm/--normes/documents/publication/wcms_123847.pdf (accessed on 27 September 2021).

6 Dong Shin "Preservation of cultural heritage of ethnic minorities in China", *Contemporary Chinese Performance Culture*, 02 December 2013, https://ccpc.asian.lsa.umich.edu/yang-lipings-efforts/ (accessed on 27 April 2022).

7 Darchula, Bajhang, Humla, Mugu, Dolpa, Mustang, Manang, Gorkha, Dhading, Rasuwa, Sindhupalchok, Dolakha, Solukhumbu, Sankhwasabha and Taplejung.

8 "Chinese development agency to aid 15 northern Nepali districts", *The Kathmandu Post*, 30 March 2019, https://kathmandupost.com/national/2019/03/30/chinese-development-agency-to-aid-15-northern-nepali-districts (accessed on 25 April 2022).

9 Ibid.

10 Prashant Jha "The message from the north" *The Hindu*, 05 October 2012, https://www.thehindu.com/opinion/op-ed/The-message-from-the-north/article12548983.ece (accessed on 27 September 2021).

11 "AI PING'S VISIT Mandarin Mission", *New Spotlight*, Kathmandu, 9 July 2012, at https://www.spotlightnepal.com/2012/07/09/ai-pings-visit-mandarin-mission/ (accessed on 27 September 2021).

12 "Chinese organisations silent after deal to make forays into Nepal", *The Kathmandu Post*, 29 October 2018, at https://kathmandupost.com/national/2018/10/29/chinese-organisations-silent-after-deal-to-make-forays-into-nepal (accessed on 27 September 2021).

13 "India slams Nepal at UN human rights body", *The Hindustan Times*, 05 November 2015, at https://www.hindustantimes.com/india/india-slams-nepal-at-un-human-rights-body/story-6QH2aBpyNTv39kx6YTfmfI.html (accessed on 27 September 2021).

14 "Milestones in India-Nepal Development Partnership", *ANI*, 30 March 2022, https://www.aninews.in/news/world/asia/milestones-in-india-nepal-development-partnership20220330225122/ (accessed on 25 April 2022).

15 India-Nepal Bilateral Brief, Northern Division, Ministry of External Affairs, Government of India, https://www.mea.gov.in/Portal/ForeignRelation/India-Nepal_2022.pdf (accessed on 17 April 2022).

16 "New policy aims to bar foreign NGOs from financing religious and political institutions", *The Kathmandu Post*, 02 June 2019, https://kathmandupost.com/national/2019/06/02/new-policy-aims-to-bar-foreign-ngos-from-financing-religious-and-political-institutions (accessed on 03 November 2024). Also see "Home ministry instructs district authorities to closely monitor religious conversions", *The Kathmandu Post*, 13 April 2024, https://kathmandupost.com/national/2024/04/13/home-ministry-instructs-district-authorities-to-closely-monitor-religious-conversions (accessed on 03 November 2024).

17 "USA to invest over $1 billion in Nepal over next 5 years", *The Economic Times*, 31 January 2023.

18 "U.S. Relations with Nepal," Bilateral Relations Fact Sheet, Bureau of South and Central Asian Affairs, U.S. Department of State, 28 July 2022, https://www.state.gov/u-s-relations-with-nepal/ (accessed on 14 October 2024).

19 "Nepal: Political Developments and U.S. Relations" Congressional Research Service, 04 December 2015, https://crsreports.congress.gov/product/pdf/R/R44303/4 (accessed on 14 October 2024).

20 "U.S. Relations with Nepal," Bilateral Relations Fact Sheet, no. 18.

21 "United States Interests and Goals in Nepal", Donald Camp, Principal Deputy Assistant Secretary Statement Before the U.S. House of Representatives Committee on International Relations, Washington, DC, 02 March 2005, https://2001-2009.state.gov/p/sca/rls/rm/2005/42910.htm (accessed on 14 October 2024).

22 "Inclusive Dialogue for Political Transition", USAID, https://2017-2020.usaid.gov/nepal/fact-sheets/inclusive-dialogue-political-transition#:~:text=Nepal's%20decade%20long %20civil%20war,sensitive%20issues%20in%20the%20Accord (accessed on 14 October 2024).

23 "United States Interests and Goals in Nepal", Donald Camp, no. 21.

24 "U.S. Relations With Nepal," Bilateral Relations Fact Sheet, Bureau of South and Central Asian Affairs, U.S. Department of State, 28 July 2022, https://www.state.gov/u-s-relations-with-nepal/ (accessed on 14 October 2024).

25 "USAID Deepens Democratic Partnership with the Government and People of Nepal" Press Release, USAID, 07 February 2023, https://www.usaid.gov/news-information/press-releases/feb-07-2023-usaid-deepens-democratic-partnership-government-and-people-nepal (accessed on 14 October 2024).

26 "2017 Report on International Religious Freedom: Nepal", U.S. Department of State, Bureau of Democracy, Human Rights, and Labor, https://www.state.gov/reports/2017-report-on-international-religious-freedom/nepal/ (accessed on 14 October 2024).

27 Krishna Hashhethu, "The European Union's Role in Democracy Building in Nepal", *International Institute for Democracy and Electoral Assistance*, 2009, Stockholm, p. 6.

28 "Nepal: Country Strategy Paper" 2007–2013, European Union, pp. 01-04, at http://eeas.europa.eu/nepal/docs/07_13_en.pdf (accessed on 12 August 2013). There is no separate data available about how much of this assistance was during the establishment of the EU (1993). Also see The EU's relations with Nepal – An Overview, at www.ec.europa.eu (accessed on 27 September 2021).

29 "EU development cooperation with Nepal", European Commission-Fact Sheet, Brussels, 04 May 2015, https://ec.europa.eu/commission/presscorner/detail/et/memo_15_4909 (accessed on 03 Novembers 2024).

30 "Nepal: Country Strategy Paper, 2007-2013," European Union, p.02. For more information, see http://eeas.europa.eu/nepal/docs/07_13_en.pdf (accessed on 12 August 2013).

31 Yam Prasad Chaulagain, "Official Development Assistance in Nepal: A Development perspective", *e-International Relations*, 28 August 2012, at http://www.e-ir.info/2012/08/28/official-development-assistance-in-nepal-a-development-perspective/ (accessed on 24 November 2012). Mr. Caulagain is a research scholar with University of Warsaw. Also see "A little help from our friends", *ekantipur*, 20 November 2012, at http://www.ekantipur.com/2012/11/20/opinion/a-little-help-from-our-friends/362949.html (accessed on 24 November 2012).

32 Media reports indicated that three donor agencies - Department for International Development (DFID), Swiss Agency for Development and Cooperation (SDC) and Finnish International Development Agency (FINNIDA) - had pledged a sum of US$61.8 million for the four-year multi-stakeholder forestry programme. For detail see "Submit documents on foreign aid, forest ministry told'," *myRepublica*, 25 March 2012, at http://www.myrepublica.com/portal/index.php?action=news_details&news_id=33221 (accessed on 24 November 2012).

33 Yam Prasad Chaulagain, no. 31.

34 "Donors not to allow use of aid for violence, political gains", *myRepublica,* 23 November 2012, at http://www.myrepublica.com/portal/index.php?action=news_details&news_id=45260 (accessed on 24 November 2012).

35 "European Initiative for Democracy and Human Rights/Non-Governmental Organisations,"

at www.ec.europa.eu. (accessed on 28 September 2021).

36 "The EU's relations with Nepal – An Overview," at www.ec.europa.eu (accessed on 27 September 2021). Also see "Nepal: EU Troika," *Press Release*, Kathmandu, 15 December 2004, Council of the European Union, at http://www.consilium.europa.eu/uedocs/cms_data/docs/pressdata/en/er/83197.pdf (accessed on 12 August 2013).

37 "MEPs Give Nepal a Helping Hand", *New Europe*, *The European Weekly*, at http://www.neurope.eu/article/meps-give-nepal-helping-hand (accessed on 12 August 2013).

38 "The Basic Operating Guidelines: A Guide for Practitioners and Signatories," 2013, for details refer https://www.ain.org.np/uploads/cmsfiles/file/BOGS-manual%20_20130304110859.pdf (accessed on 27 October 2024).

39 "Constitutional Politics and Indigenous Peoples in Nepal," IWGIA report, Prepared by Christina Nilsson and Sille Stidsen, May 2014.

40 Ibid.

41 Ibid.

42 NEFIN is an umbrella organisation of 56 ethnic communities while AJRA is a cluster of various ethnic organisations, sister wing of political parties, Janajati leaders of other political parties, experts and individuals, among others. Also see "Indigenous groups to unite for agitation", *The Kathmandu Post*, 17 November 2014, https://kathmandupost.com/miscellaneous/2014/11/17/indigenous-groups-to-unite-for-agitation (accessed on 27 September 2021).

43 "Indigenous groups to unite for agitation", *The Kathmandu Post*, 17 November 2014, https://kathmandupost.com/miscellaneous/2014/11/17/indigenous-groups-to-unite-for-agitation (accessed on 27 September 2021).

44 Switzerland (Rs 450 million), Finland (€ 2.5 million), Denmark (DKK 10 million), Norway (NOK 20 million), European Union (€ 9.5 million) and UK (£7.5million). Apart from that the EU members have offered election related technical supports by UN agencies.

45 "Bhattarai cautions UK on anti-poll initiatives", *The Himalayan Times*, Kathmandu, 7 June 2013. In fact, both the Nepali Congress and the CPN-UML share the similar views the some European countries support to the ethnic based federalism. While the Nepali Congress has been opposing the ethnic based federalism from very beginning, the formation of Federal Socialist Party by Ashok Rai, who was earlier with the CPN-UML, has made the CPN-UML critical of the ethnic based federalism.

46 "EU Nations funding for Religious Conversion in Nepal: Kamal Thapa", 23 May 2010, at http://www.telegraphnepal.com/news_det.php?news_id=7720&PHPSESSID=8e2636e8c32b7e8bff63c389bd244d9d (accessed on 12 August 2013).

47 K.B. Rokaya in *The Telegraph*, Kathmandu, 1 February 2012, at http://www.telegraphnepal.com/views/2012-01-02/nepal:-christmas-and-christianity.html (accessed on 12 August 2013). Rokaya is General Secretary of the National Council of Churches of Nepal (NCCN), Executive Committee member of United Christian Alliance of Nepal (UCAN), Founding Vice-President of Inter-Religious Council of Nepal (IRCN), President of Nepal Intellectuals Forum and member of the National Human Rights Commission of Nepal (NHRC).

48 "National Population and Housing Census 2011," National Report, Vol. 01, Central Bureau of Statistics, Government of Nepal.

49 "Nepal's First-Ever Census Reveals Good News for Christians", *Christianity Today*, 30 November 2012, at http://www.christianitytoday.com/gleanings/2012/november/nepals-first-ever-census-reveals-good-news-for-christians.html (accessed on 19 August 2013).

50 "FNCN: Christian population below actual size,' *The Kathmandu Post*, 6 December 2012, at http://www.ekantipur.com/the-kathmandu-post/2012/12/05/metro/fncn-christian-

population-below-actual-size/242499.html (accessed on 19 August 2013).

51 Prakash A. Raj, "Money for nothing", *Kathmandu Post*, 5 March 2012, at http://www.ekantipur.com/the-kathmandu-post/2012/03/05/oped/money-for-nothing/232309.html (accessed on 12 August 2013).

52 "There was no plan to meet armed groups: EU", my*Republica*, 5 May 2010, at http://www.myrepublica.com/portal/index.php?action=news_details&news_id=19227 (accessed on 12 August 2013).

53 "Donors not to allow use of aid for violence, political gains," *myRepublica*, 23 November 2012.

54 "Diplomatic headache as envoys try to reach prez', *Himalayan Times*, 7 September 2012, at http://www.thehimalayantimes.com/fullNews.php?headline=Diplomatic+headache+as+ envoys + try+to+reach+prez&NewsID=346480 (accessed on 12 August 2103).

55 "Prime Minister Oli warns EU not to undermine sovereignty of Nepal", *Nepal Foreign Affairs*, 25 March 2018, https://nepalforeignaffairs.com/prime-minister-oli-warns-eu-not-to-undermine-sovereignity-of-nepal/ (accessed on 27 September 2021).

56 "New policy aims to bar foreign NGOs from financing religious and political institutions", *The Kathmandu Post*, 02 June 2019, at https://kathmandupost.com/national/2019/06/02/new-policy-aims-to-bar-foreign-ngos-from-financing-religious-and-political-institutions (accessed on 27 September 2021).

57 Ibid.

58 "Nepal-UK Relations", https://uk.nepalembassy.gov.np/nepal-uk-relations/ (accessed on 27 April 2022).

59 "Statistics on International Development: Final UK ODA Spend 2023," UK International Development, https://assets.publishing.service.gov.uk/media/67055997080bdf716392f012/Statistics_on_International_Development_Final_UK_ODA_Spend_2023.pdf (accessed on 03 November 2024).

60 "British Embassy in Kathmandu", at www.britishembassy.gov.uk (accessed on 27 September 2021).

61 "Nepal Crisis: Mobilising International influence," Crisis Group Briefing, *International Crisis Group*, 19 April 2006, p. 5.

62 "New policy aims to bar foreign NGOs from financing religious and political institutions", no.56.

63 "British Envoy in Nepal Sparks Storm of Conversion Controversy", *Lankaweb*, (originally published in the Rising Nepal), 05 July 2015, https://www.lankaweb.com/news/items/2015/07/05/british-envoy-in-nepal-sparks-storm-of-conversion-controversy-ritu-raj-subedi/ (accessed on 03 November 2024).

64 "DFID and SDC will support through a joint programme rights, democracy and inclusion in Nepal," *News and Press Release*, Kathmandu, SDC, 22 February 2006.

65 "New policy aims to bar foreign NGOs from financing religious and political institutions", no. 56.

# *Conclusion*

Any peace process is subject to the possibility of either success or failure, with no intermediary outcomes. Any deviation from the complete success of a peace initiative, such as protracted negotiations or delays in the execution of agreements, may be regarded as a failure of the peace process, as it significantly increases the likelihood of a recurrence of conflict. Once a consensus document, such as the Comprehensive Peace Accord, is finalised, implementation should generally be straightforward. However, challenges may arise if the agreeing parties use the agreement for their strategic advantage, fail to uphold their previous commitments, or if there is a lack of a neutral and dedicated mediator.

In Nepal, the conflict seems to be being managed effectively; however, it remains unresolved. If the conflict resolution phase is extended indefinitely, the risk of relapse may increase.[1]

In the post-constitutional period, elected governments have encountered numerous challenges. They are frequently perceived as caught between the inflexible stances adopted by political parties and the dissenting marginalised groups. For instance, CPN-UML Chairman K.P. Sharma Oli asserted that the nation would face a significant crisis if all three elections—local, provincial assemblies, and federal parliament—were not conducted by January 21, 2018, as stipulated in the 2015 Constitution.[2] Conversely, Rajendra Mahato, then the Chairman of the Sadbhawana Party, asserted that the nation would enter a period of turmoil if local-level elections were conducted without delineating provincial borders, as advocated by the United Democratic Madhesi Front (UDMF).[3] The government had previously conducted two rounds of elections for local bodies across six provinces. However, the elections in Madhesh Pradesh (Province 2) were postponed due to protests organised by the UDMF. Following extensive negotiations with the principal political parties, the UDMF agreed to participate in the local body elections after receiving assurances from the then-ruling party, the NC that their proposal for amending Nepal's constitution would be presented for a vote in the legislature.

The Nepali peace process again took a nose dive after the Sanghiya Samajbadi Forum-Nepal (SSF-N), a key constituent of the agitating UDMF, withdrew support from the Prachanda-led coalition government in March 2017. The SSF-N made that decision after the government failed to address its demands,[4] which were put forward after the Saptari incident.[5] This raised concerns regarding the implementation of the constitution, as the SSF-N and other factions of the Morcha had chosen to boycott the local body elections until the passage of the amendment bill.

## New Dissenting Voices

During the constitution-making process and the subsequent prolonged dialogues that were largely unsuccessful between the ruling parties and marginalised groups, including the Terai-based political parties, there has been a growing inclination among Terai youths towards radical ideologies. They have expressed their intentions to engage in an armed struggle due to the state's inaction in addressing their demands. Reports indicate that a relatively obscure organisation known as the Alliance for Independent Madhesh (AIM) was established in 2011 under the leadership of C.K. Raut to counter state repression through armed resistance. After six years of political mobilisation to garner public support for creating a separate Madhesh and months of negotiations, AIM leader C.K. Raut signed an accord with the government on 08 March 2019. This 11-point agreement included commitments to uphold the "sovereignty," "territorial integrity," and "dignity" of the nation, as well as a pledge to adhere to democratic principles by the constitution. Subsequently, Raut founded the Janamat Party (JP) on 19 March 2022.

The manifesto of AIM asserted that Madhesh should be recognised as "a sovereign and independent nation and contended the establishment of a Madhesh Government to oversee the processes of state transition, administration, electoral conduct, and constitutional drafting. AIM characterised the Nepali security forces (comprising the Nepal Army, Armed Police Force, and Nepal Police) as "colonial" and advocated for their withdrawal from the low-lying [the Terai region] districts."[6] In addition to the AIM, various Terai-based armed organisations, such as those led by Jwala Singh and Jaya Krishna Goit, have been advocating for a sovereign Madhesh Pradesh. Security agencies have identified their presence as a significant challenge in the central Terai region of Nepal.[7]

Just after the announcement of the May 2017 two-phase local body elections, the Communist Party of Nepal (Maoist), a splinter Maoist outfit led by Netra Bikram Chand, boycotted the elections and vowed to disrupt poll-related activities. In a press release, the outfit stated: "The current parliamentary system serves the interests of the compradors. The state and the government are anti-national and anti-people. The mainstream parties were not ready to renegotiate the comprehensive peace agreement. In such a situation, [the] party believed that an armed revolution alone could ensure justice in the country."[8]

Before the establishment of the Communist Party of Nepal (Maoist), Chand served as the General Secretary of the Communist Party of Nepal-Maoist (CPN-M), which was led by Mohan Baidya, also known as Kiran. The CPN-M decided to boycott the second Constituent Assembly elections, which took place in November 2013. Notably, since the Baidya faction did not contest the local body elections, it also opted not to register with the Election Commission of Nepal. In contrast, the Chand faction adheres to Marxism-Leninism-Maoism (MLM) as its foundational ideological framework.[9]

As part of the poll boycott programme, cadres of the CPN-Maoist party reportedly attacked candidates of other political parties, the offices of mainstream political parties, the polling staff and polling stations by detonating bombs and snatching ballot boxes. Nepal Police identified the Baidya faction as a potential threat to local polls in the middle and far-west districts. At the same time, the security officials of [11-hilly] districts were asked to monitor the Chand-led Maoists' activities as a security threat for the elections.[10]

In addition to radical Maoist factions, certain extremist Hindu and royalist groups have also opposed the new constitution. For instance, pro-royalist organisations such as the Shahi Sena, Shiva Sena, Rastrabadi Nagarik, and Purano Shakti have expressed their dissent regarding local body elections, which are perceived as a preliminary step toward the implementation of the new constitutional framework.[11] In March 2022, a lesser-known new organisation called Himal Surakshya Parisad (HSP), also known as Congruent Front of Nepal, was formed.

## Leveraging the Peace Process for Tactical Gains

It can be articulated that the actors in Nepal's peace process were inclined to secure short-term gains to consolidate power rather than prioritising conflict resolution. From the Maoist perspective, the peace process represented a tactical manoeuvre designed to navigate their strategic impasse regarding the escalation of the movement. Additionally, it aimed to safeguard their cadres from a significant counteroffensive operation orchestrated by the Nepali Army with the support of the United States. Furthermore, the initiative sought to establish a united front to combat the state and abolish the monarchy, conceived as a preliminary step towards establishing a republican Nepal.

The political parties, on the other hand, required the support of the Maoists to combat the prevailing regime, which constituted a common adversary. Furthermore, they sought to protect themselves from the extensive Maoist assaults and violence. Additionally, the parties were compelled to form alliances to challenge the monarchy, mainly under the influence of India, which served as both a facilitator and stakeholder in the peace process. India actively promoted this political partnership to achieve several objectives: first, to restore democracy by diminishing the power and influence of the monarchy within the Nepali political landscape; second, to create an ideological and strategic divide between the Indian and Nepali Maoists through the process of mainstreaming the latter; and third, to mitigate the growing USA interests in the Himalayan region.

Given that these actors harboured concealed agendas for convening to sign the Comprehensive Peace Agreement, they began to undermine it subsequently following the removal of their common adversary. Their true sentiments toward one another were further unveiled after the first Constituent Assembly elections. As previously noted, the seven political parties grew increasingly apprehensive regarding the Maoists' intentions in light of their electoral success and the Maoist party's resolutions advocating the continuation of the people's movement by adopting a new revolutionary strategy.

The commitment of the political parties to endorse a framework of 'consensus politics' before the Comprehensive Peace Agreement ultimately faltered during the election of Nepal's first president. The Maoists' subsequent reversal regarding excluding non-Maoist candidates from assuming the presidency under the Interim Constitution exacerbated the existing mistrust between the negotiating parties. This pervasive suspicion was evident throughout the discussions aimed at addressing contentious political and security issues, leading to the breakdown of the consensus phase and causing significant delays in the implementation of the CPA. Although negotiations and dialogue continued, all political actors compromised on socio-political and economic issues to secure power. Consequently, the concerns of the general populace, including the demands of marginalised groups, were largely overlooked. For instance, the Maoist leaders, who initially advocated for the rights of marginalised communities and promised to implement structural reforms in Nepal—such as establishing a republican system, federalism, an inclusive constitution, and a just society—ultimately abandoned these commitments during the constitution-making process in pursuit of power. This shift significantly benefited the traditional ruling parties, which were reluctant to share power with marginalised groups.

India, initially expected to adopt a neutral stance, ultimately aligned itself with the ruling establishment in Nepal due to broader, long-term strategic interests. While there was an intention to incorporate the Maoists into mainstream politics, this was tempered by the recognition that they were not perceived as the principal political actors in Nepal. India's strategic interests in the Himalayan region significantly influenced the prevailing social and political dynamics in Nepal. Consequently, India found it necessary to support those factions that demonstrated a willingness to align with its interests.

Moreover, the Comprehensive Peace Accord lost its relevance primarily as the unity among the seven political parties deteriorated once they engaged in competitive politics, resulting in the emergence of some as opposition parties. Additionally, the CPN-Maoist experienced a fragmentation into four distinct factions during the transitional period, complicating the political landscape further. The Maoists, who were expected to advocate for marginalised communities, gradually aligned themselves with state authorities and forged alliances with elite-driven political parties.

Besides that, the CPA was arguably the first peace accord globally to be executed without a mediator. While the agreement succeeded in mitigating violence, it concurrently failed to avert the emergence of new conflicts—manifesting as regional and ethnic divisions, mistrust between hill elites and marginalised groups, the formation of anti-constitution factions, intra- and inter-party divisions, and the pursuit of external support to counter rivals. Khimlal Devkota observed that "while the promulgation of the new statute is a historic achievement, this document fails to adequately ensure the rights of Dalits, women, the ethnic nationalities, Madhesis, and Muslims."[12]

### *Other Challenges*

There were several additional challenges confronting the peace process. First, the discontent expressed by a significant number of ex-Maoist armed cadres regarding the peace initiative could prove detrimental to a post-conflict society that has yet to institutionalise this process. Media reports indicate that a considerable segment of ex-Maoists, upon leaving the cantonments with their financial packages, aligned themselves with the hardline stance advocated by Mohan Baidya concerning group integration. Furthermore, some individuals have allied themselves with the Netra Bikram Chand faction, perceiving themselves as 'abandoned by the parent party.'[13] This resentment later led to a split in the Maoist party led by Prachanda.[14] The Mohan Baidya faction pledged to combat the injustices inflicted upon its members and vehemently opposed the ongoing peace process.

Second, the integration process adopted was distinct in that the former Maoist combatants underwent rehabilitation within a relatively brief timeframe, circumventing the conventional demobilisation and reintegration processes. Demobilisation is a critical aspect of any peace strategy, as it facilitates the development of essential skills for ex-combatants, thereby enabling their successful reintegration into society.[15] However, in absence of that, a significant number were reportedly engaged in criminal activities.

Ex-women Maoist combatants, however, have been the worst off. Speaking to the media, some ex-women combatants said that the party had betrayed them along with the society for which they fought in order to bring about change. 'The party dumped us,' said Pradip Karki, a former child soldier. 'We cannot go home because we have the label of being "disqualified" hanging around our necks.'[16] Despite a new constitution, they feel that 'most of the structural factors contributing to conflict in Nepal have not been addressed.... They had joined the Maoist insurgency with the belief that these problems would be addressed promptly.'[17]

Third, around 4,000 disqualified minor Maoist combatants demanded rehabilitation as per the rehabilitation package because they wasted their childhood for the cause of the revolution. They have formed an organisation called the Discharged People's Liberation Army Struggle Committee. These combatants organised a protest rally in front of the CPN-Maoist Centre office in November 2016. They have vowed to continue their protests until the party discusses their demands with the government.

Some security experts in Nepal feel that although the reintegration of former Maoist combatants might have reached completion that had nonetheless resulted in a significant segment of these individuals feeling profoundly dissatisfied and disillusioned, thereby increasing the potential for their regrouping and the resurgence of conflict.[18] Media reports have indicated the involvement of former Maoists in some criminal activities in the post-reintegration period. The involvement of ex-Maoist combatants has been reported in the following incidents:

1. 09 November 2016: About 169 former Maoist child soldiers protested outside the party office.
2. 20 September 2016: Former Maoist combatants were found involved in planting and detonating improvised explosive devices (IED) at various schools in Kathmandu for extortion of money.
3. 10 September 2015: The National Human Rights Commission (NHRC) found the involvement of former Maoist combatants in the Tikapur incident in which eight police personnel were lynched.

Fourth, some media reports have indicated that the Netra Bikram Chand group decided to revive the armed revolution in Nepal to oppose the new constitution. He reportedly has been working hand-in-glove with other nationalist groups in Nepal, holding similar views on the new constitution. He has also formed a parallel government in many districts of the mid-western region.

Fifth, most importantly, the Baidya faction felt that except for the removal of the monarchy, none of the Maoist demands had been addressed in the new constitution. Only the institution has been done away with, but the same set of people and the same thinking concerning the marginalised groups continues. Mohan Baidya argued that the 'parliamentary system alone cannot deliver on the broader promise of the People's Democratic Republic.'[19]

Last but not least, over 16,000 people (security personnel, civilians, Maoists) were killed, while 1,300 disappeared during the decade-long Maoist conflict in Nepal.[20] Another 5,000 were physically harmed and rendered disabled, and 12,000 families were displaced after their properties were confiscated by the Maoists.[21] Therefore, the 2006-CPA sought an investigation into these charges within six months of the peace process.

### *Delay in Transitional Justice*

The Truth and Reconciliation Commission (TRC) and the Commission of Investigation on Enforced Disappeared Persons (CIEDP) were formed as part of the November 2006 CPA after a delay of around nine years due to the lack of trust between the major political parties, non-cooperation of the NA and some political parties as well as the unstable political situation. More than 58,052 cases have been filed since the formation of the TRC and CIEPD. Initially, the tenure of the two transition justice bodies was two years. The government extended their tenure till February 2018. The victims and their families want prompt justice because the investigation into these complaints has yet to begin due to the lack of proper implementation guidelines and conflict among TRC members.[22]

It is believed that there were serious differences of opinion between commission members, given their separate ideological backgrounds and affiliations to different political parties.

Some also argue that since a large number of Maoist leaders were charged with human rights violations during the insurgency period, the Maoists, who emerged as the largest party in the first CA, deliberately delayed the process to avoid prosecutions. 'Provision 7, which directs the authorities to withdraw all wartime cases before the courts and to provide amnesty to alleged perpetrators, is particularly problematic.'[23]

During the second CA, even though the Maoists landed in the third position, they still emerged as key political players in Kathmandu. They supported or forged alliances with the other two major political parties and influenced the formation of TRC and CIEPD. For example, the nine-point agreement signed in May 2016 between the CPN-UML and the Maoists to form a coalition government included the withdrawal of conflict-era cases from the court and the granting of amnesty to those involved in serious human rights violations.[24]

There are also tussles between the judiciary, ruling political parties and the TRC. While the TRC wanted to put certain cases on hold, citing insufficient evidence as per its guidelines, the Supreme Court (SC) intervened and scrapped the guidelines prepared by the TRC.[25] Earlier, the SC also rejected the proposal of granting blanket amnesty to human rights violators and transferring war crimes cases already pending before it.[26]

In such a situation, the victims' hopes of early justice are fading away. Because of disunity, the victims have failed to pressure the government and mobilise the international community to support their cause. The victims are also divided on the basis of their political inclinations.

There are at least three types of war victims in Nepal. The first category consists of those who were victimised by the former Maoist cadres. These could include both security force personnel and civilians. The second category is those victimised by the state security forces. The third category is victims of atrocities committed by both the rebels and state forces. The third category of victims is the worst affected due to delays in transitional justice because 'most of the victims of the state atrocities have already taken financial help from the state—mostly when Maoists were in the government. And those who were victimised by the Maoists have been waiting to get proper relief.'[27]

### *Weak Institutions*

Weak state institutions also contributed to the delay in the implementation of the PP. During a decade-long peace process, Nepal had ten governments and two elections to form the CA. Nepal witnessed huge governance issues due to frequent changes in government. The balance of power between the three major organs of the state—legislature, executive and judiciary—failed due to the politicisation of constitutional bodies over appointment issues. For example, in March 2016, the appointment of 11 Supreme Court judges was delayed due to differences between the Maoists and the CPN-UML.[28] Similarly, there were differences of opinion between the government and SC over the formation, role and jurisdiction of the TRC.

Furthermore, the first elected government under the constitution received jolt after two and half years in power due to intense intra-party factionalism over power sharing and leadership issues between K.P. Sharma Oli and Prachanda. This culminated in dissolution of the parliament in December 2020 and division of the NCP in March 2021.

President of Nepal Bidya Devi Bhandari, on May 22, 2021, exercising her power under Article 76(7) on the advice of the prime minister, dissolved the House of Representatives or the Lower House and announced fresh elections. This decision was taken after political parties failed to form a new government under Article 76(5) of the constitution. That was the second time the House had been dissolved in the last five months. Previously, it was dissolved in December 2020. The SC, however, reinstated the House on February 23, 2021, after hearing over a dozen writ petitions questioning the decision to dissolve the House.

Public faith in the country's constitution and political system has eroded drastically since the Oli government issued the ordinance related to the Political Party Act in April 2020. The new political system introduced by the constitution has been repeatedly misused by the ruling parties. Public disenchantment towards the new system has been manifested in a series of rallies and protests. The pro-royalist organisations even began discussing the revival of the monarchical system. During October-November 2020, a series of pro-monarchy rallies were organised across the country.

The government's policies and priorities underwent significant shifts with the establishment of new administrations in Kathmandu. Political leaders and parties predominantly concentrated on the pursuit and retention of power. Consequently, the critical initiatives of the peace process, post-earthquake reconstruction, and infrastructure development were substantially impeded.

## *New Debates on the Constitution*

The recurrent political fluctuations in Nepal since 2015 and their repercussions on the nation's development have sparked renewed discussions concerning the efficacy of the new constitution. A political interpretation suggests that the proportional representation system and the minimal threshold level have been fundamental factors contributing to political volatility, aside from "untruthful political alliances and syndication for personal and party benefits."[29]

Therefore, there are demands for "an appropriate model for PR could be either through direct voting among similar ethnicities for the lower house or through indirect voting for entire slates of party candidates for the upper house."[30] For instance, the Nepali Congress and the CPN-UML have publicly advocated for the modification of the existing mixed electoral system to promote political stability. In various forums, several senior NC leaders have called for a reassessment of the mixed electoral system.[31] The leaders of the CPN-UML have articulated analogous sentiments.[32]

In addition, certain political factions have advocated for constitutional amendments aimed at abolishing federalism and secularism. These demands for constitutional revisions could incite significant reactions from marginalised groups and have consequential political implications. In response to these debates, Prachanda declared that "it would not be accepted by the [his] party if any efforts were made to withdraw the provision of proportional representation and inclusion aiming to uplift the suppressed, marginalised, and disadvantaged communities."[33]

In conclusion, it can be observed that Nepal's peace process has only been partially successful. Social and political conflicts have remained prevalent in the period following the peace agreement, and there has been a noticeable increase in dissent concerning the new constitution. If the constitution fails to address the demands of marginalised groups, both the Hill and Terai regions may experience a resurgence of violent conflicts. Furthermore, numerous infrastructure projects in Nepal could be jeopardised during prolonged unrest. Therefore, it is imperative to cultivate a cordial atmosphere and establish political stability to facilitate meaningful dialogue with dissenting groups, ultimately fostering durable peace, progress, and prosperity.

## NOTES

1 Johan Galtung, "Institutionalized Conflict Resolution: A Theoretical Paradigm", Journal of Peace Research 2(4): 348–397, 1965.

2 "Nation will plunge into crisis if elections couldn't be held: Oli", *The Kathmandu Post,* 17 March 2017.

3 "Bad days if elections before border delineation review, warns Mahato", *The Himalayan Times,* 17 March 2017.

4 The Morcha gave a seven day ultimatum to government with address its five demands, including cancelling the local body elections. In a memorandum to Prime Minister, the United Democratic Madhesi Front demanded:
1. withdrawal of local elections announced for 14 May 2017,
2. review of the Constitution amendment bill,
3. action against those responsible for the Saptari incident,
4. declaration of the deceased as martyrs and compensation for the bereaved families
5. keeping the local level structure within provincial jurisdiction and the implementation of the three-point agreement reached during the formation of the incumbent government.

5 The five persons were killed after police opened fire at the cadres of then Samyukta Loktantrik Madhesi Morcha (SLMM), name changed again to Sanghiya Gathabandan, who had tried to disrupt the CPN-UML's Mechi Mahakali Campaign at the Gajendra Narayan Industrial area in Maleth VDC of Sapari on March 6 on 09 March 2017. https://kathmandupost.com/national/2017/05/17/5-killed-in-saptari-police-firing-declared-martyrs (accessed on 27 October 2024).

6 "CK Raut arrested in Janakpur", *The Kathmandu Post, 0*2 February 2017.

7 Ramesh Dhamala, "At Interpol conference, Nepal to dwell on armed outfits active in its flatlands, take India to task", *online khabar*, 19 January 2017.

8 "Baidhya and Chand-led Maoist parties won't be able to contest local polls: EC", *The Himalayan Times*, 28 February 2017.

9 Rishi Raj Baral, "Malkangiri fake encounter: not any responses by the Nepalese Maoists parties", *The Next Front*, an online publication of MLM supporters, 03 November 2016.

10 "Chand-led CPN Maoist main security threat for polls," *The Kathmandu Post*, 21 April 2017.

11 "Biplav "prime threat" to Kathmandu polls: Police", *Onlinekhabar*, Kathmandu, 10 May 2017.

12 Kosh Raj Koirala, "Ten years on, CPA promises largely unmet", *myRepublica*, 21 November 2016.

13 Ibid.

14 In June 2012 Mohan Baidya split from UCPN (Maoist) and formed the Communist Party of Nepal-Revolutionary Maoist. Later Netra Bikram Chand also split from Baidya faction. In 2016 again some leaders of Baidya faction reunited with the Prachanda faction and formed the CPN (Maoist centre). Baidya supports the Patriotic People's Republican Front, which is constituted under the leadership of one of its leaders, C.P. Gajurel, in local body elections.

15 Demobilisation is the formal and controlled discharge of active combatants from the armed forces or other armed groups. The first stage of demobilisation may extend from the processing of individual combatants in temporary centres to the massing of troops in camps designated for this purpose (cantonment sites, encampments, assembly areas or barracks). The second stage of demobilisation encompasses the support package provided to the demobilised, which is called reinsertion.

Reinsertion* is the assistance offered to ex-combatants during demobilisation but prior to the longer-term process of reintegration. Reinsertion is a form of transitional assistance to help cover the basic needs of ex-combatants and their families and can include transitional safety allowances, food, clothes, shelter, medical services, short-term education, training, employment and tools. While reintegration is a long-term, continuous social and economic process of development, reinsertion is short-term material and/or financial assistance to meet immediate needs, and can last up to one year.

Reintegration is the process by which ex-combatants acquire civilian status and gain sustainable employment and income. Reintegration is essentially a social and economic process with an open time-frame, primarily taking place in communities at the local level. It is part of the general development of a country and a national responsibility, and often necessitates long-term external assistance. -Secretary-General, note to the General Assembly, A/C.5/59/31, May 2005.

16 "Ex-minor ex-Maoists," Review, *Nepali Times*, 15-21 January 2016, #791, for details see http://nepalitimes.com/article/review/Ex-minor-ex-Maoists,2820 (accessed on 27 September 2021).

17 Subindra Bogati, "Assessing Inclusivity on the Post-War Army Integration Process in Nepal: Inclusive Political Settlements", Paper *11*, July 2015, Berlin: Berghof Foundation.

18 John Narayan Parajuli, "Year Ender 2016: Half-hearted Peace", *The Kathmandu Post*, 29 December 2016.

19 Bishal Thapa, "To a Maoist state?" *myRepublica*, 18 April 2017. Also see Thomas A. Marks, "Terrorism as Method in Nepali Maoist Insurgency, 1996-2016", *Small Wars & Insurgencies*, 28 (1), 2017, 81-118.

20 Nepal Conflict Report 2012, Executive Summary, United Nations Office of the High Commissioner for Human Rights, Geneva, October 2012.

21 Yubaraj Ghimire, "Politics of Human Rights," *The Indian Express*, 12 June 2016.

22 "Preliminary probe in six months: TRC," *The Himalayan Times*, 16 April 2017.

23 "Nepal: 9-Point Deal Undermines Transitional Justice, Annul Clemency for Grave Crimes," *Human Rights Watch*, 12 May 2016. Also see "Oli, Dahal sign 9-pt deal," *myRepublica*, 06 May 2016.

24 "Nepal: the uphill struggle for justice," *reliefweb*, 26 April 2017.

25 "Supreme Court invalidates TRC guidelines", *The Himalayan Times*, 02 February 2017.

26 "Nepal Supreme Court rejects amnesty for war crimes," *Reuters*, 27 February 2015.

27 Telephonic interaction with Lekhnath Pandey. Pandey is a journalist with *The Himalayan Times* and covers transitional justice issues.

28 "Tussle between UML, UCPN-M fuels conflict between judiciary, legislature", *The Himalayan Times*, 11 March 2016.

29 Hari Prasad Shrestha, "Is Proportional Representation the Cause of Frequent Government Changes in Nepal?" Opinon, *myRepublica*, date is not available, https://myrepublica.nagariknetwork.com/news/is-proportional-representation-the-cause-of-frequent-government-changes-in-nepal/ (accessed on 15 October 2024).

30 Ibid.

31 "Experts warn against hasty change in electoral system", *The Kathmandu Post*, 04 May 2024, https://kathmandupost.com/national/2024/05/04/experts-warn-against-hasty-change-in-electoral-system (accessed on 15 October 2024).

32 Ibid.

33 "Maoist Centre not against constitution amendment: Chair Dahal", *The Rising Nepal*, 08 September 2024, https://risingnepaldaily.com/news/48652 (accessed on 15 October 2024).

# APPENDICES

APPENDIX-I

## *Agreement between the Government of Nepal and the MJF*

Realising the sentiments of the movement of the Madhesi people as a continuity of the historic People's Movement of 2006/07, and in order to end all forms of discrimination against Madhesi, Adivasi/Janajatis, Dalits, women, backward classes and minorities, including the Muslim community, practised by the centralised and unitary state for a long time and to create an environment enabling all Nepalese people, inclusive of Madhesi, to join the single national mainstream and move forward by restructuring the state as an inclusive democracy and federal structure, the Government of Nepal and the Madheshi Janadhikar Forum [Madheshi Peoples' Rights Forum], Nepal, today, conclude the following agreement:

1. To immediately implement the government's decision to honour all Madhesi activists killed during the Madhesh movement and to provide compensation to their families.
2. To provide relief to those injured, rendered blind and disabled during the Madhesh movement and to provide immediate medical treatment for all injured people who are yet to receive treatment.
3. To withdraw all cases filed against the leaders and activists of the Forum during the Madhesh movement.
4. To ensure proportional representation and partnership of Madhesi, Adivasi/Janajatis, Dalits, women, backward classes, disabled people and minority communities, including Muslims, who have been excluded for generations in all organs and levels of government and in power structures, mechanisms and resources.
5. To immediately establish a commission of experts for state restructuring and ensure that its constitution is inclusive.
6. While restructuring the state, provision shall be made for a federal governance system with autonomous provinces/states, while keeping the sovereignty, national unity and integrity of Nepal intact. The rights, nature

and limits of the said autonomy will be as determined by the Constituent Assembly.

7. To accord national recognition to the dresses, languages and cultures of the Madheshis.
8. To ensure appropriate proportional representation in all political appointments made by the government and all services, including in Foreign Service and the education sector, as well as in commissions.
9. To give public holidays on major festivals of the Muslims. To enact laws to protect Madrassa Board as well as the community, language, sexes, religion, culture, and customs and traditions of the Muslims.
10. To fully guarantee human rights by ending all discriminations based on ethnicity, language, sex, religion, culture, national and social origin, political and other ideologies.
11. To establish a trilingual language policy consisting of (a) mother tongue, (b) the Nepali language, and (c) English for official transactions, education and international communication.
12. To solve the following Dalit-related problems:
    (a) Make provision for severe legal punishment for practising caste discrimination and untouchability.
    (b) Effectively implement the policy of free and compulsory education, at least up to primary level, for Dalits.
    (c) Make provision for special opportunities and reservations in education and employment.
    (d) Make provision for alternative means of livelihood for landless Dalits by providing them with land for building houses.
13. To solve problems related to citizenship by redeploying the Citizenship Distribution Teams to villages for easy and accessible distribution of citizenship certificates.
14. To adopt a balanced and just policy for the distribution of revenue and income from the State to the Madhesh and remote regions.
15. The process of returning houses, land and other property seized by the CPN (Maoist) is continuing and will be continued with urgency along with the return of weapons seized by them [CPN (M)] to their rightful owners.
16. To establish an Industrial Security Force to industrialise the country and to guarantee industrial security, as well as increasing production.
17. Both parties to stay committed to conducting the Constituent Assembly

election in an impartial, peaceful and fear-free environment. In order to ensure the impartiality of the Constituent Assembly, make necessary arrangements to prevent the misuse of the State's mechanisms, resources and power, including by the current Legislature-Parliament.

18. The Ministry of Information and Communications to appoint Madhesi media experts and journalists in all organs and levels of government-owned media, including electronic and print media, and to ensure inclusive proportional representation of Madhesi in the government communication commission, agencies and delegations.
19. To create a search team to conduct a special investigation into the abduction and disappearance of Jitendra Sah, chairperson of the Madhesi Youth Forum and to immediately make his status public.
20. To immediately establish a High-level Task Force for Inclusion to formulate policies and laws necessary for the inclusion of Madhesi, Adivasi/janajatis, Dalits, women, etc. in all organs and levels of the State.
21. To accord constitutional guarantee for the rights of ethnic, linguistic and religious minorities based on the principles upheld by the United Nations and international human rights organizations on the rights of minorities.
22. To withdraw the various movements being carried out by the Madheshi Janadhikar Forum. The GoN shall immediately fulfill those agreements that can be implemented promptly and shall fulfill other provisions in course of time. A joint Monitoring Mechanism shall be established to carry out and oversee the implementation process and to periodically review the implementation.

**Sd. Upendra Yadav,** Coordinator, Madhesi Janadhikar Forum,

**Sd. Ram Chandra Poudel,** Coordinator, GoN Talks Team

Date: August 30, 2007

*NOTE:* While still demanding the establishment of a republic and a proportional electoral system, the Madheshi Janadhikar Forum, Nepal shall give top priority to the Constituent Assembly election and shall participate in it while continuing its efforts to make it a success.

Sd.

**Upendra Yadav,** Coordinator, Madheshi Janadhikar Forum, Nepal

Date: August 30, 2007

APPENDIX-II

## *Agreement between the Government of Nepal and Samyukta Loktantrik Madheshi Morcha*

Respecting the sentiments and aspirations of the Madheshi people of Nepal, expressed during the protests and movements that they have organised time and again for equal rights, this Agreement was signed between the Government of Nepal and the Samyukta Loktantrik Madheshi Morcha [United Democratic Madheshi Front] to ensure the establishment of federal democratic republic in Nepal for multiparty democratic system of governance, to guarantee equality, freedom and justice for all, and to end all forms of discrimination. This Agreement shall be implemented at once. The points of agreement are as follows:

1. The State shall declare those killed during the Madhesh Movement as martyrs, and shall provide appropriate compensation to those maimed and yet to receive compensation. Similarly, arrangements shall be made for those injured during the Movement to receive medical expenses and those martyred shall be given due recognition and their families shall be provided with relief at the rate of Rs 1 million, and those arrested shall be immediately released.
2. Nepal shall become a federal democratic republic by accepting people's aspiration for a federal structure with autonomous regions, including the Madheshi people's aspiration for an autonomous Madhesh state. In the federal structure, power between the Centre and the states shall be divided clearly according to a list. The states shall be fully autonomous and shall enjoy full rights. The structure, full details of the lists of the Centre and the states and the division of power between them shall be determined by the Constituent Assembly, keeping Nepal's sovereignty and integrity intact.
3. The existing legal provision of 20 per cent in Sub-section 14 of Section 7 of the Election of Members to the Constituent Assembly Act 2064 shall be changed to 30 per cent.

4. The Government shall execute appointments, promotions and nominations in a manner that ensures inclusive and proportional participation of Madheshi people, Adivasi, Jananati , women, Dalits, backward regions and minority communities in all state bodies, including the security bodies.
5. Proportional, inclusive group entry of Madheshi people and other communities into the Nepal Army shall be ensured to impart national character to Nepal Army and to make it more inclusive.
6. The Government of Nepal and the United Democratic Madheshi Front together request all armed groups agitating in the Terai to begin negotiations for a peaceful political process and to find solutions to all outstanding problems through dialogue. The Government of Nepal shall take necessary steps to create an environment conducive to this purpose. We appeal everyone to help conduct the Constituent Assembly election on April 10 in an environment which is peaceful, non-violent, impartial, fair and free of fear.
7. The Government of Nepal shall immediately release all those who have been detained, withdraw cases filed against Madheshi leaders and party cadres of the Forum as well as of other parties, and immediately implement all other points of the 22-Point Agreement signed between the Government of Nepal and the Madheshi Janadhikar Forum on August 30, 2007.
8. All protest programmes called by the United Democratic Madheshi Forum shall be immediately withdrawn.

The Government of Nepal shall be responsible for the constitutional, legal, political and administrative aspects of the issues mentioned in this Agreement. The Government shall form a high-level monitoring committee, comprising, among others, members of the Front, to monitor the implementation of this agreement.

Signatories to the Agreement:

Sd.

Rajendra Mahato, National Chairperson, Sadbhavana Party

Upendra Yadav, Central Coordinator, Madheshi Janadhikar Forum, Nepal

Mahantha Thakur, Chairperson, Terai Madhesh Loktantrik Party

February 28, 2008

*Source:* "From Conflict to Peace in Nepal, Peace Agreements Database," The University of Edinburg, at https://www.peaceagreements.org/viewmasterdocument/1749, (accessed on 28 September 2021).

APPENDIX-III

## *Agreement between the Government and Janajatis*

*7 August 2007*

## Unofficial translation from the original Nepali, by UNMIN

1. While nominating candidates for the first-past-the-post electoral system arranged for the constituent assembly election in the present constitution, candidacy will be determined so as to ensure proportional representation of all castes and janajatis.
2. While preparing a proportional list, all political parties participating in the election will make arrangements to ensure representation of each of the listed indigenous janajati communities.
3. In case a listed indigenous janajati group is unable to secure its representation through both electoral systems, the Government of Nepal and the eight parties will reach a mutually acceptable conclusion in order to ensure that there is at least one representative of such a group and that the representation is legal and constitutional.
4. A state restructuring commission will soon be formed to present recommendations to the constituent assembly regarding a federal state structure based on ethnicity, language, geographic region, economic indicators and cultural distinctiveness while keeping national unity, integrity and sovereignty of Nepal at the forefront. The commission will include indigenous janajatis, Madhesis, dalits, women and eminent experts from various groups, regions and communities.
5. A commission for indigenous janajatis will be formed.
6. While so far only Nepali has been recognised as the government's official language, the constituent assembly will also make arrangements to give recognition to locally spoken mother tongues along with Nepali. The government will remain committed towards ensuring linguistic rights of its citizens.

7. Arrangements will be made for the general public to seek and receive information on matters of public importance, including the constituent assembly, in their respective mother tongues.
8. The Government of Nepal has agreed in principle that all groups, genders, communities, castes and ethnicities should be represented in political parties at all levels. A fully representative task-force will be formed immediately to conduct a study in order to ensure inclusive participation and proportional representation of all castes, ethnicities, groups, communities, genders and regions in all bodies and levels of the state.
9. All sectors will take initiatives to practically implement their legal and policy-level commitments to ensuring inclusive and proportional representation of all genders, classes, regions and communities, including indigenous janajatis in all bodies and levels of state.
10. A system will gradually be developed to receive advice and consultation from concerned groups and bodies while making important decisions regarding various groups, regions, genders and communities, including indigenous janajatis.
11. Arrangements will be made to immediately pass the proposal to ratify and adopt Convention 169 of the International Labour Organisation.
12. Appropriate steps will be immediately taken to complete the necessary legal process for adopting the United Nations Declaration on the Rights of Indigenous Peoples.
13. A District Coordination Committee for indigenous janajatis will be formed in a democratic and transparent manner. Also, high importance will be given to the involvement of the Nepal Federation of Indigenous Nationalities and the National Federation of Indigenous Women in this process.
14. In keeping with the spirit and sentiment of gender mainstreaming in development plans and programmes, including interim planning, and paying attention to women and diversity in programme implementation and profit sharing, emphasis will be laid upon participation of women from indigenous janajati, dalit and Madhesi groups.
15. As party to the Convention on Biodiversity, the country will ensure that the traditional knowledge, skills, practices and technology of indigenous janajatis are harnessed and preserved.
16. The country will honour the renowned geographer Dr. Harka Gurung.
17. Arrangements will be made to provide Rs. 1 million each as relief and

compensation to the families of all the Nepalis who died in the helicopter crash in Ghunsa, Taplejung.

18. The process started by the government to find a permanent solution to the problems faced by freed kamaiyas (bonded labourers) will be taken forward in an effective manner as per the agreement.
19. The government will make a serious effort to reach an agreement for addressing the demands of various groups and communities, including Madhesis, women and dalits through talks and discussions with the respective groups.
20. Nepal Federation of Indigenous Nationalities, Indigenous Nationalities Joint Struggle Committee and National Indigenous Women Federation request all indigenous communities in the country to unite for the success of the upcoming constituent assembly election.

- Ram Chandra Poudel, Coordinator, Government Talks Team

- Dr. Om Gurung, Coordinator, Nepal Federation of Indigenous Nationalities

- KB Gurung, Coordinator, Indigenous Nationalities Joint Struggle Committee

*Source:* ConstitutionNet is an International IDEA (an IGO headquartered in Sweden), at http://www.constitutionnet.org/sites/default/files/2007-08-07- agreement_between_ government _and_janajatis.pdf (accessed on 28 September 2021).

APPENDIX-IV

## *Madhesi Organizations: Political and Illegal Armed Groups**

1. Madhesi Janadhikar Forum (MJF, also called Madhesi People's Rights Forum or MPRF-Nepal). Leaders are Upendra Yadav and Jaya Prakash Gupta.
2. Terai Madhesh Loktrantrik Party (TMLP, also called Terai Madhes Democratic Party-Nepal). Leader, Mahendra Prasad Yadav.
3. Terai Madhesh Loktrantrik Party (TMLP, also called Terai Madhes Democratic Party), Leader, Mahantha Thakur.
4. Madhesi Janadhikar Forum-Madhes (MJF-M), Bhagyanath Prasad Gupta.
5. Madhesi Janadhikar Forum-Loktantrik (Bijay Kumar Gachhadar).
6. Nepal Sadhvawana Party (NSP). Leader, Rajendra Mahato.
7. Nepal Sadhvawana Party-Anandi Devi (NSP-A). Leader, Sarita Giri.

### Terai Political Alliances

*United Democratic Madhesi Front (UDMF),* consisting of:

1. Madhesi Janadhikar Forum
2. Terai Madhes Loktrantrik Party
3. Nepal Sadhvawana Party

### Major Illegal Armed Groups

1. Janatantrik Terai Mukti Morcha (JTMM) – Leader Nagendra Kumar Paswan alias Jwala Singh
2. Janatantrik Terai Mukti Morcha (JTMM) – Leader Jaya Krishna Goit also known as Akhil Terai Mukti Morcha (ATMM)
3. Janatantrik Terai Mukti Morcha (JTMM) – Leader Bishfot Singh faction
4. Madhesi Mukti Tigers (Maoist splinter, leader Sher Singh Rajput, chairman Rajan Mukti)

5. Nepal Janatantrik Party (pro-King, leader Rana Bahadur Chanda 'Samrat')
6. Terai Tigers (leader alias 'Arjun')
7. Tharu Mukti Morcha, leader Laxman Tharu, President
8. Chure Bhawar Ekata Samaj (demands the establishment of a Chure Bhawar state- Pro-*Pahadi*)
9. Samyukta Janatantrik Tarai Mukti Morcha (SJTMM), leader 'Mr. Pawan'
10. Liberation Tigers of Terai Elam, President Ram Lochan Singh
11. Terai Cobras (pro-Terai independence, leader Nagraj)
12. Madhesi Virus Killers, Sanket
13. Nepal Defence Army (pro-King, leader 'Parivartan')

*Home Minister Bhim Rawal on 31 July 2009 said 109 armed groups were operating in the different parts of the country in the last few years. Of these 109, around 60 outfits must be operating in the Terai region. Most of these groups have been involved in criminal activities.

APPENDIX-V

## *Terai Caste/Ethnic Groups*

| *Sl. No.* | *Recognized Terai /Madhesi caste/ethnic groups* | *Total* | *Terai* |
|---|---|---|---|
| 1 | Tharu | 1,533,879 | 21.13 |
| 2 | Muslim | 971,056 | 13.38 |
| 3 | Yadav | 895,423 | 12.33 |
| 4 | Teli | 304,536 | 4.19 |
| 5 | Chamar/Harijan/Ram | 269,661 | 3.71 |
| 6 | Koiri | 251,274 | 3.46 |
| 7 | Kurmi | 212,842 | 2.93 |
| 8 | Dhanuk | 188,150 | 2.59 |
| 9 | Musahar | 172,434 | 2.37 |
| 10 | Dusadh/Paswan/Pasi | 158,526 | 2.18 |
| 11 | Sonar | 145,088 | 1.99 |
| 12 | Kewat | 136,953 | 1.88 |
| 13 | Brahman (Terai) | 134,496 | 1.85 |
| 14 | Baniya | 126,971 | 1.74 |
| 15 | Mallah | 115,986 | 1.60 |
| 16 | Kalwar | 115,606 | 1.59 |
| 17 | Hajam/Thakur | 98,169 | 1.35 |
| 18 | Kanu | 95,826 | 1.32 |
| 19 | Rajbanshi | 95,812 | 1.32 |
| 20 | Sudi | 89,846 | 1.24 |
| 21 | Lohar | 82,637 | 1.14 |
| 22 | Tatma | 76,512 | 1.05 |
| 23 | Khatwe | 74,972 | 1.03 |
| 24 | Dhobi | 73,413 | 1.01 |
| 25 | Nuniya | 66,873 | 0.92 |
| 26 | Kumhar | 54,413 | 0.74 |
| 27 | Danuwar | 53,229 | 0.73 |

| *Sl. No.* | *Recognized Terai /Madhesi caste/ethnic groups* | *Total* | *Terai* |
|---|---|---|---|
| 28 | Haluwai | 50,583 | 0.69 |
| 29 | Rajput | 48,454 | 0.66 |
| 30 | Kayastha | 46,071 | 0.63 |
| 31 | Badhae | 45,975 | 0.63 |
| 32 | Marwadi | 43,971 | 0.60 |
| 33 | Santhal/Sattar | 42,698 | 0.58 |
| 34 | Jhangar/Dhagar | 41,764 | 0.57 |
| 35 | Bantar | 35,839 | 0.49 |
| 36 | Barae | 35,434 | 0.48 |
| 37 | Kahar | 34,531 | 0.47 |
| 38 | Gangai | 31,318 | 0.43 |
| 39 | Lodha | 24,738 | 0.34 |
| 40 | Rajbhar | 24,263 | 0.33 |
| 41 | Dhimal | 19,537 | 0.26 |
| 42 | Bing/Binda | 18,720 | 0.25 |
| 43 | Bhediyar/Gaderi | 17,729 | 0.24 |
| 44 | Nurang | 17,522 | 0.24 |
| 45 | Tajpuriya | 13,215 | 0.18 |
| 46 | Chidimar | 12,296 | 0.16 |
| 47 | Mali | 11,390 | 0.15 |
| 48 | Bengali | 9,860 | 0.13 |
| 49 | Dom | 8,931 | 0.12 |
| 50 | Kamar | 8,761 | 0.12 |
| 51 | Meche | 3,763 | 0.05 |
| 52 | Halkhor | 3,621 | 0.04 |
| 53 | Punjabi/Sikh | 3,054 | 0.04 |
| 54 | Kisan | 2,876 | 0.03 |
| 55 | Koche | 1,429 | 0.02 |
| 56 | Dhunia | 1,231 | 0.02 |
| 57 | Jaine | 1,015 | 0.01 |
| 58 | Munda | 660 | 0.00 |
| 59 | Kuswadiya/Patharkata | 552 | 0.00 |

*Source:* Central Bureau of Statistics quoted in Hari Bansh Jha, *The Economy of Terai region of Nepal: Prospects for its sustainable development,* Centre for Economic and Technical Studies, Kathmandu, 2010, p. 11.

APPENDIX-VI

# *Member Organizations (IPOs) of NEFIN*

| *Sl. No.* | *IPs* | *Organization Name* | *Address* |
|---|---|---|---|
| 1 | Kishan | Kishan Samudaya Club | Mechinagar-4, Magurmadi, Jhapa |
| 2 | Kumal | Nepal Kumal Samaj Sudhar Samiti | Anamnagar, Kathmandu |
| 3 | Gangai | Nepal Gangai Kalyan Parishad | Madhumara-11, Biratnagar, Morang |
| 4 | Gurung | Tamoo Hyul Chhanjdhi | Mitranagar, Gangabu, Kathmandu |
| 5 | Chepang | Nepal Chepang (Praja) Sangh | Pulchok, Lalitpur |
| 6 | Chhantyal | Nepal Chhantyal Sangh | Manamaiju, Kathmandu |
| 7 | Jirel | Jirel Samudaya Utthan Sangh Nepal | Jiri, Dolakha, Nepal |
| 8 | Jhangad | Nepal Jhagad (Urau) Kondrom Sudhara | Laukahi-6, Sunsari |
| 9 | Tajpuriya | Tajpuriya Samaj Kalyan Parisad | Juropani-5, Gauriganj, Jhapa |
| 10 | Tamang | Nepal Tamang Ghedung, | Bagbazar, Kathmandu |
| 11 | Tangbe | Tangbe Samaj Sewa Sangh | Mahendrapul, Pokhara |
| 12 | Topkegola | Tokpegola Welfare Society | Kathmandu, Nepal |
| 13 | Thakali | Thakali Sewa Samiti | Binayakbasti, Balaju |
| 14 | Tami | Nepal Thami Samaj | Koteshor Kathmandu |
| 15 | Tharu | Tharu Kalnyankari Sabha | Purano Baneshor, Kathmandu |
| 16 | Danuwar | Danuwar Jagaran Samiti | Purano Baneshor, Kathmandu |
| 17 | Darai | Nepal Darai Utthan Samaj | Chitawan |
| 18 | Dura | Dura Sewa Samaj | Basundhara, Kathmandu |
| 19 | Dhimal | Dhimal Jati Bikas Kendra, | Urlabari-6 Morang |
| 20 | Newar | Newa Deya Dabu, | Tamsipakha, Kathmandu |
| 21 | Pahari | Nepal Pahari Bikash Sangh | Kumaripati, Lalitpur |
| 22 | Baram | Nepal Baram Sangh | Kaldhara-16, Kathmandu |
| 23 | Bote | Nepal Bote Samaj Seaw | Bharatpur-10, Chitwan |
| 24 | Bhujel | Bhujel Samaj Sewa Samiti | Dillibazar, New Plaza, Kathmandu |
| 25 | Bhote | Nepal Bhote Janajati Sewa Samiti | Martadi, Bajura |
| 26 | Magar | Nepal Magar Sangh | Shantinagar, Kathmandu |
| 27 | Majhi | Nepal Majhi Utthan Sangh | Madhuwan-7, Sunsari |
| 28 | Mugal | Mugal Janajati Samaj Kalyan Kendra | Mugu |
| 29 | Meche | Meche Samaj Sibiyari Afat | Jorsimal, Mechinagar-12, Jhapa |

| *Sl. No.* | *IPs* | *Organization Name* | *Address* |
|---|---|---|---|
| 30 | Yakkha | Kirat Yakkha Chhumma | Mahalaxmisthan, Lalitpur |
| 31 | Limbu | Kirat Yakthung Chumlung | Mahalaxmisthan, Lalitpur |
| 32 | Rai | Kirat Rai Yayokkha | Koteshor Kathmandu |
| 33 | Rajbanshi | Rajbanshi Samaj Bikash Samiti | Biratnagar, Madhumara, Morang |
| 34 | Raji | Raji Salma Samaj | Tikapur-9, Kailali |
| 35 | Lapcha | Rong Sejum Thi | Fikkal-6, Ilam |
| 36 | Larke | Larke Samaj Kalyan Kendra | Kuleshor, Kathmandu |
| 37 | Walung | Walung Sewa Samaj | Ghattekulo, Kathmandu |
| 38 | Lhomi | Lohmi (Singsa) Kalyan Kendra | Kathmandu, Nepal |
| 39 | Sherpa | Nepal Sherpa Sangh | Kumarigal, Baudha, Kathmandu |
| 40 | Byasi | Byasi Sauka Samaj | Khalanga, Darchula |
| 41 | Santhal | Nepal Santhal Aadibashi Utthan Sangh | Majhare-8, Morang |
| 42 | Siyar | Siyar Samaj Kalyan Kendra | Swambhu, Kathmandu |
| 43 | Sunuwar | Sunuwar Sewa Samaj | Koteshor Kathmandu |
| 44 | Hayu | Bayu Gukhata Kolu Padakmi (Hayu) | Ramechhap, Nepal |
| 45 | Hyolmo | Nepal Hyolmo Samaj Sewa Sang | Baudhha, Kathmandu |
| 46 | Marfali | Marfa Thakali Samaj Sewa Sadan | Chapapani, Kaski, Pokhara |
| 47 | Tingaule Thakali | Tin Gaule Thakali Sewa Samiti | Thakalichok, Pokhara |
| 48 | Dolpo | Nepla Dolpo Janajati Bikash Kendra | Baudha, Kathmandu |
| 49 | Thudam | Thudam Sewa Samaj | Baudha, Kathmandu |
| 50 | Surel | Surel Jati Utthan Samaj | Dolakha |
| 51 | Dhanuk | Nepal Dhanuk Samaj | Gwarko Lalitpur |
| 52 | Kuchbadhiya | Kuchbadhiya Utthan sangh | Nepalganj, Banke |
| 53 | Bahragau | Bahragau samaj Sewa Samiti | Jomsom, Mustang |
| 54 | Lhopa | Lochhodun Lhopa Sangh | Lomanthang, Mustang |
| 55 | Raute | Nepal Raute Bikash Sangh | Jogbudha-1, Dadeldhura |
| 56 | Kusunda | Nepal Kusunda Bikash Samaj | Dang, Nepal |

*Source:* "Member Organizations (IPOs) of NEFIN", *NEFIN*, Kathmandu, at http://www.nefin.org.np/en/member-organization/ (accessed on 28 September 2021).

APPENDIX-VII

# *40-Point Demands by the CPN-Maoist*

*4 February 1996*

**Right Honourable Prime Minister**
**Prime Minister's Office, Singha Darbar, Kathmandu**

*Sub: Memorandum*

Sir,

It has been six years since the autocratic monarchical partyless Panchayat system was ended by the 1990 People's Movement and a constitutional monarchical multiparty parliamentary system established. During this period state control has been exercised by a tripartite interim government, a single-party government of the Nepali Congress, a minority government of UML and a present Nepali Congress-RPP-Sadbhavana coalition. That, instead of making progress, The situation of the country and the people is going downhill is evident from the fact that Nepal has slid to being the second poorest country in the world; people living below the absolute poverty line has gone up to 71 per cent; the number of unemployed has reached more than 10 per cent while the number of people who are semi-employed or in disguised employment has crossed 60 per cent; the country is on the verge of bankruptcy due to rising foreign loans and deficit trade; economic and cultural encroachment within the country by foreign, and especially Indian, expansionists is increasing by the day; the gap between the rich and the poor and between towns and villages is growing wider. On (lie other hand, parliamentary parties that have formed the government by various means have shown that they are more interested in remaining in power with the blessings of foreign imperialist and expansionist masters than in the welfare of the country and the people. This is clear from their blindly adopting so-called privatisation and liberalisation to fulfill the interests of all imperialists and from the recent 'national consensus' reached in handing over the rights over Nepal's water resources to Indian expansionists. Since 6 April, 1992, the United People's Front has been involved in various struggles to fulfill relevant demands related to nationalism, democracy and livelihood, either by itself or with others. But rather than fulfill those demands, the governments formed at different times have violently suppressed the agitators and taken the lives of hundreds; the most recent example of this is the armed police operation in Rolpa a few months back. In this context, we would like to once again present to the current coalition government demands related to nationalism, democracy and livelihood, which have been raised in the past and many of which have become relevant in the present context.

1. All discriminatory treaties, including the 1950 Nepal-India Treaty, should be abrogated.
2. The so-called Integrated Mahakali Treaty concluded on 29 January, 1996 should be repealed immediately, as it is designed to conceal the disastrous Tanakpur Treaty and allows Indian imperialist monopoly over Nepal's water resources.
3. The open border between Nepal and India should be regulated, controlled and systematised. All vehicles with Indian licence plates should be banned from Nepal.
4. The Gurkha/Gorkha Recruitment Centres should be closed. Nepali citizens should be provided dignified employment in the country.
5. Nepali workers should be given priority in different sectors. A 'work permit' system should be strictly implemented if foreign workers are required in the country.
6. The domination of foreign capital in Nepali industries, business and finance should be stopped.
7. An appropriate customs policy should be devised and implemented so that economic development helps the nation become self-reliant.
8. The invasion of imperialist and colonial culture should be banned. Vulgar Hindi films, videos and magazines should be immediately outlawed.
9. The invasion of colonial and imperial elements in the name of NGOs and INGOs should be stopped.
10. A new constitution should be drafted by representatives elected for the establishment of a people's democratic system.
11. All special privileges of the king and the royal family should be abolished.
12. The army, the police and the bureaucracy should be completely under people's control.
13. All repressive acts, including the Security Act, should be repealed.
14. Everyone arrested extra-judicially for political reasons or revenge in

Rukum, Rolpa, Jajarkot, Gorkha, Kabhrc, Sindhupalchowk. Sindhuli, Dhanusa, Ramechhap, and so on, should be immediately released. All false cases should be immediately withdrawn.

15. The operation of armed police, repression and state-sponsored terror should be immediately stopped.
16. The whereabouts of citizens who disappeared in police custody at different times, namely Dilip Chaudhary, Bhuwan Thapa Magar, Prabhakar Subedi and others, should be investigated and those responsible brought to justice. The families of victims should be duly compensated.
17. All those killed during the People's Movement should be declared martyrs. The families of the martyrs and those injured and deformed should be duly compensated, and the murderers brought to justice.
18. Nepal should be declared a secular nation.
19. Patriarchal exploitation and discrimination against women should be stopped. Daughters should be allowed access to paternal property.
20. All racial exploitation and suppression should be stopped. Where ethnic communities are in the majority, they should be allowed to form their own autonomous governments.
21. Discrimination against downtrodden and backward people should be stopped. The system of untouchability should be eliminated.
22. All languages and dialects should be given equal opportunities to prosper. The right to education in the mother tongue up to higher levels should be guaranteed.
23. The right to expression and freedom of press and publication should be guaranteed. The government mass media should be completely autonomous.
24. Academic and professional freedom of scholars, writers, artists and cultural workers should be guaranteed.
25. Regional discrimination between the hills and the tarai should be eliminated. Backward areas should be given regional autonomy. Rural and urban areas should be treated at par.
26. Local bodies should be empowered and appropriately equipped.
27. Land should be belong to 'tenants'. Land under the control of the feudal system should be confiscated and distributed to the landless and the homeless.
28. The property of middlemen and comprador capitalists should be confiscated and nationalised. Capital lying unproductive should be invested to promote industrialisation.

29. Employment should be guaranteed for all. Until such time as employment can be arranged, an unemployment allowance should be provided.
30. A minimum wage for workers in industries, agriculture and so on should be fixed and strictly implemented.
31. The homeless should be rehabilitated. No one should be ' relocated until alternative infrastructure is guaranteed.
32. Poor farmers should be exempt from loan repayments. Loans taken by small farmers from the Agricultural Development Bank should be written off. Appropriate provisions should be made to provide loans for small farmers.
33. Fertiliser and seeds should be easily available and at a cheap rate. Farmers should be provided with appropriate prices and markets for their produce.
34. People in flood and drought-affected areas should be provided with appropriate relief materials.
35. Free and scientific health services and education should be available to all. The commercialisation of education should be stopped.
36. Inflation should be checked. Wages should be increased proportionate to inflation. Essential goods should be cheaply and easily available to everyone.
37. Drinking water, roads and electricity should be provided to all villagers.
38. Domestic and cottage industries should be protected and promoted.
39. Corruption, smuggling, black marketing, bribery, and the practices of middlemen and so on should be eliminated.
40. Orphans, the disabled, the elderly and children should be duly honoured and protected.

We would like to request the present coalition government to immediately initiate steps to fulfil these demands which are inextricably linked with the Nepali nation and the life of the people. If there are no positive indications towards this from the government by 17 February, 1996, we would like to inform you that we will be forced to adopt the path of armed struggle against the existing state power.

Thank you.

Dr Baburam Bhattarai, Chairman, Central Committee, United People's Front, Nepal

*Source:* "40 Point Demand", *South Asia Terrorism Portal*, New Delhi, at https://www.satp.org/satporgtp/countries/nepal/document/papers/40points.htm(last accessed on 28 September 2021)

APPENDIX-VIII

## *The 12-Point Agreement by the Seven Party Alliance and the Maoists*

*22 November 2005*

A rough translation of the twelve point agreement is given:

1. Peace and Prosperity of the country is impossible without ending autocracy and establishing absolute monarchy. All anti regressive forces have decided to focus their attack against the autocratic monarchy independently.
2. The seven party alliance would go for a road map by reinstatement of parliament first, followed by formation of an all party government with full executive power, talks with the Maoists and election to the constituent assembly in that order. The Maoists on the other hand, would prefer a road map with the formation of an interim government formed after a national conference of agitating parties which then will oversee an election to the constituent assembly.
3. While both parties are committed to a constituent assembly, the Maoists are committed to follow a 'new' peaceful political outlook. Once the autocratic monarchy is ended (not the monarchy as such!), the arms of both the RNA and the Maoists will be supervised by the UN or a dependable international body to ensure free and fair election to the constituent assembly. Both parties expect involvement of a credible international community in the dialogue process.
4. CPN-M (Maoists) is committed to a competitive multi party system, fundamental rights of the people, human rights, rule of law, democratic principles and values and to act accordingly.
5. Maoists will create a conducive atmosphere for all leaders and cadres of democratic forces and people to return to their homes and would return the physical properties and houses seized unjustifiably. People will be

allowed to take part in political activities without hindrance.

6. The Maoists have agreed to criticise itself for the past mistakes with a promise not to repeat them.
7. The political parties of the alliance will also not repeat the mistakes after introspection.
8. Human rights principles and freedom of press will be fully respected during the peace process.
9. The Municipal and Parliamentary Polls will be boycotted and made unsuccessful.
10. Both sides have expressed their commitment to protect their independence, national unity, and sovereignty and safeguarding geographical integrity. They have also declared their responsibility to maintain cordial relationship with all nations of the world, especially the neighbours, India and China.
11. Both sides called on all to actively support the people's movement launched under the common agreement based on democracy, peace, prosperity, social transformation, and the nation's sovereignty.
12. Past incidents will be probed and action will be taken against the guilty.

# *Index*